REVISE
GERMAN

A COMPLETE REVISION COURSE FOR
GCSE

John Davies, MA

Headmaster, Beauchamps Grant Maintained School,
Wickford, Essex

THIS BOOK BELONGS
TO
SAMANTA SASENARINE

BPP Letts Educational Ltd

First published 1983
Revised 1987, 1990, 1993
Reprinted 1988, 1991

Illustrations: Ian David Baker

© Text: John Davies 1983, 1987, 1990, 1991, 1993
© Illustrations: BBP (Letts Educational) Ltd 1987, 1990, 1991, 1993

BPP (Letts Educational) Ltd
Aldine House
Aldine Place
142-144 Uxbridge Road
London W12 8AW

Photos by permission of *The Daily Telegraph,* p. 87, and
Ace Photo Agency, pp. 61, 66, 69, 78, 88, 92, 97 and 102.

The University of London Examinations and Assessment
Council accepts no responsibility whatsoever for the accuracy
or method of working in the answers given.

Printed and bound in Great Britain by
WM Print Ltd, Frederick Street, Walsall, West Midlands WS2 9NE

British Library Cataloguing in Publication Data

Davies, John
  Revise English: a complete revision course
  for GCSE.–3rd ed.–(Letts study aids)
  1. German language–Examinations,
  questions, etc.
  I. Title
  438 PF3112

  ISBN 1 85758 016 8

CONTENTS

PREFACE

This book is designed as a revision guide for candidates studying for GCSE examinations in German. It has been written after analysing the requirements of all the Examining Groups in England, Northern Ireland, Scotland and Wales. A summary of these requirements is given in tabular form.

The book contains a revision of all the major grammatical points required for GCSE and includes hints on revision and examination technique. It also includes questions for you to answer taken from actual GCSE papers. I would like to thank the University of London Examinations and Assessment Council and the Southern Examining Group for permission to use these questions.

With careful and consistent use, this book should help candidates gain confidence in all the skills which are tested in GCSE German examinations. All Examining Groups test the four skills of listening, speaking, reading and writing German. This book shows you what emphasis is laid on each skill by the different Examining Groups and provides you with an opportunity to practise those skills and improve your chances of success by so doing.

John H. Davies

INTRODUCTION AND GUIDE TO USING THIS BOOK

This book has been written to help you revise for the GCSE examination in German. The key to success in these examinations lies in your ability to convince the examiner that you have mastered the four basic skills which all the Examining Groups test in one form or another. The skills are listening and reading comprehension, speaking and writing German.

The first thing you need to find out before you plan your revision programme is exactly what will be expected of you in the examination itself. The analysis of the syllabuses of each of the Examining Groups on page vi will help you do this. If you are a mature student it can be used to give you guidance on which Group's examination will suit you best. The analysis and summary of the Groups' requirements indicate the emphasis each Group gives to the different skills and how they are tested. You should concentrate on the types of question your Group sets and ensure that you are given the fullest possible information about the grammar, vocabulary and topic areas which your particular Group expects you to have studied. If you cannot obtain this information from your teacher, you can always write to the Examining Group for your own copy. The addresses of the Examining Groups are listed on page xv.

Success at GCSE in German means having a good knowledge of vocabulary and the grammar of the language. This is not a text book or a vocabulary book, but if you use it wisely as an aid to revision and in conjunction with your course books and specimen examination materials, there should not be any difficulty in achieving success in your Examining Group's tests. This book assumes that you have studied German for at least two years. You should use it to help plan your revision programme over the last twelve months or so leading up to your examination. You should work systematically through the grammar sections in Section 1 and follow the advice and hints on how to tackle the tests which you will be expected to take in your examination. Finally you can practise the types of question which you will have to do.

Remember, there is a good deal of distilled experience and advice contained in the hints on examination technique in Sections 4–7. So if you know your vocabulary, you know your grammar and you follow the advice given and improve your examination technique you should find that the reward for your efforts will be the success you are anxious to achieve. Enjoy your revision and good luck in your German examinations.

Analysis of examination syllabuses

Examining Group	ULEAC		MEG			NEA		SEG		NISEAC		SEB			WJEC	
Level	Basic	Higher	Basic	Higher I	Higher II	Basic	Higher	General	Extended	Basic	Higher	Foundation	General	Credit	Basic	Higher
Listening																
Questions	T/Ge	T/Ge	T/Ge	T/Ge	T/Ge	T/Ge	T/Ge	T/Ge/V	T/Ge/V	T/Ge	T/Ge	T/Ge	T/Ge	T/Ge	T/Ge/W	T/Ge/W
Answers	E	E	MCE or E	E	E	MCE or E	MCE or E	E	E	E	E	E	E	E	E/W	E/W
Time	30 mins	30 mins	20 mins	20 mins	20 mins	30 mins	30 mins	30 mins	35 mins	30 mins	30 mins	25 mins	25 mins	30 mins	30 mins	40 mins
Reading												††	††	††		
Questions	Ge/V	Ge/V	Ge/V	Ge/V	Ge/V	Ge/V	Ge/V	Ge/V	Ge	Ge/V	Ge/V	Ge	Ge	Ge	V/Ge/W	V/Ge/W
Answers	E	E	MCE or E	MCE or E	MCE or E	MCG or E	MCG or E	E	E	E	E	E	E	E	E/W	E/W
Time	30 mins	30 mins	25 mins	25 mins	25 mins	25 mins	40 mins	30 mins	40 mins	45 mins	40 mins	45 mins	45 mins	60 mins	30 mins	40 mins
Oral/Speaking												*				
Role-play	2	3	2	3	3	2/V	4/V	2	2	2	2	5			2	4
Conversation	Gu	Gu + Gen	Gu	Gu	Gu + V	Gen	Gen	Gu	Gen	Gu	Gen				Gu	Gen
Time	10 mins	20 mins	10 mins	12 mins	15 mins	5-10 mins	10-15 mins	10 mins	12 mins	10 mins	15 mins	15 mins			10 mins	15 mins
Taped	T	T	T	T	T	T	T	T	T	T	T				T	T
Writing													††	††		
Forms & Lists	Op		●							●					●	
Postcards	Op		●			●				●					●	
Letters	●	Op		●		●	●	●	Op	●	●				●	●
Messages	Op		●			●		●		●			†●		●	
Visual/Pictures		Op			●	●	●		Op		●					Op
Topic		Op			●		●		Op V	●	●			†●		Op
Time	45 mins	60 mins	25 mins	30 mins	35 mins	25 mins	50 mins	30 mins	60 mins	45 mins	50 mins		30 mins	45 mins	30 mins	70 mins

Key

E	English
E/W	English and Welsh
Ge	Material in German with English questions
Gen	General
Gu	Guided
MCE	Multiple choice English
MCG	Multiple choice German
Op	You have a choice
T	Taped
V	Visual material may be used in this test, e.g. pictures, diagrams, plans, etc.

● Any or all of these may be included in the test

† The writing element is an optional endorsement to General and Credit levels only.

†† Dictionaries are allowed in these SEB examinations.

* In Scotland the speaking skill will be assessed by on-going assessment during S4 as well as the final oral proficiency test.

THE GCSE

The General Certificate of Secondary Education replaced GCE O level and CSE in the summer of 1988. the examination is administered by five examining groups in England and Wales and monitored by the Secondary Examinations and Assessment Council (SEAC), soon to be merged with the National Curriculum Council (NCC) and be known as the School Curriculum and Assessment Authority (SCAA). This is in preparation for the merging of Key Stage 4 assessment of the National Curriculum with GCSE which will begin in the summer of 1994.

In 1994 grades will be awarded on the basis of the National Curriculum levels 4–10. At present there is a single seven-point scale: A, B, C, D, E, F and G for GCSE. The relationship between National Curriculum (NC) levels and the existing grades is expected to be as shown in the table below.

NC Level	GCSE Grade
10	A+ (i.e. super A)
9	A
8	B
	C
7	D
6	E
5	F
4	G

National Curriculum levels 1–3 will not qualify candidates for an award at GCSE. Up until the summer of 1994 the system of grading at GCSE will continue as now and as described in the following pages for each of the examining groups.

The system of grading for GCSE continues to be objective and criteria-related. Grades will continue to be awarded according to the extent to which candidates have demonstrated particular levels of attainment as defined in the published 'grade criteria' or in accordance with the levels of the National Curriculum (Key Stage 4) from the summer of 1994. In effect this means that candidates will be assessed positively on what they know, understand and can do.

Differentiation or Differentiated Assessment

One of the principles of ensuring that 90 per cent of all pupils can be positively assessed is contained in the statement on differentiated assessment which is part of the general national criteria for this examination.

'All examinations must be designed in such a way as to ensure proper discrimination, so that candidates across the ability range are given opportunities to demonstrate their knowledge, abilities and achievements–that is, to show what they know, understand and can do. Accordingly differentiated papers or differentiated questions within papers will be required in all subjects. In many subjects a mixture of common and differentiated elements will be appropriate.'

In modern languages differentiation is achieved by setting at least two papers at different levels in all four skill areas of listening, reading, speaking and writing. In most cases these different levels are described as 'basic' and 'higher' and the relationship between them and the awarding of grades needs explanation in detail and varies slightly from one Examining Group to another. It is essential to realize that the tasks set at 'Higher' Level are more taxing and demanding than those at 'Basic' Level.

ULEAC

The scheme of assessment for ULEAC German examinations is as follows. All papers are numbered 1–8. Papers 1, 3, 5 and 7 represent the Basic Level in listening, reading, oral and writing. Papers 2, 4, 6 and 8 are the higher-level papers in each skill area. Each of the four areas has the same weighting of 25 per cent of the marks awarded.

The list of papers is therefore:

Paper 1   Basic listening comprehension
Paper 2   Hither listening comprehension
Paper 3   Basic reading comprehension
Paper 4   Higher reading comprehension
Paper 5   Basic oral
Paper 6   Higher oral
Paper 7   Basic writing
Paper 8   Higher writing

The maximum GCSE grade which may be awarded for any particular combination of papers is as follows:

Combination of papers	Highest grade available
1, 3, 5	E
1, 3, 5 plus at least one paper from 2, 4, 6, 7	D
1, 3, 5, 7 plus at least one paper from 2, 4, 6, 8	C
1, 3, 5, 7, 8 plus one papers from 2, 4, 6	B
1, 3, 5, 7, 8 plus two papers from 2, 4, 6	A
1, 3, 5, 7, 2, 4, 6, 8	

MEG

The scheme of assessment for MEG is more complicated. There are three compulsory elements. These three common-core elements must be taken by all candidates. They are: Basic Listening, Speaking and Reading.

All other elements in this examination are optional additional elements. Please note that Higher Writing can only be offered if the candidate is also entered for Basic Writing. As can be seen from the analysis of syllabuses on page vi, there are four papers at Basic Level and each Higher Level is divided into two parts. The full scheme of assessment is therefore:

Listening	Reading	Speaking	Writing
Basic	Basic	Basic	Basic
Higher	Higher	Higher	Higher
Part 1	Part 1	Part 1	Part 1
Part 2	Part 2	Part 2	Part 2

The four skills of Listening, Reading, Speaking and Writing are equally weighted. All candidates must do Basic Listening, Speaking and Reading and will then choose additional elements according to their ability. Each higher-level element will be in two parts. Part 1 of any higher-level element must be attempted if entered for any higher-level examination. Part 2 is therefore an optional extra. Candidates will be able to decide on the day of the examination whether or not to attempt Part 2 although it is assumed in most cases that candidates and their teachers will have decided in the weeks prior to the examination whether Part 2 is to be attempted on the day. It will not be necessary to indicate on your entry form whether Parts 1 and 2 are both to be attempted.

The minimum number of elements which must be offered to qualify for the award of each of the Grades A–G is summarised below. It is assumed that candidates will attempt as many elements of the examination as is consistent with their likelihood of success.

Summary

Grades	Papers to be attempted (minimum number of elements)
G, F, E	Basic Listening, Reading, Speaking
D	Basic Listening, Reading, Speaking
plus either Basic Writing
or Part 1 of any two higher-level elements
or Parts 1 and 2 of any one higher-level element
C	Basic Listening, Reading, Speaking, Writing
plus Part 1 of any two higher-level elements
or Parts 1 and 2 of any one higher-level element
B	Basic Listening, Reading, Speaking, Writing
plus higher-level Writing (Parts 1 and 2)
plus one additional higher-level element (Parts 1 and 2)
A	Basic Listening, Reading, Speaking, Writing
plus higher-level Writing (Parts 1 and 2)
plus two additional higher-level elements (Parts 1 and 2)

NEA

The NEA scheme of assessment is similar to the LEAG scheme. All candidates must be entered for what are called the common-core basic-level tests in Listening, Reading and Speaking. Candidates may be entered for any combination of additional tests considered appropriate by the centre. Please note higher-level Writing can only be entered if the candidate is also doing basic-level Writing.

The minimum entry requirements for the different grades can be summarised as follows:

Maximum Grade	Minimum entry requirements
G, F, E	Basic Listening, Reading, Speaking
D	Basic Listening, Reading, Speaking *plus* any one other test
C	Basic Listening, Reading, Speaking, Writing *plus* any one other test
B	Basic Listening, Reading, Speaking, Writing, Higher Writing *plus* any one other test
A	Basic Listening, Reading, Speaking, Writing, Higher Writing *plus* any two other tests

It must be stressed that these are the *minimum* requirements to achieve the different grades and that in each case a very high level of competence in the stated number of tests will be required in order to achieve the maximum grade available. It is expected, therefore, that candidates aiming at a particular grade will normally attempt a wider range of tests than the minimum number on which the grade can be awarded. There will be equal weighting for each of the skill areas within any one level.

SEG

SEG describes its assessment pattern in terms of general- and extended-level tests. There will be one of each in all four skill areas of Speaking, Listening, Reading and Writing. The minimum entry will be for the three tests of Speaking, Listening and Reading at General Level. These three are to be known as the common-core tests. The relationship between the award of grades and the level of tests entered is similar to the other Examining Groups and can be summarised as follows:

Maximum Grade	Minimum entry requirements
G, F, E	Three common-core tsts
D	Three common-core tests *plus* at least one Extended Level excluding Extended Writing or General Writing
C	Three common-core tests *plus* General Writing *plus* at least one extended-level test
B	Three common-core tests *plus* General Writing *plus* Extended Writing *plus* any one other extended-level test
A	Three common-core tests *plus* General Writing *plus* Extended Writing *plus* any two other extended-level tests

Equal weighting will be given to each of the skills attempted. Entry cannot be made to any extended-level test in any of the four skill areas unless it is also made at General Level in that skill. The only exception to this is Speaking, where candidates may enter for *either* General Level or Extended Level, since the extended-level test includes the general-level test.

WJEC

As with the other Examining Groups the Welsh Board has basic-and higher-level tests in each of the four skill areas. Basic Listening, Reading and Oral tests are known as the *compulsory core*, which all candidates must enter. All other tests are described as additional elements.

Maximum Grade	Minimum entry requirements
E	Compulsory core
D	Compulsory core *plus* one additional element
C	Compulsory core *plus* Basic Writing *plus* one additional element
B	Compulsory core *plus* Basic and Higher Writing *plus* one additional higher element
A	Compulsory core *plus* Basic and Higher Writing *plus* two additional higher elements

It should be noted that these are the minimum entry requirements and that to achieve the grades listed the overall level of competence required within the elements expected will be very high. Equal weighting will be given in assessment and grading to the various skill areas within each of the two levels.

In addition to the five Examining Groups in England and Wales the Northern Ireland Schools Examinations and Assessment Council (NISEAC) is now offering GCSE, while in Scotland the Scottish Examining Board (SEB) introduced a revised Standard Grade in the Scottish Certificate of Education in 1990.

NISEAC

NISEAC describes its assessment objectives in a similar way to those of the Examining Groups in England and Wales. There are three common-core objectives: Basic Listening, Reading and Speaking. Additional assessment objectives are Basic Writing and Higher Listening, Reading, Speaking and Writing. Equal allocations of marks are given to the skill areas within each of the differentiated levels. In each of the skill areas the proportion of marks awarded to the basic- and higher-level components will be in the ratio of four to three. The relationship between assessment objectives and grades is summarised below:

Maximum Grade	Minimum number of elements required
E	Three common-core elements
D	Three common-core elements *plus* one additional element
C	Three common-core elements *plus* Basic Writing *plus* any one higher-level additional element
B	Three common-core elements *plus* Basic Writing *plus* Higher Writing *plus* any one additional higher-level element
A	Three common-core elements *plus* Basic Writing *plus* Higher Writing *plus* any two additional higher-level elements

SEB

The SEB Standard examination became fully operational in 1990. However, SEB proposals are complex for the awarding of a Scottish Certificate of Education at Standard Grade. There are three levels described as Foundation, General and Credit. Grades are awarded on a seven-point scale: 1, 2, 3, 4, 5, 6 and 7. The terms 'Foundation', 'General' and 'Credit' relate only to particular ranges of grades: Foundation covering grades 7 to 5, General grades 5 to 2 and Credit covering grades 2 and 1. All candidates are assessed in the three elements of Reading, Listening and Speaking. Writing is an optional test. The assessment procedures for each skill area are as follows:

Reading: weighting 25 per cent

There will be three papers, Foundation, General and Credit. Candidates will be entered for one or two of the papers. The grade awarded will depend upon the highest grade at which the candidate shows competence on the papers entered. Candidates will be allowed to use a dictionary.

Listening: weighting 25 per cent

Three papers will be available. As with the assessment for reading, candidates can be entered for one or two papers only and the grade awarded will depend on the highest grade at which the candidate shows competence. This examination will be recorded on tape. The examination centre will be required to provide an estimated grade for Listening for each candidate.

Speaking: weighting 50 per cent

Speaking: on-going internal assessment

Schools will be required to monitor, for each candidate, a number of short speaking activities which will arise out of normal class work. For certification purposes this will be done over a period of one year during what is known as S4 in Scotland. A record in terms of grades will be kept by the teacher of individual performances and these grades will be used to form the basis of a final rating based on the grade-related criteria and giving evidence of the normal performance of each candidate in speaking activities. The whole process will be internally moderated within the school. The rating for the on-going internal assessment will have to be based on a wide variety of speaking activities and these activities should have a reasonable spread as far as the topic areas of the syllabus are concerned.

The examination centre will be required to provide an interim grade for Speaking, based on the on-going assessment, for each candidate.

Speaking: final proficiency test

This will take place in March of the S4 year and will comprise a formal oral test for each candidate. Up to five tasks will be set by the Board which all candidates will be expected to attempt. This final proficiency test in speaking will normally be carried out by the candidate's own teacher. A number of these oral tests will be observed by a moderator appointed by the Board who will agree levels of performance and award of appropriate grades with the teachers conducting the tests. Some of these tests will also need to be taped for future moderation exercises.

Optional endorsement in writing – General and Credit levels only

There will be two papers lasting 30 minutes for the General level and 45 mins for the Credit level. At General level the candidate will be asked to write a number of short, simple messages in German. These will be linked in English by context. At Credit level the stimulus will be a passage or passages requiring a personal response in German from the candidate in some 200 words. The use of a dictionary is allowed in both writing examinations.

Examination centres will be required to provide an estimated grade for each candidate taking the written option.

Grade Related Criteria (GRC)

GRC are defined at three levels of performance: Foundation, General and Credit.

Awards will be reported on six grades, two grades being distinguished at each level – Foundation: grades 6 and 5, General: grades 4 and 3, and Credit: grades 2 and 1. The grades at each level will be awarded in accordance with the stated criteria and on how each candidate meets these criteria. Grade 7 will be awarded to candidates who complete the course but fail to meet the criteria for any level.

Summary

Finally some general points about all the seven Examining Groups and their examination tests in German.

(a) All seven have similar aims such as developing the ability to use the language effectively for the purposes of practical communication, forming a basis for further study, work and leisure, providing enjoyment and intellectual stimulation and promoting learning skills of a more general application (e.g. analysis, memorizing, drawing of inferences).

(b) The material used in all examination tests must be authentic and relevant.

(c) The syllabus content of each Examining Group is now defined under topic areas and settings. A composite list of these topic areas is included in Section 2 of this book where it is made clear at what level the vocabulary listed there will be used in the examinations.

DEVISING A REVISION PROGRAMME FOR GERMAN

Organizing your revision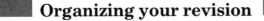

You cannot expect to remember all the grammar and vocabulary that you have learned over a period of three or four years unless you are prepared to revise. You need to be able to recall the vocabulary and rules of grammar from your memory during any part of the examination.

Organize your revision by making a timetable. Choose a time when you are at your most receptive. It might be best to revise in the early evening before you get too tired, or early in the morning after a good night's sleep. Having decided when to revise, put the times on to your revision timetable.

You also need a suitable place to revise. Find a quiet, or fairly quiet room away from distractions like TV or loud music. You need a table, a chair, adequate light (a table lamp will often help you to concentrate) and a comfortable temperature. It is better to revise when sitting at a table than when lying down. It is more effective to revise inside the house rather than basking in the sun.

How to revise for German

When revising vocabulary do not just keep reading the words and their meanings through aimlessly. Try to learn the words in context. Remember you need to know the gender and the plural of all nouns.

Learn lists of words in short spells at a time and always give yourself a written test. In other words you must review the words you have learned. Without this review you will forget what you have learned very quickly.

When revising grammar points you should make notes on a post card, which will then help you to do some light revision on the night before the exam. Look for the important key facts about German grammar and make notes on them as you revise. Use the test yourself section of this book to test what you have revised. If you have not understood and are still getting it wrong then go back to the relevant grammar section and look at it again.

The reviewing of what you have revised is very important. You should try to carry out this testing and retesting of what you have learned during a revision session after 24 hours, then after a week and maybe again after a month. You should keep your summary notes for use just before the exam.

Plan all your revision in short bursts, depending on your span of concentration.

(1) You learn most by studying for 20-40 minutes and then testing yourself to see how much you remember.

(2) Take regular breaks. On your timetable you could split a two-hour session into four shorter periods, like this: revise for 25 minutes; break for 10 minutes; work another 25 minutes; then stop, have a longer break (20-30 minutes) and then work for another 35-40 minutes. Give yourself a reward at the end of the revision period, e.g. watch TV, read a book, listen to a record or the radio, or go and see a friend.

(3) Have a definite start time and finish time. Learning efficiency tends to fall at the beginning of a revision session but rises towards the end.

(4) Allow two hours each day for revision at the beginning of your programme and build up to three hours a day or more during the last three or so weeks of revision before the examinations start. Make sure German has a weekly session in your revision programme.

Some other tips:

Don't waste revision time

(a) Recognize when your mind begins to wander.

(b) If you have things on your mind deal with them first; or make a list of the 'things you need to do' then go back to your revision.

(c) Get up and move about – do something different, make a cup of tea, etc.

(d) Think with your daydream – it will probably go away.

(e) Change your revision subject – move to another subject, then come back to German revision.

Work in pairs

(a) Learning vocabulary is easy this way; you can test one another.

(b) Practise talking German with a friend.

(c) Listen to German radio broadcasts together.

Understand the work

Learning grammar 'parrot fashion' can lower recall. Remember: *work, test, rest, reward.*

Do not give up

You may feel irritable and depressed, but recognize that this is a common problem. Do not give up.

Use 'tricks' to help you remember

Things like *mnemonics* help you to remember groups of prepositions which take a particular case, e.g. BUD GO FEW gives you the initial letters of the prepositions which take the accusative only: **bis**, **um**, **durch**, **gegen**, **ohne**, **für**, **entlang** and **wider**.

Here is the 'Ladder to Success' which can help you understand how to prepare properly not only for your German examinations but other examinations as well.

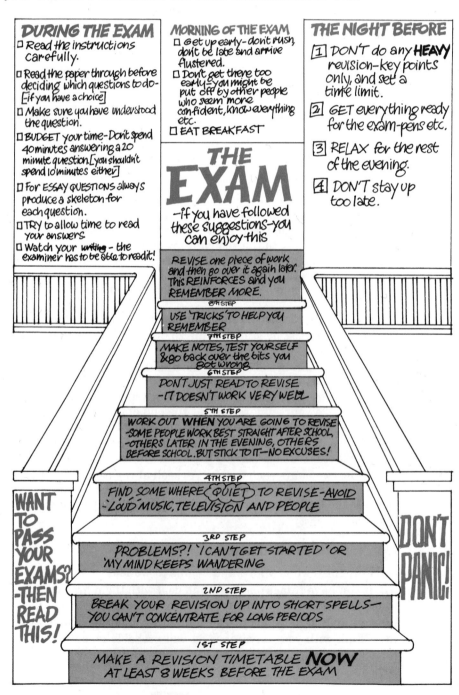

Examination Boards: Addresses

To obtain syllabuses, past examination papers and further details, write to your Examining Group.

Northern Examination Association (NEA)

JMB	Joint Matriculation Board Devas Street, Manchester M15 6EU
ALSEB	Associated Lancashire Schools Examining Board 12 Harter Street, Manchester M1 6HL
NREB	Northern Regional Examinations Board Wheatfield Road, Westerhope, Newcastle upon Tyne NE5 5JZ
NWREB	North-West Regional Examinations Board Orbit House, Albert Street, Eccles, Manchester M20 0WL
YHREB	Yorkshire and Humberside Regional Examinations Board Harrogate Office – 31-33 Springfield Avenue, Harrogate HG1 2HW Sheffield Office – Scarsdale House, 136 Derbyshire Lane, Sheffield S8 8SE

Midland Examining Group (MEG)

Cambridge	University of Cambridge Local Examinations Syndicate Syndicate Buildings, 1 Hills Road, Cambridge CB1 2EU
O & C	Oxford and Cambridge Schools Examination Board Purbeck House, Purbeck Road, Cambridge CB2 1PU and Elsfield Way, Oxford OX2 7BZ
WMEB	West Midlands Examinations Board Mill Wharf, Mill Street, Birmingham B6 4BU
EMREB	East Midland Regional Examinations Board Robins Wood House, Robins Wood Road, Aspley, Nottingham NG8 3NR

London East Anglian Group (LEAG)
(now known as University of London Examinations and Assessment Council)

London	Stewart House, 32 Russell Square, London WC1B 5DN
Colchester	The Lindens, Lexden Road, Colchester CO3 3RL

Southern Examining Group (SEG)

AEB	The Associated Examining Board Stag Hill House, Guildford GU2 5XJ
UODLE	University of Oxford Delegacy of Local Examinations Ewert House, Ewert Place, Summertown, Oxford OX2 7BZ
SEG	Southern Regional Examinations Board Unit 23, Monksbrook Industrial Park, Chandlers Ford, Eastleigh SO5 3RA
	South-East Regional Examinations Board Beloe House, 2-10 Mount Ephraim Road, Tunbridge Wells TN1 1EU
	South-Western Examinations Board 23-29 Marsh Street, Bristol BS1 4BP

Wales

WJEC	Welsh Joint Education Committee 245 Western Avenue, Cardiff CF5 2YZ

Northern Ireland

NISEAC	Northern Ireland Schools Examinations and Assessment Council Beechill House, 42 Beechill Road, Belfast BT8 4RS

Scotland

SEB	Scottish Examination Board Ironmills Road, Dalkeith, Midlothian EH22 1BR

1 GRAMMAR REVISION

The aim of this section of the book is to set out in simple terms the essential details of German grammar which every GCSE candidate is expected to know. At first sight, German with its formal sentence construction seems difficult to understand, but it need not be. What you have to do is to make a determined effort to learn certain fundamental rules and then apply them carefully and conscientiously. Once these basics have been absorbed and understood, you will have much more confidence in your own ability to write and speak clear and accurate German. Similarly, you will find it much easier to understand both spoken and written German.

At the beginning of each section which follows there is a brief explanation of the equivalent English grammar so that you will be able to understand the terms being used to explain the structure of the German language.

1 Nouns

Nouns are words which are used for the names of things, ideas or living creatures.

Here are some examples of English nouns chosen at random, with their German equivalents:

book	**das Buch**	(¨er)	(*n*)	day	**der Tag**	(-e)	(*m*)
chair	**der Stuhl**	(¨e)	(*m*)	night	**die Nacht**	(¨e)	(*f*)
dog	**der Hund**	(-e)	(*m*)	school	**die Schule**	(-n)	(*f*)
cat	**die Katze**	(-n)	(*f*)	dining-room	**das Eßzimmer**	(-)	(*n*)
baker	**der Bäcker**	(-)	(*m*)	truth	**die Wahrheit**	(-en)	(*f*)
teacher	**der Lehrer**	(-)	(*m*)	fear	**die Angst**	(¨e)	(*f*)

There are a number of things which are immediately apparent from this short list. The first is that the German is more complicated than the English; the second is that German nouns have to be learned with their gender and plural; and the third is that all German nouns are written with a capital letter.

Here are some very common German nouns written out in the four cases – nominative (**N**), accusative (**A**), genitive (**G**) and dative (**D**).

	Masculine	*Plural*			*Feminine*	*Plural*
N	der Mann	die Männer		**N**	die Frau	die Frauen
A	den Mann	die Männer		**A**	die Frau	die Frauen
G	des Mannes	der Männer		**G**	der Frau	der Frauen
D	dem Mann	den Männern		**D**	der Frau	den Frauen

	Neuter	*Plural*
N	das Kind	die Kinder
A	das Kind	die Kinder
G	des Kindes	der Kinder
D	dem Kind	den Kindern

Points to note:

(i) In the singular genitive case, masculine and neuter nouns add the ending **-es** (or **-s** if the noun has more than one syllable).
(ii) Feminine nouns do not change in the singular.
(iii) All nouns in the dative plural end in **-n** or **-en**.

The only exception to this rule is the group of nouns of foreign origin which form their plural by adding **-s**, e.g. das Auto (-s), das Hotel (-s), der Klub (-s).

These nouns do not have the dative plural **-n** or **-en**:

	Singular	*Plural*
N	das Auto	die Autos
A	das Auto	die Autos
G	des Autos	der Autos
D	dem Auto	den Autos

All nouns fall into groups which are sometimes called **declensions**. These groups are identified by the gender of the noun and the formation of the plural.

GROUP 1

This group consists of nouns which do not change in the plural. Most masculine and neuter nouns which end in **-el, -en**, and **-er** belong to this group. In fact the majority of this group are masculine in gender and many of the masculine nouns that end in **-er** are formed by adding this ending to the stem of the verb, giving you nouns like **der Bäcker**, baker; **der Diener**, servant; **der Leser**, reader; **der Arbeiter**, worker; **der Wärter**, keeper and many more which follow the same pattern.

Example: **der Onkel**, uncle

	Singular	Plural
N	der Onkel	die Onkel
A	den Onkel	die Onkel
G	des Onkels	der Onkel
D	dem Onkel	den Onkeln

Here are some of the commonest **masculine nouns** that belong to this group:

Ärmel	sleeve	**Fehler**	mistake	**Felsen**	rock
Deckel	lid	**Flieger**	airman	**Haken**	hook
Enkel	grandson	**Gegner**	opponent	†**Husten**	cough
Esel	donkey	**Gletscher**	glacier	**Knochen**	bone
Flügel	wing	**Jäger**	hunter	**Kuchen**	cake
Gipfel	summit	**Keller**	cellar	**Rahmen**	frame
Gürtel	belt	**Kellner**	waiter	**Rasen**	lawn
Himmel	sky	**Koffer**	trunk	†**Regen**	rain
Hügel	hill	**Körper**	body	**Reifen**	tyre
Kessel	kettle	**Meister**	master	**Rücken**	back
Löffel	spoon	**Pfarrer**	parson	†**Schatten**	shade
Nebel	fog	†**Puder**	powder	†**Schinken**	ham
Schlüssel	key	**Schäfer**	shepherd	**Schlitten**	sledge
Sessel	armchair	**Schaffner**	conductor	†**Schnupfen**	cold
Stengel	stalk	**Schalter**	booking office	**Spaten**	spade
Stiefel	boot	**Schneider**	tailor	**Streifen**	stripe
Titel	title	**Teller**	plate	**Wagen**	car
Zettel	(slip of) paper	**Tiger**	tiger	**Weizen**	wheat
Zweifel	doubt			†**Norden**	north
		Balken	beam	†**Süden**	south
		Besen	broom	†**Osten**	east
Bettler	beggar	**Brunnen**	well	†**Westen**	west
Bürger	citizen	**Braten**	roast		
Eimer	bucket				

NB Nouns which end in **-en** do not add an extra **-n** in the dative plural.

Neuter nouns belonging to this group include:

(i) **Bündel**, bundle   **Kapitel**, chapter
     Dunkel, darkness   **Möbel**, (piece of) furniture
     Exempel, example   **Segel**, sail

(ii) The fractions: **Drittel**, third; **Viertel**, quarter

(iii) All neuter nouns ending in **-chen** and **-lein**: **Mädchen**, girl; **Fräulein**, young lady

(iv) Neuter nouns ending in **-en** and **-er**:

Becken	basin	**Feuer**	fire	**Semester**	University term
†**Eisen**	iron	†**Fieber**	fever	†**Silber**	silver
Examen	examination	†**Leder**	leather	**Theater**	theatre
Kissen	cushion	**Messer**	knife	**Ufer**	shore, bank
Zeichen	sign	**Muster**	model	†**Wasser**	water
Abenteuer	adventure	**Orchester**	orchestra	**Wetter**	weather
Alter	age	†**Pulver**	powder	**Wunder**	wonder
Fenster	window	**Ruder**	oar	**Zimmer**	room

(v) Neuters that begin with **Ge-** and end in **-e** do not change in the plural except for the dative plural **-n**.

Example: **Gebirge**, range of mountains

	Singular	Plural
N	das Gebirge	die Gebirge
A	das Gebirge	die Gebirge
G	des Gebirges	der Gebirge
D	dem Gebirge	den Gebirgen

† These nouns are rarely used in the plural.

GROUP 1(a)

Nouns which take an Umlaut in the plural and end in **-el**, **-er**, or **-en**.
Example: **der Nagel**, nail

	Singular	Plural
N	der Nagel	die Nägel
A	den Nagel	die Nägel
G	des Nagels	der Nägel
D	dem Nagel	den Nägeln

N.B. Nouns ending in **-en** do not add an extra **-n** in the dative plural. To this group belong:
(i) Two very common feminine nouns, **die Mutter** (ᐨ), mother, and **die Tochter** (ᐨ), daughter, plus one neuter, **das Kloster** (ᐨ), monastery.
(ii) The following masculines:

Apfel	apple	**Hammer**	hammer	**Schaden**	damage
Boden	ground	**Laden**	shop	**Schnabel**	beak
Bruder	brother	**Mantel**	cloak	**Vater**	father
Garten	garden	**Nagel**	nail	**Vogel**	bird
Graben	ditch	**Ofen**	stove		
Hafen	harbour	**Sattel**	saddle		

GROUP 1(b)

This group is really the same as Group 1. The **-n** is missing in the nominative singular, otherwise it is exactly like Group 1.
Example: **der Name**, name

	Singular	Plural
N	der Name	die Namen
A	den Namen	die Namen
G	des Namens	der Namen
D	dem Namen	den Namen

To this group belong:
 (i) **das Herz**, heart, which does not have the **-en** in the accusative singular.
(ii) The following masculines:

Buchstabe	letter of the alphabet	**Gedanke**	thought	**Same**	seed
Friede	peace	**Glaube**	faith	**Wille**	will

Do not confuse this group with the other masculines which end in **-e** (see page 6). There is one masculine noun that ends in **-e** which does not belong to either group: **der Käse**, cheese. The usual plural is **die Käsesorten**, kinds of cheese. In the singular it behaves like a regular masculine noun.

GROUP 2

Example: **der Sohn**, son

	Singular	Plural
N	der Sohn	die Söhne
A	den Sohn	die Söhne
G	des Sohnes	der Söhne
D	dem Sohn	den Söhnen

(i) This group contains most of the masculine single-syllable nouns. There are therefore a very large number of nouns which belong to this group and form their plural by adding **-e** and modifying the vowel with an Umlaut. Some obvious examples are: **der Arzt** (ᐨe), doctor; **der Stuhl** (ᐨe), chair; and there are many more.
(ii) To this group also belong the following masculines with more than one syllable.
   Bischof, bishop **Palast**, palace **Kanal**, channel
(iii) One neuter noun belongs to this group: **das Floß**, raft.

GROUP 2(a)

Example: **das Jahr**, year

	Singular	Plural
N	das Jahr	die Jahre
A	das Jahr	die Jahre
G	des Jahres	der Jahre
D	dem Jahr	den Jahren

Nouns in this group add **-e** in the plural but do *not* take an Umlaut.

(i) To this group belong most neuters, except for those mentioned as belonging to **Group 3**. Neuter nouns ending in **-chen, -lein, -e, -el, -er, -en, -tum** and **-um** also do *not* belong to this group.

Here is a list of the commonest neuter nouns of one syllable which belong to this group:

Bein	leg	**Jahr**	year	**Riff**	reef
Bier	beer	**Kinn**	chin	**Rohr**	tube
†**Blut**	blood	*****Knie**	knee	†**Salz**	salt
Boot	boat	**Kreuz**	cross	**Schaf**	sheep
†**Brot**	bread	**Mahl**	meal	**Schiff**	ship
Ding	thing	**Mal**	time	**Schilf**	reed
†**Eis**	ice	**Maß**	measure	**Schwein**	pig
Erz	ore	**Meer**	sea	**Seil**	rope
Fell	skin	†**Moos**	moss	**Spiel**	game
Fest	festival	**Netz**	net	†**Stroh**	straw
°**Fleisch**	meat	°**Obst**	fruit	**Stück**	piece
Gas	gas	†**Öl**	oil	**Tier**	animal
Gift	poison	**Paar**	pair	**Tor**	gate, goal
†**Glück**	fortune	**Pferd**	horse	†**Vieh**	cattle
†**Gold**	gold	**Pfund**	pound	**Werk**	work (of art)
Haar	hair	**Pult**	desk	*****Wrack**	wreck
Heft	exercise book	**Recht**	right	**Zelt**	tent
†**Heu**	hay	**Reh**	deer	†**Zeug**	stuff, material
Heim	home	**Reich**	realm	**Ziel**	aim

Some other neuters of more than one syllable also form their plural this way by adding **-e**. Here are a few of them:

Alphabet	alphabet	**Manuskript**	manuscript	**Talent**	talent
Dutzend	dozen	**Paket**	parcel	**Telegramm**	telegram
†**Elend**	misery	**Problem**	problem	**Telephon**	telephone
Gegenteil	contrast	**Programm**	programme	**Verbot**	prohibition
Institut	institute	**Prozent**	percentage		
Konzert	concert	**System**	system		

(ii) To this group belong also most masculine nouns of more than one syllable (not listed elsewhere) and the following masculines of one syllable which are quite commonly used:

Arm	arm	**Laut**	sound	†**Schmuck**	finery, jewellery
Dom	cathedral	**Mond**	moon	**Schuh**	shoe
Forst	forest	**Ort**	place	**Stoff**	stuff, material
Grad	degree	**Pfad**	path	**Tag**	day
Huf	hoof	**Puls**	pulse	**Thron**	throne
Hund	dog	**Punkt**	point		
Kurs	course	**Ruf**	call		

GROUP 2(b)

Example: **die Hand**, hand

	Singular	Plural
N	die Hand	die Hände
A	die Hand	die Hände
G	der Hand	der Hände
D	der Hand	den Händen

This sub-group contains all feminine nouns which do *not* follow the normal pattern of feminine nouns in the formation of their plural. They are mostly very common feminine nouns and are often favourites with examiners because they do not follow the usual pattern, so learn them carefully.

Axt	axe	**Haut**	skin	**Maus**	mouse
Bank	bench	**Kraft**	strength	**Nacht**	night
Braut	bride	**Kuh**	cow	**Nuß**	nut
Brust	breast	**Kunst**	art	**Schnur**	string
Faust	fist	**Luft**	air	**Stadt**	town
Frucht	fruit	**Lust**	pleasure	**Wand**	wall
Gans	goose	**Macht**	power	**Wurst**	sausage
Hand	hand	**Magd**	maid		

* The plural of **Knie** can also be **Knie**, i.e. no change. The plural of **Wrack** can also be **Wracks**.
† These nouns are rarely used in the plural.
° The plural of these nouns is usually **-sorten**, hence **Fleischsorten**, kinds of meat; **Obstsorten**, kinds of fruit.

GROUP 3

Example: **das Dorf**, village

	Singular	*Plural*
N	das Dorf	die Dörfer
A	das Dorf	die Dörfer
G	des Dorfes	der Dörfer
D	dem Dorf	den Dörfern

To this group belong:

(i) Nouns ending in **-tum**, e.g. **der Irrtum**, error.

(ii) The following group of common masculines:

Gott	God	**Leib**	body	**Wald**	wood
Geist	spirit	**Rand**	edge	**Wurm**	worm
Mann	man	**Strauch**	shrub		

(iii) The following group of neuters of one syllable and five neuters of more than one syllable. There is no Umlaut in the plural if the vowel is not an **a**, **o**, **u** or **au**.

Amt	office	**Haupt**	head	**Rad**	wheel
Bad	bath	**Haus**	house	**Rind**	ox
Bild	picture	**Holz**	wood	**Schild**	signboard
Blatt	leaf	**Horn**	horn	**Schloß**	castle
Brett	plank	**Huhn**	chicken	**Schwert**	sword
Buch	book	**Kalb**	calf	**Tal**	valley
Dach	roof	**Kind**	child	**Volk**	people
Dorf	village	**Kleid**	dress	**Weib**	woman
Ei	egg	**Korn**	grain	**Gehalt**	salary
Fach	compartment, subject	**Kraut**	herb	**Gemüt**	mind
Feld	field	**Lamm**	lamb	**Gesicht**	face
Geld	money	**Lid**	eyelid	**Gespenst**	ghost
Glas	glass	**Lied**	song	**Gewand**	garment
Glied	limb	**Loch**	hole		
Grab	grave	**Maul**	mouth		
Gras	grass (*plural very rarely used*)		(*of animals*)		
		Nest	nest		

GROUP 4

Example: **die Blume**, flower

	Singular	*Plural*
N	die Blume	die Blumen
A	die Blume	die Blumen
G	der Blume	der Blumen
D	der Blume	den Blumen

These nouns form their plural by adding **-n** or **-en**. They are nearly all feminines. There are very few feminine nouns which do not form their plural this way. (See Group 2(b)). A small point to note is that feminines which end in **-in** (e.g. **die Lehrerin**, schoolmistress) add **-nen** in the plural, so schoolmistresses=**die Lehrerinnen** in German. Most nouns that end in **-e**, except those listed in Groups 1(b) and 4(a), are in fact feminine and form their plural this way. A few examples are: **die Ecke**, corner; **die Farbe**, colour; **die Straße**, street; **die Welle**, wave; **die Wolke**, cloud. There are of course many more feminine nouns which belong to this group.

The following is a mixed list of feminines which all belong to this group and are mostly listed by the examining groups.

Antwort	answer	**Gabel**	fork	**Schrift**	writing
†**Arbeit**	work	**Gegend**	district	**Schuld**	debt
Art	sort, kind	†**Jugend**	youth	**See**	sea
Bahn	track, path	**Kartoffel**	potato	**Stirn**	forehead
Bai	bay	**Kur**	cure	**Tat**	deed
Bucht	bay	**Last**	burden	**Tür**	door
Burg	castle	**Leiter**	ladder	**Uhr**	clock
Eisenbahn	railway	**List**	cunning	**Wahl**	choice
Fahrt	journey	**Mauer**	wall	**Welt**	world
Feder	feather, pen	†**Milch**	milk	**Zahl**	number
Feier	celebration	**Nadel**	needle	**Zeit**	time
*****Firma**	firm	**Pflicht**	duty	**Zwiebel**	onion
Flut	flood	**Post**	post		
Frau	woman	**Saat**	seed		

* Plural = **die Firmen**.
† **Arbeit**, **Jugend** and **Milch** do not have a plural.

GROUP 4(a)

This group is usually known as the 'weak declension' because the letter -n is added in all cases except the nominative singular.

Example: **der Junge**, boy

	Singular	Plural
N	der Junge	die Jungen
A	den Jungen	die Jungen
G	des Jungen	der Jungen
D	dem Jungen	den Jungen

(i) To this group belong most masculines ending in -e. The exceptions are **der Käse**, cheese, and those listed under Group 1(b). The difference is that these do not have an -s in the genitive singular. Here are some of the commonest examples of masculine nouns which belong to this group:

Affe, monkey; **Franzose**, Frenchman; **Hase**, hare; **Löwe**, lion; **Matrose**, sailor; **Neffe**, nephew; **Russe**, Russian; **Schotte**, Scotsman.

(ii) To this group also belong many masculines of foreign origin, mainly denoting persons: **Dentist**, dental technician; **Elefant**, elephant; **Kamerad**, comrade; **Präsident**, president; **Soldat**, soldier; **Student**, student.

(iii) The following masculine nouns also belong to this group:

Bär	bear	***Herr**	gentleman	**Prinz**	prince
Bauer	peasant, farmer	**Mensch**	human being	**Spatz**	sparrow
Graf	count	**Narr**	buffoon	**Tor**	fool
Held	hero	**Ochs**	ox		

GROUP 5

Example: **der Staat**, state

	Singular	Plural
N	der Staat	die Staaten
A	den Staat	die Staaten
G	des Staates	der Staaten
D	dem Staat	den Staaten

(i) There are not many nouns which belong to this group. The following masculines are worth learning:

Direktor	headmaster	**Papagei**	parrot	**°Stachel**	sting
Doktor	doctor	**Professor**	professor	**Strahl**	ray
Dorn	thorn	**Schmerz**	pain	**Vetter**	cousin
†°Nachbar	neighbour	**°See**	lake		
Pantoffel	slipper	**Staat**	state		

(ii) The following neuters belong to this group:

Auge	eye	**Hemd**	shirt	**Leid**	sorrow
Bett	bed	**Insekt**	insect	**Ohr**	ear
Ende	end	**Interesse**	interest	**Statut**	statute

Note **das Museum**, museum, and **das Studium**, study, have the plurals **Museen** and **Studien**.

GROUP 6

Example: **das Auto**, car

	Singular	Plural
N	das Auto	die Autos
A	das Auto	die Autos
G	des Autos	der Autos
D	dem Auto	den Autos

* **Herr** is worth special note because it only adds -n in the singular: **Herrn**, and -en in the plural: **Herren**.
° **Nachbarn, Stacheln** and **Vettern** are the plurals, i.e. only -n is added.
† **Des Nachbarn** ending in -n is the usual genitive singular.

Points to note about this group are that they are all foreign nouns and because the plural is with **-s** there is no **-n** in the dative plural. Here is a short list of some of the commonest nouns in this group:

das Auto	car	**die Kamera**	camera	**der Streik**	strike
der Bankier	banker	**der Klub**	club	**der Tunnel**	tunnel
das Hobby	hobby	**der Park**	park		
das Hotel	hotel	**das Restaurant**	restaurant		

2 The gender of nouns

One of the most vexing problems that students of German at any level have to grapple with is the learning of the gender of all nouns. It is essential to learn all nouns with their gender and the plural.

Here are a few hints which will help you to learn the gender of nouns:

(a) Masculines

(i) Names of seasons, months, days of the week and points of the compass are all masculine: **der Frühling**, spring (etc.); **der Januar**, January (etc.); **der Sonntag**, Sunday (etc.); **der Norden**, north (etc.).

(ii) Persons carrying out a profession or trade; these nouns end in **-er: der Arbeiter**, worker or workman; **der Lehrer** teacher; **der Fleischer**, butcher (etc.).

(iii) Most nouns formed from the stem of a verb are masculine: **der Besuch**, visit; **der Rat**, advice (etc.).

(b) Feminines

Nouns which end in the syllables **-ei, -heit, -keit, -in, -schaft, -ung** are all feminine: **die Bäckerei**, bakery; **die Krankheit**, illness; **die Einsamkeit**, loneliness; **die Lehrerin**, schoolmistress; **die Freundschaft**, friendship; **die Wohnung**, flat.

(c) Neuters

(i) Infinitives of verbs used as nouns are all neuter.
e.g. **das Rechnen**, calculating, arithmetic; **das Singen**, singing.

(ii) All names of towns and most names of countries are neuter in German.
(Countries which *are not* neuter include: **die Schweiz**, Switzerland; **die Türkei**, Turkey.)

(iii) All nouns which end in **-chen, -lein, -ment, -sal** and **-um**.
e.g. **das Mädchen**, girl; **das Fräulein**, young lady; **das Element**, element; **das Schicksal**, fate; **das Studium**, study.

N.B. There are two nouns ending in **-tum** which are not neuter but masculine:
der Irrtum, error; **der Reichtum**, wealth.

(d) Nouns with two genders

There are some nouns which have two genders and mean different things according to the gender. The commonest of these are listed below:

der Band	volume	**das Band**	ribbon
der Bund	alliance	**das Bund**	bundle
der Erbe	heir	**das Erbe**	inheritance
der Flur	entrance hall	**die Flur**	field
der Gehalt	contents	**das Gehalt**	salary
der Hut	hat	**die Hut**	guard
der Kunde	customer	**die Kunde**	knowledge
der Leiter	guide	**die Leiter**	ladder
der Marsch	march	**die Marsch**	marsh
der Messer	measurer, meter	**das Messer**	knife
der Reis	rice	**das Reis**	twig
der Schild	shield	**das Schild**	signboard
der See	lake	**die See**	sea
die Steuer	tax	**das Steuer**	rudder
der Tau	dew	**das Tau**	rope
der Tor	fool	**das Tor**	gate
die Wehr	defence	**das Wehr**	weir

3 Proper nouns

Proper nouns include actual names like George, Henry and Mary, and the names of geographical features such as rivers and towns. In German as in English they have a capital letter.

(a) Proper nouns usually remain unchanged except in the genitive case where an **-s** is added as in English, but without the English apostrophe:

George's book, Georgs Buch
Mary's pencil, Maries Bleistift
Mr Smith's car, Herrn Schmidts Auto

Note that feminine names add the genitive **-s** in the same way as the others do.

(b) To form the plural of a surname, it is usual to add an **-s**, e.g. The Dinkelborgs=**die Dinkelborgs,** just as in English.

(c) Geographical names usually add **-s** in the genitive if they are masculine or neuter, but remain unchanged if they are feminine:

die Ufer des Rheins, the banks of the Rhine
die Geschichte Deutschlands, the history of Germany
but **die Ufer der Donau,** the banks of the Danube

4 The articles

There are two articles, known in English as the **definite article** and the **indefinite article**.

THE DEFINITE ARTICLE

In English, the definite article is 'the', and it is invariable. In German, however, the definite article changes to show the gender of the noun and also the case.
Here is the full declension of the definite article in German:

	Masculine	*Feminine*	*Neuter*	*Plural*	
N	der	die	das	die	*the*
A	den	die	das	die	*the*
G	des	der	des	der	*of the*
D	dem	der	dem	den	*to the*

Some forms of the definite article are usually contracted when used with certain prepositions. **Der, das** and **dem** contract as follows:

an das	becomes	**ans**	**in das**	becomes	**ins**
an dem	becomes	**am**	**in dem**	becomes	**im**
auf das	becomes	**aufs**	**um das**	becomes	**ums**
bei dem	becomes	**beim**	**von dem**	becomes	**vom**
durch das	becomes	**durchs**	**zu der**	becomes	**zur**
für das	becomes	**fürs**	**zu dem**	becomes	**zum**

There are some special uses of the definite article which should be noted:

(a) The definite article is used in German with names of days, months and seasons. It is usually omitted in English.

am Montag, *on Monday*   am Dienstag, *on Tuesday*
im August, *in August*   im Januar, *in January*
im Sommer, *in summer*   im Frühling, *in spring*

(b) The definite article is also used in German with masculine and feminine names of countries, rivers and streets. Remember most countries are neuter in gender.
Wir fahren in die Schweiz. *We are going to Switzerland.*
Er wohnt in der Friedrichstraße. *He lives in Friedrich Street.*
Es gibt ein Denkmal auf dem Potsdamer Platz. *There is a monumemt in Potsdam Square.*
Der Rhein fließt durch Köln. *The Rhine flows through Cologne.*
London liegt an der Themse. *London is on the Thames.*

(c) The definite article is used with proper names when they are preceded by an adjective:
der kleine Peter, *little Peter*
das heutige Deutschland, *present-day Germany*

(d) It is also used in expressions with parts of the body and clothes where in English we would usually use the possessive adjective:

Er hob den Arm. *He raised his arm.*
Die Schwestern schüttelten den Kopf. *The sisters shook their heads.*
Sie zog den Mantel aus. *She took off her coat.*
Er wusch sich die Hände. *He washed his hands.*
Er wusch ihr die Hände. *He washed her hands.*
Er hielt den Hut in der Hand. *He held his hat in his hand.*

(e) It is also used when talking about meals and in common phrases of transport, where in English it is omitted:

beim Frühstück, *at breakfast*   mit dem Zug, *by train*
in die Stadt gehen, *to go to town*   mit dem Flugzeug, *by air*
nach dem Mittagessen, *after lunch*   in die Kirche gehen, *to go to church*
in die Schule gehen, *to go to school*

(f) An important use is in phrases where the indefinite article 'a' or 'an' is used in English:
(i) drei Mark das Pfund, *three marks a pound*
zwei Mark das Kilo, *two marks a kilo*
(ii) zweimal in der Woche, *twice a week*
einmal im Monat, *once a month*

(g) A further case where the definite article is omitted in English but not in German is with abstract nouns:
Die Zeit ist für uns. *Time is on our side.*

OMISSION OF THE DEFINITE ARTICLE

The definite article is omitted in German in the following types of phrase or construction:

(a) Where pairs of nouns occur which are closely linked in one idea:
Wind und Wetter, *wind and weather*
Hand in Hand, *hand in hand*
Lesen und Schreiben, *reading and writing*
Mit Auto und Zug geht es schneller als mit dem Fahrrad.
It is quicker by car and by train than by bicycle.

(b) With **weder** and **noch** meaning 'neither . . . nor':
Er hat weder Vater noch Mutter. *He has neither father nor mother.*

THE INDEFINITE ARTICLE

This ('a' or 'an' in English) indicates that no particular one is meant. There is no plural form of the indefinite article. So **ein Buch**, a book, becomes **Bücher**, books, in the plural.

	Masculine	Feminine	Neuter	
N	ein	eine	ein	*a(n)*
A	einen	eine	ein	*a(n)*
G	eines	einer	eines	*of a(n)*
D	einem	einer	einem	*to a(n)*

The indefinite article is omitted in the following kinds of phrase or construction where we might expect to use the article in English:

(a) With nationalities or professions:
Er ist Arzt. *He is a doctor.*
Sie ist Französin. *She is a Frenchwoman.*

(b) Before a noun in apposition after **als** (*as*):
Er sprach als Freund. *He spoke as a friend.*

(c) With some prepositional phrases. Here are a few common examples:
ein Land ohne König, *a country without a king*
mit schwerem Herzen, *with a heavy heart*
mit lauter Stimme, *in a loud voice*

KEIN

Be careful when using 'not a' or 'not any' in German. **Nicht ein** means 'not one'; 'not a' is **kein**. The endings of **kein** are exactly the same as for **ein**. There is also a plural form, meaning 'not any'.

Er hat keine Tomaten gegessen. *He has not eaten any tomatoes.*
Er hat keine Lust nach Hause zu gehen. *He has no desire to go home.*

The full declension of **kein** – 'not a, no, not any' is:

	Masculine	*Feminine*	*Neuter*	*Plural*
N	kein	keine	kein	keine
A	keinen	keine	kein	keine
G	keines	keiner	keines	keiner
D	keinem	keiner	keinem	keinen

Note the differences and the similarities between the declensions of **der** and **ein**. The endings of both words are really very similar. Note that the neuter of **ein** is different because there is no ending in the nominative and the accusative. Similarly the masculine form of the nominative has no ending and looks exactly like the neuter. This means that when using the indefinite article without an adjective, the gender of the noun is not shown, as it is with the definite article. **Ein Mann** (a man) is obviously masculine, but **ein Vogel** (a bird) could apparently be masculine or neuter. In fact, it is masculine, but **ein Kind** (a child) on the other hand is neuter. Apart from the masculine and neuter nominative and the neuter accusative of **ein** the two declensions are identical. This is worth remembering because it establishes a set of endings which are repeated over and over again. The full declension of **kein** (not a) shows that this also holds true for the plural forms. Learn these two patterns very carefully. Learn to recognize the case and the endings associated with each case in the three genders and in the plural of the definite article.

5 The cases

Already in this unit we have given examples of nouns and articles showing how they change, and how different endings are used to show the case, the gender and the plural.

The idea of the different cases used in German can at first be difficult to understand, as very little use is made of case endings in English. However, there are some English words, e.g. personal pronouns, which *do* change according to the case in which they are being used within a sentence. 'I' sometimes becomes 'me', 'he' becomes 'him', and 'she' becomes 'her'. The change depends on the job that the word is doing in the sentence. This is really what cases are – they indicate the role of the word in the sentence.

Let us look at this in a little more detail. First of all we need to understand the structure of a sentence. The simplest sentences contain just a subject and a verb, e.g. 'He dreamed.' 'We left.' 'The clock struck.' The subject of a verb can be either a noun or a pronoun and its job is to show who or what did the action. The action is explained by the verb.

Here is a slightly more elaborate sentence, but it is still simple because it only contains one subject and one verb: 'The girl stayed at home with her brother.' This sentence consists of a subject – 'the girl', a verb – 'stayed', and two prepositional phrases, one of place – 'at home', and the other of manner – 'with her brother'.

Now let us look at some sentences which show the main use of each of the four cases that occur in German:

(a) The man gives the son the brother's pencil.
(b) The woman gives the sister the daughter's handbag.
(c) The child gives the girl the young lady's book.
(d) The parents give the friends the children's toys.

These sentences have been deliberately chosen because in German the nouns used in sentence (a) are all masculine. In (b) they are all feminine. In (c) they are all neuter and in (d) plural.

By learning these four sentences off by heart the case endings of nouns and of the definite article in all three genders plus the plural will be known. The pattern will have been established and this knowledge can then be applied over and over again in different contexts.

Each of these sentences contains the same five elements: a subject, a verb, a direct object, an indirect object and a genitive, which is the phrase which shows possession or ownership. It is important to be able to recognize these elements and the role they have in the sentence. If you know what the role is you will know which case is required in German and you can then use the appropriate ending.

The four cases in German are the nominative, the accusative, the genitive and the dative – N, A, G, D for short.

Here are the four sentences again, this time with the German as well as the English:

(a) The man gives the son the brother's pencil.
   Der Mann   gibt   dem Sohn   den Bleistift   des Bruders.
     (N)   (verb)   (D)   (A)   (G)

(b) The woman gives the sister the daughter's handbag.
   Die Frau   gibt   der Schwester   die Handtasche   der Tochter.
     (N)   (verb)   (D)   (A)   (G)

(c) The child gives the girl the young lady's book.

Das Kind	**gibt**	**dem Mädchen**	**das Buch**	**des Fräuleins.**
(N)	(verb)	(D)	(A)	(G)

(d) The parents give the friends the children's toys.

Die Eltern	**geben**	**den Freunden**	**die Spielzeuge**	**der Kinder.**
(N)	(verb)	(D)	(A)	(G)

The four nouns in these sentences each show one of the four cases in German and represent the main use of that case. Note that, except where the noun changes in the masculine and neuter genitive singular and the dative plural, it is the definite article which shows the case.

N: The **nominative** case is used for the **subject** of the verb.

A: The **accusative** case is used for the **direct object** of the verb. The direct object is the noun or pronoun which receives the action of the verb directly. In the examples above, 'what is given' in each sentence is the direct object, i.e. 'the pencil', 'the handbag', 'the book' and 'the toys'.

G: The **genitive** case is the one which shows **ownership** or **possession**, often indicated in English by 's or s'. In our four examples the words in the genitive are: 'the brother's', 'the daughter's', 'the young lady's' and 'the children's'.

D: The **dative** case is used for the **indirect object** of the verb. Indirect objects only occur with certain types of verb like 'give', 'show', 'buy'. The indirect object is the person or thing to whom or to which the action of the verb is done. In our four examples we could have changed the word order in the English and used the word 'to' before the indirect objects:

(a) The man gives the brother's pencil *to the son.*
(b) The woman gives the daughter's handbag *to the sister.*
(c) The child gives the young lady's book *to the girl.*
(d) The parents give the children's toys *to the friends.*

This is the best way to check for an indirect object. Insert the word 'to' and alter the word order. If this does not change the meaning of the sentence, the noun or pronoun with the 'to' in front of it is the indirect object and therefore in German it is in the dative case.

The other special uses of the four cases are dealt with elsewhere in this unit.

6 Adjectives

An adjective is a word used to describe a noun or a pronoun, e.g. a *small* chair, the *long journey,* an *old* friend; or: Clothes are *expensive.* She is *fat.* The road is *clear.*

From these examples you can see that an adjective can be used in two different ways, either immediately *before* the noun it describes ('small', 'long', 'old' in the examples given), or *after* the verb ('expensive', 'fat', and 'clear' above). The adjectives 'small', 'long' and 'old' are used *attributively,* while 'expensive', 'fat' and 'clear' are used *predicatively.*

It is the first kind of use – 'attributive' – which causes problems for students of German. In English, although we use adjectives in both these ways, they do not change. We say both 'The man is *tall*' and 'He is a *tall* man'. In German, however, there is a distinct difference: 'Der Mann is **groß**' (predicative use of **groß** – no ending, just like English), *but:* 'Er ist ein **großer** Mann' (attributive use of **groß**, where there has to be an ending on the *adjective* – in this sentence -**er**).

Part of the problem is that there are three different sets of adjective endings in German when adjectives are used attributively. (When an adjective is used predicatively in German, it is invariable – there are no endings.)

Here for reference are the three declensions of adjective endings in full, followed by some tips on how to remember them.

(a) Weak declension

This is used after **der** (the) and words declined like **der**, i.e. **dieser** (this), **jeder** (each, every), **jener** (that), **solcher** (such), **welcher** (which) and **alle** (all).

	Masculine	*Feminine*	*Neuter*	*Plural*
N	der gute Mann	die gute Frau	das gute Kind	die guten Eltern
A	den guten Mann	die gute Frau	das gute Kind	die guten Eltern
G	des guten Mannes	der guten Frau	des guten Kindes	der guten Eltern
D	dem guten Mann(e)	der guten Frau	dem guten Kind(e)	den guten Eltern

This really is very easy to remember, as there are only two endings: **-e** or **en**. Make a careful note of where the **-e** endings are used – they are above the line drawn through the declension.

(b) Mixed declension

This is used after **ein** (a, an), **kein** (not a/any), and the possessive adjectives, **mein** (my), **dein** (your), **sein** (his), **ihr** (her), **unser** (our), **euer** (your), **Ihr** (your formally) and **ihr** (their).

Using **kein** as the introductory word because **ein** has no plural form, here is the full declension:

	Masculine	*Feminine*	*Neuter*	*Plural*
N	kein gut**er** Wein	keine gute Milch	kein gut**es** Bier	keine gut**en** Eltern
A	kein**en** gut**en** Wein	keine gute Milch	kein gut**es** Bier	keine gut**en** Eltern
G	kein**es** gut**en** Wein**es**	keiner gut**en** Milch	kein**es** gut**en** Biers	keiner gut**en** Eltern
D	kein**em** gut**en** Wein	keiner gut**en** Milch	kein**em** gut**en** Bier	kein**en** gut**en** Eltern

This declension is very similar to the weak declension, and the main ending for the adjectives is again **-en**, as seen below the line.

(c) Strong declension

These endings are used when there is no preceding determining word like **der** or **ein**.

	Masculine	*Feminine*	*Neuter*	*Plural*
N	gut**er** Wein	frisch**e** Milch	kalt**es** Bier	frisch**e** Eier
A	gut**en** Wein	frisch**e** Milch	kalt**es** Bier	frisch**e** Eier
G	gut**en** Wein**es**	frisch**er** Milch	kalt**en** Bier(e)s	frisch**er** Eier
D	gut**em** Wein	frisch**er** Milch	kalt**em** Bier	frisch**en** Eiern
	(good wine)	*(fresh milk)*	*(cold beer)*	*(fresh eggs)*

The most important point about this declension is that as there is no determining word like **der** or **ein** the adjective follows the pattern of endings of **der** and **dieser**, except in the masculine and neuter genitive singular, where the ending is **-en**.

Secondly, these endings are used after the cardinal numerals (except **ein**), e.g. **zwei gute Bücher**, *two good books*, and after the words **viele**, **wenige**, **einige** and **mehrere**, e.g.:

viele kleine Kinder, *many small children*
wenige frische Eier, *a few fresh eggs*
ein Haus mit einigen großen Zimmern, *a house with some large rooms*
mehrere englische Touristen, *several English tourists*

If you now look at these three adjective declensions very carefully you will notice that the function of the determining word or article – **der** or **ein** – and of the adjective is simply to ensure that the number, gender and case of the noun are clear.

Let us take the strong declension first. Here the adjective has the same endings as **dieser** except in the masculine and neuter genitive singular. So if you know how to say 'these boys' – 'diese Jungen', you also know how to say 'good boys' – 'gut**e** Jungen' and so on in any other example you might like to test for yourself.

Comparing the weak and the mixed declensions you will see that the adjective always ends in **-en** in the genitive and dative cases, in the accusative of the masculine singular and throughout the plural. Therefore you should concentrate on the differences between these declensions in the other cases. These occur only in the masculine nominative singular and in the neuter nominative and accusative singular. So learn the following with special care.

(a) *Weak declension*   **(b)** *Mixed declension*
dieser gut**e** Mann   ein gut**er** Mann   (masculine nominative singular)
dieses gut**e** Kind   ein gut**es** Kind   (neuter nominative and accusative singular)

Here are some examples:

Der kleine Mann hat diesen grünen Hut.
   (N)   **(A)**

The small man has this green hat.

Die schöne Frau sieht ihre kleine Tochter.
   (N)   **(A)**

The beautiful woman sees her small daughter.

Das gute Kind findet ein rotes Buch.
   (N)   **(A)**

The good child finds a red book.

Die guten Freunde meines alten Onkels haben ein großes Haus.
   (N)   **(G)**   **(A)**

The good friends of my old uncle have a large house.

Ein guter Freund wohnt in Bonn.
   (N)

A good friend lives in Bonn.

Meine kleine Tochter liest ein altes Buch.
   (N)   **(A)**

My small daughter is reading an old book.

Sein schönes Haus liegt an einem kleinen See.
   (N)   **(D)**

His beautiful house is situated by a small lake.

To sum up:

(a) Strong declension adjective endings are like the endings of **dieser**.

(b) Mixed declension adjective endings show the gender in the masculine, feminine and neuter nominative singular and in the feminine and neuter accusative singular, i.e. **-er**, **-e**, **-es**, otherwise they are **-en** in all cases – not a lot to learn once you know how the cases work.

Other points about adjectives

(a) Almost all adjectives can be used as nouns. To do this simply write the adjective with a capital letter and decline it as above.

Der Alte sitzt im Gras. *The old man is sitting on the grass.*
Ein Alter kam ins Hotel. *An old man came into the hotel.*

(b) Some adjectives have a slightly different form when they are inflected:

dunkel (dark) loses the 'e': **ein dunkles Haus**, a dark house.
hoch (high) loses the 'c': **ein hoher Berg**, a high mountain.

(c) Adjectives can be formed from the names of towns by adding **-er**. These adjectives are indeclinable (invariable).

die Berliner Kaufhäuser, the department stores of Berlin
der Hamburger Hafen, the port of Hamburg

7 The comparative and superlative of adjectives

In English the comparative and superlative of adjectives are formed in two ways:

Basic	*Comparative*	*Superlative*
small	smaller	smallest
beautiful	more beautiful	most beautiful

The **-er/-est** endings are usually used with short adjectives, whereas the **more/most** combination is nearly always used with longer adjectives of several syllables.

In German, adjectives add **-er** or **-st**. The other form does not exist. In addition, some single syllable adjectives take an Umlaut where possible in the comparative and superlative forms (see the list below).

Basic	*Comparative*	*Superlative*	
klein	kleiner	der/die/das kleinste	(*small*)
stark	stärker	der/die/das stärkste	(*strong*)
intelligent	intelligenter	der/die/das intelligenteste	(*intelligent*)

Note

(a) Adjectives ending in **-e** only add **-r** in the comparative:
weise   weiser   der/die/das weiseste   (wise)

(b) Adjectives ending in **-el, -en, -er** usually drop this **-e** in the comparative:
dunkel   dunkler   der/die/das dunkelste   (dark)

(c) Adjectives ending in **-d, -t** or a sibilant add **-est** in the superlative:
hart   härter   der/die/das härteste   (hard)
heiß   heißer   der/die/das heißeste   (hot)

(d) The following adjectives modify the vowel by taking an Umlaut in the comparative and superlative:

alt	old	**hart**	hard	**scharf**	sharp
arg	bad	**jung**	young	**schwach**	weak
arm	poor	**kalt**	cold	**schwarz**	black
dumm	stupid	**klug**	clever	**stark**	strong
gesund	healthy	**krank**	ill	**warm**	warm
grob	coarse	**kurz**	short		
groß	big	**lang**	long		

(e) The following comparisons are irregular:

groß	**größer**	**der/die/das größte**	(big)
gut	**besser**	**der/die/das beste**	(good)
hoch	**höher**	**der/die/das höchste**	(high)
nah	**näher**	**der/die/das nächste**	(near)
viel	**mehr**	**der/die/das meiste**	(much)

(f) The comparative and superlative of all adjectives have to be declined like any other adjective, using the appropriate endings.

Er ist ein kleinerer Mann als ich. (attributive use) *He is a smaller man than I.* Er ist kleiner als ich. (predicative use) *He is smaller than I.*

(g) Be careful about the superlative. It must be a true comparison:

(i) *The coldest month is January.* Der kälteste Monat ist Januar.

(ii) *That book is good, but this book is the best.*

Jenes Buch ist gut, aber dieses Buch ist das beste.

But:

(iii) *That is a most interesting book.* Das ist ein sehr interessantes Buch.

In this third example the word 'most' is an adverb of degree intensifying the interesting quality of the book. In English, 'most' can be replaced by 'very' in such examples, without changing the meaning.

(h) Be careful when using 'most' in German:

most (of the) books, die meisten Bücher

most of my friends, die meisten meiner Freunde

These examples are with plural nouns. With a singular noun you have to 'get round' it as in the following example:

most of the book, der größte Teil des Buches

(i) The repeated comparative is translated by **immer** in German:

The holidays are getting shorter and shorter. Die Ferien werden immer kürzer.

(j) Other comparisons involving adjectives:

(Eben) so ... wie is used for comparisons of equals:

Hans is as tall as Fritz. Hans ist (eben) so groß wie Fritz.

Als is used for 'than' in a comparison of unequals:

Hans is taller than Fritz. Hans ist größer als Fritz.

Weniger ... als is used for comparisons of inferiority:

Hans is less clever than Fritz. Hans ist weniger klug als Fritz.

'Hans ist nicht so klug wie Fritz' is also possible.

Je ... desto (or **umso**) are used with comparatives as in this example:

Je früher die Sonne aufgeht, desto (or umso) später geht sie unter.

The earlier the sun rises, the later it sets.

8 Possessive adjectives

The following are the possessive adjectives seen in relation to the corresponding personal pronouns:

Pronoun	Possessive adjective	Pronoun	Possessive adjective
ich, *I*	mein, *my*	wir, *we*	unser, *our*
*du, *you*	dein, *your*	*ihr, *you*	euer, *your*
er, *he*	sein, *his*	sie, *they*	ihr, *their*
sie, *she*	ihr, *her*	*Sie, *you*	Ihr, your
es, *it*	sein, its		

*Note that there are three different forms of 'you' and 'your' in German. **Du** and **dein** should only be used when addressing one person who is familiar to the speaker or the writer, usually when addressing one close friend, one child, one member of the family or one animal. Similarly, **ihr** and **euer** are familiar forms, this time used when addressing more than one person. Always use **Sie** and **Ihr** for 'you' and 'your' when addressing any other person or persons (both singular and plural). Remember that **Sie** and **Ihr** *always* begin with a capital letter. They are called the 'polite' or 'formal' forms. The important thing to remember is to decide whether to use the familiar or the formal words for 'you' and 'your' and to stick to your choice without mixing the two. Also, do not forget to link the correct words for 'you' and 'your'–**du** with **dein** and so on. There are some examples illustrating the use of possessive adjectives on page 15.

First of all we need to look at the declension of the possessive adjectives. These are all declined the same way and have the same endings as **kein**. It is important to remember that **unser** (our) and **euer** (your), although they look like **dieser** (this), do not have the **der** declension endings, because they are **ein** words.

	Masculine	Feminine	Neuter	Plural
N	mein	meine	mein	meine
A	meinen	meine	mein	meine
G	meines	meiner	meines	meiner
D	meinem	meiner	meinem	meinen

All possessive adjectives take their number, gender and case ending from the noun they are describing and the role that noun plays in the sentence:

Jeden Tag fährt mein Vater mit seinem Auto in die Stadt.
Every day my father goes to town in his car.
Wie alt bist du, Hans? Dein Onkel ist Arzt, nicht wahr?
How old are you, Hans? Your uncle is a doctor, isn't he?
Lotte, Uschi, kommt herunter! Euer Frühstück ist auf dem Tisch.
Lotte, Uschi, come down! Your breakfast is on the table.
Ihr Bleistift ist rot, sein Füllfederhalter ist auch rot.
Her pencil is red, his pen is also red.

Note: although the English 'her' refers to a female, '**Ihr Bleistift**' is masculine singular nominative case, because the possessive adjective agrees in number, gender and case with *the noun it qualifies.*

Guten Morgen, Herr Schmidt! Ihr Kaffee ist schon bereit.
Good morning, Mr Smith! Your coffee is ready.

Remember adjectives after a possessive adjective have the mixed declension endings, e.g. unser alt**er** Großvater, *our old grandfather.*

9 Demonstrative adjectives

These are the words 'this', 'that' and 'such' in English. In German, **dieser** can be used for either 'this' or 'that'. **Jener** is usually used in contrast to **dieser**, and means 'that'. It is heard much less frequently than **dieser**. **Solcher** is the word for 'such', but see the examples below. **Dieser** and **jener** are declined like **der** (the), as follows:

	Masculine	*Feminine*	*Neuter*	*Plural*
N	dieser Mann	diese Frau	dieses Kind	diese Eltern
A	diesen Mann	diese Frau	dieses Kind	diese Eltern
G	dieses Mannes	dieser Frau	dieses Kindes	dieser Eltern
D	diesem Mann(e)	dieser Frau	diesem Kind	diesen Eltern

Diese Frage ist schwer, jene Frage ist aber ganz leicht zu beantworten.
This question is difficult, but that question is very easy to answer.
There are two ways of using **solcher** *meaning* 'such':

(a) Ein solcher Mann, *such a man* (**Solcher** is here declined like an adjective after **ein** – mixed declension endings).

(b) Solche Männer, *such men* (**Solcher** is here declined like **dieser**).

NB 'Such a' can also be translated by **solch ein** or **so ein**:
Such a pretty girl = **solch ein** hübsches Mädchen *or* **so ein** hübsches Mädchen *or* **ein so** hübsches Mädchen.

10 Interrogative adjectives

These are adjectives used in asking questions. There are basically two of them in German: **welcher** (which) and **was für** (what sort of).

(a) **Welcher** (which) is declined exactly like **dieser** (see above) and takes its number, gender and case from the noun it is describing in the usual way.
Welches Buch ist das? *Which book is that?*
Welchen Bleistift hat er in der Hand? *Which pencil has he in his hand?*
Mit welchem Zug fährt er nach Köln? *By which train is he travelling to Cologne?*

(b) Was für Blumen sind das? *What sort of flowers are those?* (plural)
Was für ein Hund ist das? *What sort of dog is that?* (singular)
Mit was für einem Kugelschreiber schreibt er?
What sort of ballpoint pen is he writing with? (singular)

Note that **was für** is uninflected – i.e. it does not change, but with singular words **ein** must be used in the appropriate case with the corresponding case ending, agreeing with the noun it describes.

11 Adverbs

Adverbs are words which describe or amplify the action of a verb. They fall into groups describing *when*, *where* or *how* things happen, e.g. 'always', 'upstairs', 'quickly'.
There are also adverbs which are used to qualify an adjective or another adverb. These could be described as 'adverbs of degree', e.g. He arrived *very* late. He did it *extremely* badly. He worked *surprisingly* long hours.

Very often you can recognize an adverb in English because it ends in '**-ly**'. In German, adverbs are used in much the same way as in English. They are particularly important words in examinations because they are so often overlooked by candidates. They are not used enough in productive writing, when you consider that they are much easier to use correctly than adjectives.

The most common adverbs are listed here:

also (then, therefore, so) NB It does *not* mean 'also'.
Also blieb ich in der Schule. *So I stayed at school.*

auch (also, too)
Er mußte auch nach Hause gehen. *He also had to go home.*

bald (soon)
Sein Vater kommt bald. *His father is coming soon.*

damals, dann, denn (then)

damals means 'then' in the sense of 'at that time' in the past.
Wir wohnten damals in Bonn. *We were then living in Bonn.*

dann means 'then' in the sense of 'after that' or 'next'.
Wir aßen unser Frühstück, und gingen dann zur Arbeit.
We ate our breakfast and then went to work.

denn means 'then' in the sense of 'well then' or 'so'.
Was ist denn los? *So what's the matter?*

doch (yet, however, but, after all, you know; also used for emphasis). It is clear that **doch** has many shades of meaning. The following illustrate a few of the commonest uses:
Er ist doch nicht gekommen. *He has not come after all.*
Er kann doch singen. *He can sing.* (emphatic use)
Aber er hat es doch selber gesagt. *But he said so himself, you know.*
Öffne doch das Paket! *Do open the parcel!*
Und doch habe ich nichts gemacht. *And yet I did nothing.*

doch is also used like 'si' in French, contradicting a negative question and meaning 'yes'.
Hast du ihn nicht gesehen? *Haven't you seen him?*
Doch, ich habe ihn gestern gesehen. *Yes, I saw him yesterday.*

eben (just, exactly – it does *not* mean 'even' as an adverb).
Das ist es eben, was er sagte. *That is just what he said.*

erst (not until, only)
Sie kam erst um vier Uhr an. *She did not arrive until four o'clock.*
Er ist erst zwanzig Jahre alt. *He is only twenty years old.*

fast (almost)
Er schlief fast ein. *He almost fell asleep.*

ganz (quite, completely)
Der Himmel war ganz schwarz. *The sky was quite black.*

genug (enough)   Used like 'enough' in English.
Er lief nicht schnell genug. *He did not run fast enough.*

gerade (just)   Used like **eben**.

gern (shows liking)
Ich trinke gern Bier. *I like drinking beer.*

immer (always, still)
Er kommt immer spät an. *He always arrives late.*

jetzt (now), and **nun** ('now' or 'well' without reference to time)
Es ist jetzt halb acht. *It is now half past seven.*
Nun, wie geht es dir? *Well, how are you?*

kaum (hardly, scarcely)
Er konnte kaum sehen. *He could scarcely see.*

lange (for a long time)
Der Mann stand lange vor dem Haus. *The man stood for a long time in front of the house.*

leider (unfortunately)
Heute abend kann ich leider nicht kommen. *Unfortunately I cannot come this evening.*

mal (just – reducing the emphasis in a command).
Sagen Sie mir mal, was geschah! *Just tell me what happened.*

noch (yet, still – but other meanings are possible).
Er schläft noch. *He is still asleep.*
Sonst noch etwas? *(Would you like) anything else?*
Noch ein Glas Milch, bitte. *Another glass of milk please.*

nur (only – do not confuse with **erst**, see above).
Ich wollte nur schlafen. *I only wanted to sleep.*

oft (often)
Sie fuhr oft in die Schweiz. *She often went to Switzerland.*

plötzlich (suddenly)
Er wurde plötzlich krank. *He suddenly became ill.*

schon (already)
Es regnet schon. *It is already raining.*

sehr (very, very much – used with verbs to denote degree, not quantity).
Danke sehr. *Thank you very much.*
Ich liebe ihn sehr. *I love him very much.*
Er ist sehr klug. *He is very clever.*

sofort, **sogleich** (immediately)
Wir gehen sofort nach Hause. *We are going home immediately.*

sogar (even)
Er wollte sogar meine Adresse haben. *He even wanted to have my address.*

sonst (otherwise)
Du mußt es mir sagen, sonst kann ich nicht mitkommen.
You must tell me, otherwise I am not able to come with you.

vielleicht (perhaps)
Sie haben vielleicht recht. *You are perhaps right/You may be right.*

wieder (back, again)
Er kam wieder nach Hause. *He came back home again.*

wohl (in the sense of 'I suppose').
Sie wissen wohl, was geschieht. *I suppose you know what is happening.*

ziemlich (rather)
Das kostet ziemlich viel. *That costs rather a lot.*

Many adjectives can also be used as adverbs. When used as adverbs, they do not have any case endings. They always remain the same in the basic form.
The commonest adjectives that are used as adverbs include the following. Note that the meaning changes sometimes from adjective to adverb.

früh, early (*adjective and adverb*)
gut, good (*adjective*), well (*adverb*)
einfach, simple (*adjective*), simply (*adverb*)
langsam, slow (*adjective*), slowly (*adverb*)
leicht, light, easy (*adjective*), lightly, easily (*adverb*)
schnell, fast, quick (*adjective*), quickly (*adverb*)
spät, late (*adjective and adverb*)
vollkommen, complete (*adjective*), completely (*adverb*)

Note these examples of an adjective, a present participle and a past participle being used as adverbs:

(a) ein schnell geschriebener Brief, a quickly written letter
(b) eine überraschend langsame Reise, a surprisingly slow journey
(c) er sprach sehr aufgeregt, he spoke very excitedly

Note also the formation of adverbs by adding **-erweise** to an adjective. Obvious examples are:
glücklicherweise (fortunately) and
unglücklicherweise (unfortunately)

Adverbs of place

Adverbs of place are very common.

oben, above, upstairs   **dort**, there   **mitten**, *plus preposition*, in the middle of
unten, below, downstairs   **da**, there   **hier**, here

Er ging nach oben. *He went upstairs.*
Mitten in der Nacht. *In the middle of the night.*

Hin and **her** are also very common as prefixes indicating 'place where to' and 'place where from':

Er ging die Treppe hinunter. *He went downstairs.*
Er kam die Treppe herunter. *He came downstairs.*

Hin implies motion *away from* the speaker.
Her implies motion *towards* the speaker.

Adverbs which ask a question

There are four of these in German that GCSE candidates should know. They are:

wo, where   Wo liegt das Buch? *Where is the book?*
wann, when   Wann beginnt die Schule? *When does school begin?*
wie, how   Wie alt ist er? *How old is he?*
warum, why   Warum spielt er Fußball? *Why does he play football?*

Wie can be combined with **viel(e)**
Wieviel Geld hat er? *How much money has he got?*
Wieviele Geschwister hat sie? *How many brothers and sisters does she have?*

The position of adverbs

Normally the adverb is placed next to the word it affects in German, but do not forget the other rules of word order, which must also be applied (see pages 47–9).

Er lief schnell die Straße entlang. *He ran quickly along the street.*
Er mußte den Brief von seiner Tante schnell lesen.
He had to read the letter from his aunt quickly.

12 The comparative and superlative of adverbs

This is similar to the comparison of adjectives except that the superlative has a different form – using **am** at the beginning and ending in **-sten**:

scharf (sharply), **schärfer** (more sharply), **am schärfsten** (most sharply)
klar (clearly), **klarer** (more clearly), **am klarsten** (most clearly)
schnell (quickly), **schneller** (more quickly), **am schnellsten** (most quickly)

In the use of the superlative it is very important to be able to distinguish between a true superlative and an expression of degreee or intensity. This is explained by the following examples:

Er spricht sehr klar. *He speaks most/very clearly.*
(i.e. an indication of how clearly he speaks)
Er spricht am klarsten in der Klasse. *He speaks the most clearly in the class.*
(i.e. a true superlative)

The superlative ending, **-st**, is sometimes used with certain words without any further ending, e.g. **höchst** and **äußerst** (extremely), **möglichst schnell** (as quickly as possible), **längst** (long since).

By adding **-ens** to certain words you form the other common adverbial expressions like **höchstens** (at the most), **meistens** (for the most part), **spätestens** (at the lastest), **mindestens** and **wenigstens** (at least).

There are a few irregular comparisons that ought to be known because they occur so frequently in examinations.

bald (soon), **früher** (earlier), **am frühesten** (at the earliest)
gern (willingly), **lieber** (more willingly), **am liebsten** (most willingly)
gut (well), **besser** (better), **am besten** (best)

The second example, **gern** (etc.) is particularly important because of its use in the idiom **gern haben**, to like.

Ich habe Mathematik gern. *I like maths.*
Ich habe Englisch am liebsten. *I like English best.*
Ich habe Deutsch lieber. *I prefer German.*

Remember **gern** (etc.) can be used with other verbs to show liking, e.g.
Ich trinke gern. *I like drinking.*   Ich trinke lieber. *I prefer drinking.*
Note the position of **gern** (etc.) at the end of the clause.

13 Negatives

Most of the following negatives are used adverbially:

nicht	not	**nein**	no
gar nicht	not at all	**nichts**	nothing
nicht mehr	no more, no longer	**niemand**	nobody
nie	never	**nichts als**	nothing but
noch nicht	not yet	**nirgendwo**	nowhere
nicht einmal	not even	**gar nichts**	nothing at all
noch nie	never yet	**weder . . . noch**	neither . . . nor

nicht . . . sondern . . .   not . . . but . . .
nicht wahr   isn't it, etc. – used as *n'est-ce pas* in French

Ich habe ihn nicht gesehen. *I have not seen him.*
Ich habe gar nichts gegessen. *I have eaten nothing at all.*
Er ist noch nicht gekommen. *He has not come yet.*
Er spricht nichts als die Wahrheit. *He speaks nothing but the truth.*
Er hat den Brief geschrieben, nicht wahr? *He has written the letter, hasn't he?*
Wir können nicht mehr ins Kino gehen. *We cannot go to the cinema any more.*
Er ist nicht klein, sondern groß. *He is not small, but tall.*
Sie kann weder singen noch tanzen. *She can neither sing nor dance.*

14 Personal pronouns

Pronouns are words which are used in place of nouns, but not all of the personal pronouns (see below) actually replace a noun. Like nouns in German, pronouns are used in the appropriate case according to their role in the sentence. In the third person they agree in number and gender with the noun they are replacing.

The chart below shows the forms of the personal pronouns. You will notice that the genitive case has been omitted. This is because pronouns in the genitive case are rarely used in German and are not expected to be known for GCSE. The layout of this chart is also slightly different because you need to know which pronouns are first person, second person and third person in both the singular and the plural.

		First person singular	*First person plural*
N	(*Subject*)	**ich**, I	**wir**, we
A	(*Direct object*)	**mich**, me	**uns**, us
D	(*Indirect object*)	**mir**, to me	**uns**, to us

		Second person singular	*Second person plural*
N	(*Subject*)	**du**, you (familiar)	**ihr**, you (familiar)
A	(*Direct object*)	**dich**, you (familiar)	**euch**, you (familiar)
D	(*Indirect object*)	**dir**, to you (familiar)	**euch**, to you (familiar)

		Third person singular			*Third person plural*
		Masculine	*Feminine*	*Neuter*	
N	(*Subject*)	**er**, he, it	**sie** she, it	**es**, it	**sie**, they
A	(*Direct object*)	**ihn**, him, it	**sie**, her, it	**es**, it	**sie**, them
D	(*Indirect object*)	**ihm**, to him, it	**ihr**, to her, it	**ihm**, to, it	**ihnen**, to them

The 'polite' form of 'you' in German is **(N) Sie, (A) Sie, (D) Ihnen**. These are all written with a capital letter and can all be either singular or plural.

Points to note are that the first and second person pronouns are basically new endings, but the third person pronouns are very similar to the endings of **dieser** (this). It is worth remembering to associate in the singular the ending **-n** or **-en** for the masculine accusative – **diesen** and **ihn**; the **-m** or **-em** ending for the dative singular of both the masculine and neuter – **diesem** and **ihm**; the **-r** or **-er** in the feminine dative singular – **dieser** and **ihr**; and the dative plural **-n** or **-en** – **diesen** and **ihnen**. Once again the pattern of endings is basically very similar to the one you already know.

It is comparatively easy to use first and second person pronouns correctly because they are used in a very similar way in English.
He sees me at the butcher's. Er sieht mich beim Metzger.
She gives us a book. Sie gibt uns ein Buch.
The **uns** in this example is dative (indirect object).

The third person pronouns need a little more care and thought when they are used, especially in the singular when you have to be sure you have not only the right case but also the right gender. Look at the following two passages carefully. Ask yourself which pronouns you ought to use for the nouns which are printed in dark type in the first passage. Then check to see if you picked the right one by looking at the second passage.

Passage 1

Liesel und Hans standen **im Krankenhaus** und sprachen mit **einer Krankenschwester**.
„Hatte **der Mann** nichts bei sich?" fragte **Liesel** endlich.
„Nein", antwortete **die Krankenschwester.**
Hans stand auf und trat an den kleinen Tisch an der Wand.
Da war eine alte Brieftasche. Er nahm **die Brieftasche** in die Hand, aber sie enthielt nichts.
Liesel öffnete **die Brieftasche** wieder und zog **ein kleines Stück Papier** heraus.
Sie nahm **einen Bleistift** und begann zu schreiben.

Passage 2

Sie (*they*) standen **darin** (*in it*) und sprachen mit **ihr** (*her*).
„Hatte **er** (*he*) nichts bei sich?" fragte **sie** (*she*) endlich.
„Nein", antwortete **sie** (*she*).
Er (*he*) stand auf und trat an den kleinen Tisch an der Wand.
Da war eine alte Brieftasche. Er nahm **sie** (*it*) in die Hand, aber sie enthielt nichts. **Sie** (*she*)
öffnete **sie** (*it*) wieder und zog **es** (*it*) heraus.
Sie nahm **ihn** (*it*) und begann zu schreiben.

How many did you get right? Did you spot the catch question where **darin** (see **(b)** below) had to be used instead of a pronoun? Did you remember that **Brieftasche** is feminine and therefore required **sie** in the accusative (er nahm **sie** *and* sie öffnete **sie**) and that **Bleistift** is masculine and had to be replaced by **ihn** because it is the direct object?

Three more points need to be made about personal pronouns.

(a) The uses of **es**:
 (i) In phrases like 'It is I', the word order is reversed in German and you say **'Ich bin es'**.
(ii) **Es** is used to mean 'there' in phrases like:
There are a lot of people going by. **Es** gehen viele Leute vorbei.
(iii) **Es gibt**='there is' or 'there are' in a general sense.
Es gibt Bücher in einer Buchhandlung. *There are books in a bookshop.*
But **es ist** and **es sind** mean 'there is' or 'there are' in phrases which are more specific:
Es sind zwei Bücher auf dem Tisch. *There are two books on the table.*

(b) Third person pronouns referring to things are replaced by **da-** or **dar-** when the pronoun is being used with a preposition (see **darin** above):
Er weiß nichts davon. *He knows nothing about it.*
Das Buch liegt darauf. *The book is lying on it.*
But: Wir wissen nichts von ihm. *We know nothing about him.*
In this last example the pronoun stands for a person and **ihm** is used. In the other examples **dar-** plus preposition is used when the preposition begins with a vowel.

(c) **Du, ihr** and **Sie** are the words for 'you'. Every student must know the difference between the formal **Sie** and its associated words and the familiar **du** (singular) and **ihr** (plural). See page 14.

When writing informal letters, which you are asked to do in almost all written papers in GCSE, **Du** and **Ihr** (you), **Dein** and **Euer** (your) should be used and written with capital letters:
Liebe Uschi,
Wie geht's Dir? Danke sehr für Deinen Brief, den ich gestern gelesen habe . . .

Reflexive pronouns

For the use of reflexive pronouns, please see the paragraph on reflexive verbs (page 37).

15 Relative pronouns

The relative pronouns cause some difficulty for English students because we do not always use them in sentences and constructions where they have to be included in German.

Basically a relative pronoun introduces a clause in a sentence which describes the noun for which the relative pronoun stands. Look at these examples:

 (i) The man sitting on the grass is my father.
 (ii) The man whom I saw yesterday left the hotel this morning.
(iii) The book which I read last year is on the table.
 (iv) Here is the letter I cannot read.
 (v) Where is the woman who was living here last year?

Three of these sentences contain the relative pronouns 'who', 'whom', and 'which' in English. In the other two the pronouns have been omitted. In English we also use 'that' instead of 'which' when referring to things, so the third example could have been written: 'The book *that* I read last year is on the table'.

The relative pronouns in English are 'who', 'whom', 'whose' and 'to whom' referring to people, or 'which' ('that') and 'of which' referring to things. In German the relative pronouns are declined as follows:

	Masculine	*Feminine*	*Neuter*	*Plural*	
N	der	die	das	die	*who, which*
A	den	die	das	die	*whom, which*
G	dessen	deren	dessen	deren	*of whom, of which, whose*
D	dem	der	dem	denen	*to whom, to which*

The most obvious thing about this declension is that it looks like the declension of the definite article ('the') with some additional endings in the genitive and in the dative plural. There is therefore very little that is new to learn about the relative pronouns as far as their formation is concerned.

How do we choose, then, which one to use in a given context? The rules in German are these:

(a) The relative pronoun takes its number and gender from the noun (or pronoun) for which it stands. This word is called grammatically the *antecedent*.

(b) The case of the relative pronoun is determined by the role it plays within the relative clause which it introduces.

(c) The finite verb in a relative clause in German must be placed at the end of the clause (see word order rules, pages 47–8).

(d) The relative clause must be separated from the rest of the sentence by a comma.

Let us now have another look at the five examples given earlier.

(i) The man sitting on the grass is my father.
We know that the relative pronoun has been omitted here so we should begin by thinking of the sentence as:
The man *who* is sitting on the grass is my father.
The relative pronoun is 'who' and the antecedent (i.e. the noun it stands for) is 'the man'. We know that 'the man' is masculine singular, so immediately we have narrowed the choice in German to **der**, **den**, **dessen**, or **dem**. Now comes the tricky bit. Which case is 'who' in the clause 'who is sitting on the grass?' In fact 'who' is the subject of the verb 'is sitting', so in German it must be the nominative. We therefore know for certain that the word for 'who' in this sentence will be **der**, which is masculine singular nominative. The complete sentence in German therefore is:
Der Mann, **der** auf dem Gras sitzt, ist mein Vater.
Note that **sitzt** comes at the end of the clause and the clause is separated from the rest of the sentence by commas.

By using the same technique and asking the same question we can work out the correct relative pronoun in the other four examples.
(ii) The man *whom* I saw yesterday left the hotel this morning.
Der Mann, **den** ich gestern sah, verließ heute morgen das Hotel.
(antecedent = the man, masculine singular; case = direct object, accusative)
(iii) The book *which* I read last year is on the table.
Das Buch, **das** ich letztes Jahr gelesen habe, ist auf dem Tisch.
(antecedent = the book, neuter singular; case = direct object, accusative)
(iv) There is the letter I cannot read. (relative pronoun missing)
There is the letter *which* I cannot read. (relative pronoun supplied)
Da ist der Brief, **den** ich nicht lesen kann.
(antecedent = the letter, masculine singular; case = direct object, accusative)
(v) Where is the woman *who* was living here last year?
Wo ist die Frau, **die** letztes Jahr hier wohnte?
(antecedent = the woman, feminine singular; case = subject, nominative)

Now look at these examples:
(i) Er nahm aus einem Loch in der Steinmauer einen Koffer, den er vor zwei Tagen dort versteckt hatte.
He took out of a hole in the stone wall a case, which he had hidden there two days before.
(masculine singular accusative)
(ii) Der Freund, mit dessen Bruder ich spreche, wohnt in Berlin.
The friend with whose brother (or with the brother of whom) I am speaking lives in Berlin.
(masculine singular genitive)

(iii) Sie gingen die Straße entlang, die zu ihrem Dorfe führte.
They went along the street which led to their village.
(feminine singular nominative)

(iv) Brigitte hatte eine Freundin, mit der sie oft den Abend verbrachte.
Brigitte had a friend with whom she often spent the evening.
(feminine singular dative)

(v) Ich wohne bei meinen Eltern, mit denen meine Schwester und ihre Katze auch wohnen.
I live with my parents, with whom my sister and her cat also live.
(dative plural)

Other points about relative pronouns

(a) der, **die**, **das** (etc.) can be replaced by:

	Masculine	*Feminine*	*Neuter*	*Plural*
N	welcher	welche	welches	welche
A	welchen	welche	welches	welche
G	(dessen)	(deren)	(dessen)	(deren)
D	welchem	welcher	welchem	welchen

Welcher, **welche**, **welches** (etc.) are much less frequently used than **der**, **die**, **das** (etc.), but can be used to avoid too much repetition.
Die, welche die Geschichte hörten . . . *Those who heard the story* . . .

(b) Wo- or **wor-** plus a preposition may be used instead of prepositions plus the relative pronoun when referring to things, not to people.
Der Tisch, worauf viele Bücher lagen . . . *The table on which there were many books* . . . Der Zug, womit er ankommt, . . . *The train by which he is arriving* . . .

(c) Wo also replaces the relative pronoun on occasions in expressions of place and time.
Die Stadt, wo ich wohne . . . *The town where (in which) I live* . . . Der Tag, wo ich sie das erste Mal sah, . . . *The day when (on which) I first saw her* . . .

(d) After **alles** and **nichts** the relative is **was**:
Alles, was ich habe . . . *All (that) I have* . . .
Nichts, was ich sage . . . *Nothing (that) I say* . . .

16 Interrogative pronouns

These are pronouns which are used in asking questions. They are especially important for students studying for GCSE because they are frequently used in the parts of the examinations where questions are asked in German.

In German as in English there are two kinds of interrogative pronouns, those referring to people and those referring to things. As you would expect in German, there are four cases and the case endings are familiar, this time being very similar to the relative pronouns **der**, **die**, **das**, etc. There is no plural form of these pronouns.

	Referring to people (m. and f.)		*Referring to things*	
N	wer	*who*	was	*what*
A	wen	*whom*	was	*what*
G	wessen	*whose*	wessen	*of what*
D	wem	*to whom*	(wem)	*(to what)* (rarely used)

The dative neuter form is rarely used because it would usually be required after a preposition, when it is replaced by **wo-** plus preposition, or **wor-** where the preposition begins with a vowel.
e.g. Womit schreibst du? *What are you writing with?*
This construction is used with prepositions whatever the case when the pronoun refers to a thing.

(a) Referring to people:
Wessen Buch ist das? *Whose book is that?*
Wer wohnt in diesem Haus? *Who lives in this house?*
Wen sah er gestern abend? *Whom did he see yesterday evening?*
Mit wem sprach er? *To whom was he speaking?*
Wem gab sie das Heft? *To whom did she give the exercise book?*
Wer sind deine Freunde? *Who are your friends?*

Also in indirect questions:
Ich fragte ihn, wen er gestern gesehen habe. (See pages 43–4 for the uses of the subjunctive.)
I asked him whom he saw yesterday. (NB verb at end of clause)

(b) Referring to things:
Was liegt auf dem Tisch? *What is on the table?*
Worauf liegt das Buch? *On what is the book?*
Was kann er sehen? *What can he see?*
Wovon spricht er? *What is he talking about?*
Woran denkst du? *What are you thinking of?*

17 Possessive pronouns

These should not be confused with possessive adjectives, although they look just like them in German. In English they are equally similar to the possessive adjectives (see pages 14–15).

meiner	mine	**ihrer**	hers	**Ihrer**	yours (*formal*)
deiner	yours (*familiar*)	**uns(e)rer**	ours	**ihrer**	theirs
seiner	his, its	**eu(e)rer**	yours (*familiar*)		

The endings of these pronouns are exactly the same as those of **dieser** (see page 15). They must agree in number and gender with the noun for which they stand and the case ending is determined by the role in the sentence or clause.

Er hat sein Buch verloren, ich habe meines auch verloren.
He has lost his book, I have lost mine too.
Ich habe meinen Kugelschreiber vergessen, er hat seinen auch vergessen.
I have forgotten my ballpoint pen, he has forgotten his too.
Note the phrase **ein Freund von mir** – a friend of mine.

18 Demonstrative pronouns

These are not very important in GCSE, except for **dieser** and **jener** which mean 'this one' and 'that one', and on occasions 'the latter' and 'the former'.

Dies and **das** can also be used for 'this' and 'that', and occasionally 'those', as pronouns.
Das ist meine Mutter. *That is my mother.*
Das sind meine Freunde. *Those are my friends.*
Herr und Frau Kittel sprachen miteinander; diese wollte einen Spaziergang machen.
Mr and Mrs Kittel were talking to each other; the latter wanted to go for a walk.

Derselbe, dieselbe, dasselbe, the same one
This declines as if it were two words: **der, die, das** (etc.) plus **selbe** as an adjective. It is, of course, written as one word.
Dieses Buch ist dasselbe, das ich gestern kaufte.
This book is the same one that I bought yesterday.

Like all pronouns, the demonstrative pronouns agree in number and gender with the noun for which they stand and take their case ending from the role they play in their part of the sentence.

19 Indefinite pronouns

There are two groups of indefinite pronouns:

(a) Those used only as pronouns:
man, one, someone
jedermann, everyone
jemand, someone
keiner, none, nobody
nichts, nothing
niemand, nobody

(b) Those used as pronouns and adjectives:
all, all
ander, other
beide, both
ein bißchen, a little
ein paar, a few
einige, some (*plural*)
etwas, some (*singular*)
genug, enough
jeder, each
mancher, many a
mehrere, several
viel, much
wenig, little

GROUP (a)

Man is used like 'on' in French. It can only be used in the nominative. If you need to use an accusative, genitive or dative, they are **einen, eines** and **einem** respectively:
Wenn einem nicht wohl ist, bleibt man besser zu Hause.
If one is not feeling well, it is better to stay at home.
The possessive adjective 'one's' is **sein**:
Man muß arbeiten, um sein Geld zu verdienen. *One must work to earn one's money.*
Keiner is declined like **dieser** and is used instead of **niemand**.
Nichts can be used with an adjective, in which case the adjective has to have a capital letter:
Ich habe nichts Neues gesehen. *I have seen nothing new.*

GROUP (b)

all, **alles**, **alle**, all
Ist alles da? *Is everything there (here)?*
all diese Leute, *all these people*
Alle sind gekommen *Everybody (all) has (have) arrived.*
alle zwei Wochen, *every other week, every second week.*

beide, both
meine beiden Schwestern, *both my sisters* or *my two sisters*
Alle beide sind schon weg. *They have both gone already.*

ein bißchen, **ein paar**, **einige**, **etwas**
ein bißchen Brot, *a little bread*
ein paar Blumen, *a few flowers* (i.e. *very few*)
einige Freunde, *a few friends* (i.e. *some*)
Ich will dir etwas sagen. *I want to say something to you.*
etwas Gutes, *something good* (for use with adjective, see **nichts**)

genug
Ich habe Zeit genug. Ich habe genug Zeit. *I have enough time.*
Note that **genug** can either follow or precede the noun it qualifies in German.

Mancher is declined like **dieser**.
manche alte Kirche, *many an old church*

Mehrere is declined like the plural of **dieser**:
mehrere grüne Äpfel, *several green apples*

Viel and **wenig** can be pronouns, adjectives or adverbs:
das wenige Geld, *the little money* (adjective)
Viele sind gekommen. *Many came.* (pronoun)
vielen Dank, *thank you very much* (adjective)
Viel Glück! *Good luck!* (adjective)
Er arbeitet viel. *He works a great deal.* (adverb)
mit ein wenig Geduld, *with a little patience* (adjective)
There is no hard and fast rule about whether they are declined or not.

20 Prepositions

Prepositions are usually small words which indicate *where, how* or sometimes *when* something is happening. In both English and German prepositions are used in many different ways, and the rules governing their use are very diverse. Consequently, no attempt has been made to give an exhaustive list of the uses of prepositions in German in this section, but those uses which candidates for GCSE examinations are expected to know are covered.

The case of nouns following prepositions depends on the preposition. Prepositions in German must therefore be learned in groups according to the case they govern.

PREPOSITIONS GOVERNING THE ACCUSATIVE ONLY

bis, till, as far as	**für**, for, by	**um**, round, exactly at
durch, through, by	**gegen**, against, towards, about	**wider**, against
*****entlang**, along	**ohne**, without	

bis:
Er bleibt bis nächsten Montag. *He is staying till next Monday.*
Bis morgen! *See you tomorrow!*
NB Before an article or a demonstrative or interrogative adjective, **bis** is usually followed by another preposition: the case is determined by the other preposition:
Sie ging bis an die Tür. *She went as far as the door.*
Wir gingen bis zum Ufer des Rheins. *We walked up to the bank of the Rhine.*

durch:
Er ging durch den Wald. *He walked through the wood.*
Er wurde durch eine Erkältung gewarnt. *He was warned by a cold.*
(For the explanation of **durch**, 'by' in the passive, see page 42.)

entlang:
Er fuhr die Straße entlang. *He drove along the street.*

* *NB* **entlang** follows the noun it governs.

für:
Er arbeitet für sie. *He works for her.*
Tag für Tag, *day by day*
(*NB* **für** is not usually used in expressions of time.)

gegen: ⎫ Both mean 'against', but **wider** suggests hostility. **Gegen** also means 'towards'
wider: ⎭ (place and time).
Er tat es wider meinen Willen. *He did it against my will.*
Wir laufen gegen den Wind. *We are running against the wind.*
Er fährt gegen Osten. *He is driving towards the East (eastwards).*
Gegen acht Uhr muß ich abfahren. *I must leave about eight o'clock.*

ohne:
Er kam ohne mich. *He came without me.*

um:
Sie saßen um den Tisch. *They were sitting round the table.*
um halb zehn, *at half past nine*

PREPOSITIONS GOVERNING THE GENITIVE ONLY

(an)statt, instead of   **während**, during   **innerhalb**, inside
trotz, in spite of   **wegen**, on account of, because of   **oberhalb**, above
um . . . willen, for the sake of   **außerhalb**, outside   **unterhalb**, below

anstatt/statt:
Both mean exactly the same thing.
statt meines Bruders, *instead of my brother*

trotz:
trotz des schlechten Wetters, *in spite of the bad weather*

um . . . willen:
Um Himmels willen! *For Heaven's sake!*
Um meiner Schwester willen. *For my sister's sake.*
Note: **um meinetwillen**, for my sake, **um seinetwillen**, for his sake, etc.

während:
während der Sommerferien, *during the summer holidays*

wegen:
Wegen seines Vaters habe ich nichts gesagt. *Because of his father I said nothing.*
Note: **meinetwegen**, on my account, etc., as **um . . . willen**.

außerhalb:
außerhalb der Stadt, *outside the town*

oberhalb:
oberhalb des Dorfes, *above the village*

innerhalb:
innerhalb eines Monats, *inside a month*

unterhalb:
unterhalb der Brücke, *below the bridge*

PREPOSITIONS GOVERNING THE DATIVE ONLY

aus, out of   **mit**, with   **zu**, to, at
außer, outside; except   ***nach**, to, after, according to   ***gegenüber**, opposite
bei, near   **seit**, since, for (*length of time*)   **von**, from, of, by

aus:
Er lief aus dem Haus. *He ran out of the house.*
Er kommt aus Bonn. *He comes from Bonn.*
Es ist aus Leder. *It is made of leather.*

außer:
Keiner außer ihm. *Nobody except him.*

* Both **nach**, when it means according to, and **gegenüber** follow the noun they govern.

bei:
Potsdam bei Berlin, *Potsdam near Berlin*
Er stand beim Fenster. *He was standing by/near the window.*
Er wohnt bei mir. *He is living at my house (with me).*
Ich habe kein Geld bei mir. *I have no money on me.*
beim Frühstück/Mittagessen, *at breakfast/lunch*
bei schlechtem Wetter, *in bad weather*

gegenüber: (often follows the noun it governs)
dem Rathaus gegenüber, *opposite the town hall*
der Kirche gegenüber, *opposite the church*

mit:
Er kam mit ihr. *He came with her.*
Sie winkte mit der Hand. *She waved her hand.*
mit der Zeit, *in (the course of) time*
Meaning 'by' in phrases of transport:
mit dem Zug, *by train*
mit dem Auto, *by car*
mit dem Dampfer, *by steamer*
mit dem Flugzeug, *by plane*

nach: = *to (somewhere)*
Er fuhr nach Berlin, nach Italien. *He went to Berlin, to Italy.*
Er ging nach Hause. *He went home.*
= *after*
Er kam nach mir. *He came after me.*
nach einer Weile, *after a while.*
= *according to* (when it usually follows the word it governs)
meiner Meinung nach, *in my opinion (according to my opinion).*
Seinem Brief nach ist er krank. *According to his letter he is ill.*

seit:
seit dem Krieg, *since the war*
Er wohnt seit vier Jahren in Köln. *He has been living in Cologne for four years.*
Seit einem Jahr wohnte er bei uns. *He had been living with us for a year.*

von:
von Zeit zu Zeit, *from time to time*
ein Mann von zwanzig Jahren, *a man of twenty years of age*
eine Frau von kleiner Gestalt, *a woman of small stature*
Wir sind von Paris nach Berlin gefahren. *We travelled from Paris to Berlin.*
Dieser Brief wurde von ihm geschrieben. *This letter was written by him.*
(For using 'by' in the passive, see page 42.)

zu: = *to*
Er ging zum Arzt. *He went to the doctor.*
Er ging zum Bahnhof. *He went to the station.*
Er ging zu Bett. *He went to bed.*
= *at*
zu Ostern, *at Easter*
zu Weihnachten, *at Christmas*
Briefmarken zu 60 Pfennig, *60-Pfennig stamps*

Other useful phrases:
zu Fuß, on foot
zu Pferd, on horseback
zum Beispiel, for example
zum Spaß, for a joke
zu Ende, at an end
zum Glück, fortunately

PREPOSITIONS GOVERNING THE ACCUSATIVE OR THE DATIVE

an, by, on, at, to	**in**, in, into	**unter**, under
auf, on	**neben**, beside, near	**vor**, in front of, before
hinter, behind	**über**, over, above	**zwischen**, between

These prepositions in their literal meanings refer mainly to places. The general rule as to which case should be used after them is straightforward. If the prepositional phrase explains 'where' something is happening, then the *dative* case must be used. If it indicates place 'whereto', 'motion towards', then the *accusative* case must be used.

Er ging **an die** See. (accusative) *He went to the seaside.*
Er wohnt **an der** See. (dative) *He lives by the sea/at the seaside.*
Das Buch liegt **auf dem** Tisch. (dative) *The book is on the table.*
Er legt das Buch **auf den** Tisch. (accusative) *He puts the book on (to) the table.*
Er fährt **in die** Stadt. (accusative) *He goes into town.*
Er wohnt **in der** Stadt. (dative) *He lives in town.*
Der Tunnel liegt **unter der** Elbe. (dative) *The tunnel is under the Elbe.*
Er schob den Stuhl **unter den** Tisch. (accusative) *He pushed the chair under the table.*
Sie sitzt **auf einer** Bank. (dative) *She is sitting on a bench.*
Sie setzt sich **auf eine** Bank. (accusative) *She sits down on a bench.*

an (plus accusative):
Er ging ans Fenster. *He went to the window.*
Sie kommen an die Reihe. *It is your turn.*

an (plus dative):
Er stand an der Tür. *He was standing at the door.*
Das Bild ist an der Wand. *The picture is on the wall.*
am nächsten Morgen, *the next morning*
am ersten Februar, *on February the first*
Er ging/fuhr am Postamt vorbei. *He went past the post office.*
am Wochenende, *at the weekend*
an der Mosel, *by/on the Mosel*
am Himmel, *in the sky*
an Bord, *on board*
an seiner Stelle, *in his place*

auf (plus accusative):
Er ging auf die Post/die Bank/die Universität.
He went to the post office/the bank/the university.
Er lief auf die Straße. *He ran into the street.*
Er ging aufs Land. *He went into the country.*
Er fährt auf eine Woche an die See. *He is going to the seaside for a week.*
auf diese Weise, *in this way*
auf jeden Fall, *in any case*
auf eigene Kosten, *at his own expense*
auf deutsch, *in German*

auf (plus dative):
Er war auf dem Markt. *He was at the market.*
Er stand auf dem Platz. *He was standing in the square.*
Er ist auf dem Lande. *He is in the country.*
auf der Straße/der Bank, *in the street/at the bank*
auf dem Rückweg, *on the way back*
Er wurde auf frischer Tat ertappt. *He was caught in the act.*

in (plus accusative):
Er reiste ins Ausland. *He travelled abroad.*
Er fuhr in die Schweiz. *He went to Switzerland.*
Er ging ins Theater/ins Kino/ins Büro. *He went to the theatre/the cinema/the office.*
Ich schnitt mich in den Finger. *I cut my finger.*
in die Schule/die Kirche/die Stadt gehen, *to go to school/church/town*

in (plus dative):
Er ist in der Nähe. *He is nearby (in the neighbourhood).*
Er arbeitet im Freien. *He works in the open air/out of doors.*
Er lebt im Ausland. *He lives abroad.*
im Fernsehen/im Radio, *on television/on the radio*
in der Schule/in der Kirche/im Konzert, *at school/at church/at the concert*
im ersten Stock, *on the first floor*
in diesem Augenblick, *at that moment*
im Stich lassen, *to leave in the lurch*
heute in acht Tagen, *a week today*

über (plus accusative):
Er fuhr über Ostende. *He went via Ostend.*
Er blieb über Nacht. *He stayed overnight.*
Er schwamm über den Fluß. *He swam across the river.*
Kinder über acht Jahre, *children over eight*

unter (plus dative):
Unter Freunden geschieht das nicht. *That does not happen among friends.*
unter meinen Sachen, *among my things*
unter diesen Umständen, *in these circumstances*
Das Paket wiegt unter einem Kilo. *The parcel weighs less than a kilo.*

vor (plus dative):
vor vielen Jahren, *many years ago*
vor allem, *above all*
vor kurzem, *a short time ago*
vor dem Krieg, *before the war*
Sie tanzte vor Freude. *She danced for joy.*
Er stand vor der Tür. *He stood in front of the door.*

21 Prepositions used with verbs, nouns and adjectives

an (plus accusative):
sich erinnern an, to remember
Ich kann mich an meine Großmutter nicht erinnern.
I cannot remember my grandmother.
sich gewöhnen an, to get accustomed to
Er gewöhnt sich an seine neue Schule. *He is getting used to his new school.*
denken an, to think of
Ich denke an die Sommerferien. *I am thinking of the summer holidays.*
schreiben an, to write to
Er schrieb an seinen Freund. *He wrote to his friend.*

an (plus dative):
leiden an, to suffer from
Er litt an der Grippe. *He was suffering from flu.*
sterben an, to die of
Er starb an der Grippe. *He died of flu.*
teilnehmen an, to take part in
Er nahm am Theaterstück teil. *He took part in the play.*
vorbeigehen an, to go past
Er ging an mir vorbei. *He went past me.*

auf (plus accusative):
antworten auf, to answer
Er antwortete nicht auf meine Frage. *He did not answer my question.*
blicken auf, to look at
Er blickte auf das hübsche Mädchen. *He looked at the pretty girl.*
sich freuen auf, to look forward to
Wir freuen uns auf die Ferien. *We are looking forward to the holidays.*
hoffen auf, to hope for
Sie hofft auf ein neues Kleid. *She is hoping for a new dress.*
warten auf, to wait for
Wir warten auf den nächsten Bus. *We are waiting for the next bus.*
zugehen auf, to go up to
Er ging auf sie zu. *He went up to her.*
zukommen auf, to come up to
Sie kam auf mich zu. *She came up to me.*
böse auf, angry with
Sie ist böse auf ihren Chef. *She is angry with her boss.*
stolz auf, proud of
Wir sind stolz auf unseren Hund. *We are proud of our dog.*

aus (plus dative):
bestehen aus, to consist of
Das besteht aus Holz. *That is made of wood.*

für (plus accusative):
halten für, to consider
Er hielt ihn für einen Verbrecher. *He considered him a criminal.*
sich interessieren für, to be interested in
Ich interessiere mich für Briefmarken. *I am interested in stamps.*

in (plus accusative):
einsteigen in, to get into
Sie stiegen in den Zug ein. *They boarded the train.*
übersetzen in, to translate into
Er übersetzte das Buch ins Deutsche. *He translated the book into German.*

in (plus dative):
ankommen in, to arrive at/in
Wir kamen in der Stadt an. *We arrived in the town.*

nach (plus dative):
schicken nach, to send for
Wir schickten nach dem Arzt. *We sent for the doctor.*
schmecken nach, to taste of
Das schmeckt nach Obst. *That tastes of fruit.*

über (plus accusative):
sich freuen über, to be pleased about
Wir freuten uns über seinen Brief. *We were pleased about his letter.*
lachen über, to laugh about
Er lachte über seine Fehler. *He laughed about his mistakes.*

um (plus accusative):
bitten um, to ask for
Er bat um Hilfe. *He asked for help.*
sich handeln um, to be a question of
Es handelt sich um die Freiheit. *It is a question of freedom.*

von (plus dative):
abhängen von, to depend on
Das hängt vom Wetter ab. *That depends on the weather.*

vor (plus dative):
sich fürchten vor, to be afraid of
Er fürchtete sich vor seinem Vater. *He was afraid of his father.*

Prepositions which govern verbs in infinitive constructions

(an)statt, instead of
ohne, without
um, in order to
All three are used with infinitives preceded by **zu**:
Anstatt sein Buch zu lesen, . . . *Instead of reading his book . . .*
Ohne nach Hause zu gehen, . . . *Without going home . . .*
Um ins Kino zu gehen, . . . *In order to go to the cinema . . .*

22 Verbs

Verbs are the most important words in any sentence. Without a finite verb there can be no sentence. The verb shows the action or the state of being in the sentence. For a verb to be finite it has to have a subject.

In German there are basically two types of verb, *weak verbs* and *strong verbs*. There is also a group of verbs called *auxiliary verbs*. As their name suggests, these are used to help form tenses or moods. The biggest group of verbs in German is that of the weak verbs.

Using **sagen**, to say, let us now look at the formation of all the tenses of a weak verb.

Sagen is the *infinitive* or the name of the verb. It is made up of a stem, **sag-** and an ending, **-en**.

The other parts of the verb are the two *participles*. The *present participle* always ends in **-d**. This ending is added to the infinitive to form **sagend**, *saying*. The *past participle* of a weak verb is usually formed by **ge-** + stem + **-t**, making **gesagt**, *said*. The past participle is used in the compound tenses in the past.

To conjugate a verb we need to know what endings are required in the six parts of each tense, as follows:

Present tense

	Singular		*Plural*	
1st person	ich sage	(I say)	wir sagen	(we say)
2nd person	du sagst	(you say)	ihr sagt	(you say)
3rd person	er/sie/es sagt	(he/she/it/says)	sie sagen	(they say)

2nd person (*singular or plural*) Sie sagen (you say)
All weak verbs have these endings in the present tense.

Imperfect tense or **Simple past tense**
Meaning: I said (etc.)

Singular	*Plural*
ich sagte	wir sagten
du sagtest	ihr sagtet
er/sie/es sagte	sie sagten
Sie sagten	

Perfect tense – formed with the present tense of **haben** plus the past participle.
Meaning: I have said (etc.)

Singular		*Plural*	
ich habe		wir haben	
du hast	} gesagt	ihr habt	} gesagt
er/sie/es hat		sie haben	
Sie haben gesagt			

Pluperfect tense – formed with the imperfect tense of **haben** plus the past participle.
Meaning: I had said (etc.)

Singular		*Plural*	
ich hatte		wir hatten	
du hattest	} gesagt	ihr hattet	} gesagt
er/sie/es hatte		sie hatten	
Sie hatten gesagt			

Future tense – formed with the present tense of **werden** plus the infinitive.
Meaning: I shall say, you will say (etc.)

Singular		*Plural*	
ich werde		wir werden	
du wirst	} sagen	ihr werdet	} sagen
er/sie/es wird		sie werden	
Sie werden sagen			

Future perfect tense – formed with the future of **haben** plus the past participle.
Meaning: I shall have said (etc.)

Singular		*Plural*	
ich werde		wir werden	
du wirst	} gesagt haben	ihr werdet	} gesagt haben
er/sie/es wird		sie werden	
Sie werden gesagt haben			

Conditional tense – formed with the imperfect subjunctive of **werden** plus the infinitive. (For the subjunctive, see page 43.)
Meaning: I should say, you would say (etc.)

Singular		*Plural*	
ich würde		wir würden	
du würdest	} sagen	ihr würdet	} sagen
er/sie/es würde		sie würden	
Sie würden sagen			

Conditional perfect tense – formed with the conditional tense of **haben** plus the past participle.
Meaning: I should have said, you would have said (etc.)

Singular		*Plural*	
ich würde		wir würden	
du würdest	} gesagt haben	ihr würdet	} gesagt haben
er/sie/es würde		sie würden	
Sie würden gesagt haben			

The imperative or command forms

sage!	say! (*familiar singular*)
sagt!	say! (*familiar plural*)
Sagen Sie!	say! (*polite form singular or plural*)
sagen wir!	let us say!

From this complete list of the indicative tenses of the verb **sagen**, to say, it becomes clear that there are two auxiliary verbs which are very important and which need to be known very carefully. These are **haben**, to have, and **werden**, to become. We can add a third auxiliary verb, **sein**, to be, because not all verbs form the perfect tenses with **haben** – some are conjugated with **sein**.

Here are the tenses of each of these important auxiliary verbs in full, omitting the subjunctive forms (see page 43).

Haben, to have

Present participle: **habend**, having

Past participle: **gehabt**, had

Present: I have (etc.)

ich habe	wir haben	
du hast	ihr habt	
er/sie/es hat	sie haben	
	Sie haben	

Imperfect: I had (etc.)

ich hatte	wir hatten
du hattest	ihr hattet
er/sie/es hatte	sie hatten
	Sie hatten

Perfect: I have had (etc.)

ich habe
du hast ⎫ gehabt
er/sie/es hat ⎭

wir haben
ihr habt ⎫ gehabt
sie haben ⎭

Sie haben gehabt

Pluperfect: I had had (etc.)

ich hatte
du hattest ⎫ gehabt
er/sie/es hatte ⎭

wir hatten
ihr hattet ⎫ gehabt
sie hatten ⎭

Sie hatten gehabt

Future: I shall have (etc.)

ich werde
du wirst ⎫ haben
er/sie/es wird ⎭

wir werden
ihr werdet ⎫ haben
sie werden ⎭

Sie werden haben

Future perfect: I shall have had (etc.)

ich werde
du wirst ⎫ gehabt haben
er/sie/es wird ⎭

wir werden
ihr werdet ⎫ gehabt haben
sie werden ⎭

Sie werden gehabt haben

Conditional: I should have (etc.)

ich würde
du würdest ⎫ haben
er/sie/es würde ⎭

wir würden
ihr würdet ⎫ haben
sie würden ⎭

Sie würden haben

Conditional perfect: I should have had (etc.)

ich würde gehabt haben (etc.)

Imperative:

habe! habt! haben Sie! haben wir!

Sein, to be

Present participle: **seiend**, being (very rarely used)

Past participle: **gewesen**, been

Present: I am (etc.)

ich bin	wir sind
du bist	ihr seid
er/sie/es ist	sie sind
	Sie sind

Imperfect: I was (etc.)

ich war	wir waren
du warst	ihr wart
er/sie/es war	sie waren
	Sie waren

Perfect: I have been (etc.)

ich bin			wir sind	
du bist	} gewesen		ihr seid	} gewesen
er/sie/es ist			sie sind	

Sie sind gewesen

Pluperfect: I had been (etc.)

ich war			wir waren	
du warst	} gewesen		ihr wart	} gewesen
er/sie/es war			sie waren	

Sie waren gewesen

Future: I shall be (etc.)

ich werde			wir werden	
du wirst	} sein		ihr werdet	} sein
er/sie/es wird			sie werden	

Sie werden sein

Future perfect: I shall have been (etc.)

ich werde gewesen sein (etc.)

Conditional: I should be (etc.)

ich würde			wir würden	
du würdest	} sein		ihr würdet	} sein
er/sie/es würde			sie würden	

Sie würden sein

Conditional perfect: I should have been (etc.)

ich würde gewesen sein (etc.)

Imperative:

sei! seid! seien Sie! seien wir!

Werden, to become

Present participle: **werdend**, becoming

Past participle: **geworden**, become

Present: I become (etc.)		**Imperfect**: I became (etc.)	
ich werde	wir werden	ich wurde	wir wurden
du wirst	ihr werdet	du wurdest	ihr wurdet
er/sie/es wird	sie werden	er/sie/es wurde	sie wurden
Sie werden		Sie wurden	

Perfect: I have become (etc.)

ich bin			wir sind	
du bist	} geworden		ihr seid	} geworden
er/sie/es ist			sie sind	

Sie sind geworden

Pluperfect: I had become (etc.)

ich war			wir waren	
du warst	} geworden		ihr wart	} geworden
er/sie/es war			sie waren	

Sie waren geworden

Future: I shall become (etc.)

ich werde			wir werden	
du wirst	} werden		ihr werdet	} werden
er/sie/es wird			sie werden	

Sie werden werden

Future perfect: I shall have become (etc.)

ich werde geworden sein (etc.)

Conditional: I should become (etc.)

ich würde			wir würden	
du würdest	} werden		ihr würdet	} werden
er/sie/es würde			sie würden	

Sie würden werden

Conditional perfect: I should have become (etc.)

ich würde geworden sein (etc.)

Imperative:

werde! werdet! werden Sie! werden wir!

23 The formation of tenses

From the charts above giving the full conjugations of the indicative tenses of **sagen** and **haben** (weak verbs), and **sein** and **werden** (strong verbs), we can draw up some rules for the formation of the tenses of virtually all the verbs any candidate for GCSE is likely to need to know. Because **sein** and **werden** are irregular strong verbs, **trinken**, to drink, has been chosen as the example of a regular strong verb.

It is worth noting that we have weak and strong verbs in English. The differences between the two sorts of verb lie in the formation of tenses and the fact that in a strong verb the stem changes. In a weak verb the stem remains the same whatever the tense. For example, 'to play' is a weak verb in English. The stem is 'play' and it occurs in all tenses and in the two participles. The present participle is 'playing'. The past partciple is 'played'. The simple past tense is 'I played' (etc.).

'To drink' is a strong verb in English. The stem is 'drink' in the present tense, but it changes to 'drank' in the simple past tense and the past participle is 'drunk'.

Weak and strong verbs in German show the same kind of differences.
Spielen, to play, is a weak verb. The principal parts of **spielen** are:

Infinitive	*Present tense*	*Imperfect*	*Perfect*
spielen	spielt	spielte	hat gespielt

The present participle is **spielend** and the past participle is **gespielt**.
Trinken, to drink, is a strong verb. The principal parts of **trinken** are:

Infinitive	*Present tense*	*Imperfect*	*Perfect*
trinken	trinkt	trank	hat getrunken

The present participle is **trinkend** and the past participle is **getrunken**.
For a full list of the principal parts of strong verbs see pages 52–4.

24 The present tense

For both strong and weak verbs the endings are:

-e, -st, -t, -en, -t, -en.

These endings are added to the stem of the infinitive:

spielen → ich spiele (etc.)
trinken→ ich trinke (etc.)

Some strong verbs have special forms in the present tense.
(a) Stem vowel **a** or **au**.
Most of these modify the vowel in the 2nd and 3rd persons singular, e.g. **fallen**, to fall, **laufen**, to run:

ich falle, du fällst, er/sie/es fällt, wir fallen, ihr fallt, sie fallen, (Sie fallen)
ich laufe, du läufst, er/sie/es läuft, wir laufen, ihr lauft, sie laufen, (Sie laufen)

(b) Stem vowel **e** (short) or **e** (long)
In most of these e (short) changes to **i**, e (long) changes to **ie**, e.g. **sprechen**, to speak, **lesen**, to read:
ich spreche, du sprichst, er/sie/es spricht, wir sprechen, ihr sprecht, sie sprechen, (Sie sprechen)
ich lese, du liest, er/sie/es liest, wir lesen, ihr lest, sie lesen, (Sie lesen)

25 The imperfect or simple past tense

Weak verbs add the following endings to the stem:

-te, -test, -te, -ten, -tet, -ten

e.g. ich spielte (etc.)
Strong verbs have a change of stem vowel. There are no endings added to the stem in the 1st and 3rd persons singular. The endings are therefore:

-, -st, -, -en, -t, -en

e.g. ich trank, du trankst, er/sie/es trank, wir tranken, ihr trankt, sie tranken, (Sie tranken)

26 The perfect tense

Both weak and strong verbs form this tense with the present tense of either **haben** or **sein**, plus the past participle of the verb concerned.

The past participle of most weak verbs begins with **ge-** and ends in **-t**, with the stem of the verb in between:

spielen→**gespielt.**

The past participle of most strong verbs begins with **ge-** and ends in **-en**, with the stem of the verb in between:

trinken→**getrunken.**

The past participle must be placed at the end of the clause in which it is used (see pages 47–8).

Gestern habe ich Fußball gespielt, aber ich habe nichts getrunken.
Yesterday I played football, but I did not drink anything.

The choice of **haben** or **sein** as the auxiliary verb causes problems for students. However, it is really comparatively easy if you understand the difference between a *transitive* and an *intransitive* verb.

The best way to distinguish between transitive and intransitive verbs is to remember that a verb can only be transitive if it can take a direct object, i.e. the accusative in German. All these transitive verbs, which are by far the bigger group, form their perfect tenses with **haben**.

The following verbs are intransitive in German. They form their perfect tenses with **sein**.

(a) **sein,** to be; **bleiben,** to remain

(b) verbs denoting a change of condition, e.g.:
   aufwachen, to wake up   **sterben,** to die
   einschlafen, to fall asleep   **werden,** to become

(c) some verbs which take the dative, e.g.:
   begegnen, to meet   __*__**gelingen,** to succeed
   folgen, to follow   __*__**geschehen,** to happen

(d) verbs of movement, e.g.:
   gehen, to go   **erscheinen,** to appear
   kommen, to come   **verschwinden,** to disappear

An important difference between French and German concerns reflexive verbs. In German they are transitive and use **haben** as the auxiliary verb in forming the perfect tenses. In French all reflexive verbs use *être* to form the perfect tenses.

27 The future tense

Use the present tense of **werden** together with the infinitive of the verb, which must be placed at the end of the clause in which it is used.
(weak)   Ich werde spielen.   *I shall play.*
(strong) Ich werde trinken.   *I shall drink.*

28 The conditional tense

Use the imperfect subjunctive of **werden** together with the infinitive, placed at the end of the clause in which it is used. (Note: The formation of the subjunctive is explained on page 43.)
(weak)   Ich würde spielen.   *I should play.*
(strong) Ich würde trinken.   *I should drink.*

29 The pluperfect tense

Use the imperfect of **haben/sein** plus the past participle of the verb concerned. Remember past participles are placed at the end of the clause in which they are used.
(weak)   Ich hatte gespielt. *I had played.*
(strong) Ich hatte getrunken. *I had drunk.*
(weak)   Ich war gereist. *I had travelled.*
(strong) Ich war gekommen. *I had come.*

__*__**Gelingen** and **geschehen** are only used in the 3rd person singular and are consequently known as *impersonal* verbs.
   Es ist mir gelungen. *I have succeeded.*
   Es ist früh am Morgen geschehen. *It happened early in the morning.*

30 The future perfect tense

Use the future of **haben/sein** together with the past participle. Note the word order. The infinitive (**haben/sein**) follows the past participle at the end of the clause.

(weak)   Ich werde gespielt haben. *I shall have played.*
(strong) Ich werde getrunken haben. *I shall have drunk.*
(weak)   Ich werde gereist sein. *I shall have travelled.*
(strong) Ich werde gekommen sein. *I shall have come.*

31 The conditional perfect tense

Use the conditional of **haben/sein** together with the past participle. The word order is the same as for the future perfect.

(weak)   Ich würde gespielt haben. *I should have played.*
(strong) Ich würde getrunken haben. *I should have drunk.*
(weak)   Ich würde gereist sein. *I should have travelled.*
(strong) Ich würde gekommen sein. *I should have come.*

32 The imperative

The imperative is used for giving commands. Four forms of the imperative are essential for GCSE. Three of them are the 2nd person forms connected with **du, ihr** and **Sie**. The fourth is the 1st person plural form 'Let us . . .'.

The 2nd person singular (familiar form) adds **-e** to the stem of weak verbs and most strong verbs except for those mentioned below.

The 2nd person plural (familiar form) is the same as the **ihr** form of the present tense without the **ihr**. It ends in **-t**.

The 2nd person polite form (singular or plural) is the same as the **Sie** form of the present tense with the **Sie** written after the verb.

The 1st person plural form is like the **wir** form of the present tense, similarly inverted.

When written, all forms require an exclamation mark to indicate that it is the imperative that is being used.

The examples which follow show all four forms of the imperative in a weak verb (**spielen**) and a strong verb (**trinken**).

spielen, to play
du form: **Spiele!** Play! (*2nd person singular familiar*)
ihr form: **Spielt!** Play! (*2nd person plural familiar*)
Sie form: **Spielen Sie!** Play! (*2nd person singular/plural polite*)
wir form: **Spielen wir!** Let us play! (*1st person plural*)

trinken, to drink
du form: **Trinke!** Drink!
ihr form: **Trinkt!** Drink!
Sie form: **Trinken Sie!** Drink!
wir form: **Trinken wir!** Let us drink!

The **-e** of the familiar form singular is dropped in strong verbs where the stem vowel changes from **e** to **i** or **e** to **ie**, as in the present tense (see page 33). It is also frequently dropped in conversation and in writing with certain very common verbs like **kommen, gehen, stehen, lassen.**

Geben, to give (**e→i**)
Gib mir das Buch! *Give me the book!*
Gebt mir das Buch! *Give me the book!*
Geben Sie mir das Buch! *Give me the book!*
Geben wir ihm das Buch! *Let us give him the book!*

Lesen, to read (**e→ie**)
Lies das Buch! *Read the book!*
Lest das Buch! *Read the book!*
Lesen Sie das Buch! *Read the book!*
Lesen wir das Buch! *Let us read the book!*

Steh auf! *Get up!*
Geh weg! *Go away!*
Komm schnell! *Come quickly!*

The 2nd person forms of the imperative of **lassen**, to let, can be used to translate 'let us . . .' (1st person plural). The phrase always includes **uns**, us, and has the infinitive of the verb concerned placed at the end:

Laß uns ins Kino gehen! *Let us go to the cinema.* (singular)
Laßt uns ins Kino gehen! *Let us go to the cinema.* (plural)
Lassen Sie uns ins Kino gehen! *Let us go to the cinema.* (singular/plural)

33 Simple and continuous tenses

A sentence such as:

Herr Braun geht nach Hause (present tense of **gehen**, 3rd person singular)
could be translated in three ways in English:

Mr Braun goes home, *or*
Mr Braun is going home, *or*
Mr Braun does go home.

This is because in English we have both simple tenses (e.g. he goes) and continuous tenses (e.g. he is going). We can also use the word 'do' to emphasize another verb (e.g. he does go).

In German, there is only one form of each tense. There are no continuous tenses in German, so to say e.g. 'He is drinking', you simply say 'Er trinkt'.

34 Addition of 'e'

Some verbs add an extra **-e** before certain endings. These are:
(a) weak verbs with a stem ending in **-d** or **-t**, e.g. **baden**, to bathe, **arbeiten**, to work.
(b) weak verbs with a stem ending in **-m** or **-n** preceded by another consonant, e.g. **atmen**, to breathe, **rechnen**, to reckon.
These all add an **-e** before the **-st** and **-t** endings of the present tense, throughout the imperfect tense and in the past participle.
e.g. **arbeiten**
Present tense:
ich arbeite   wir arbeiten
du arbeitest   ihr arbeitet
er/sie/es arbeitet sie arbeiten
        Sie arbeiten

Imperfect tense: ich arbeitete   Past participle: gearbeitet

Similarly: ich badete, du atmest, er atmete, gerechnet (etc.)

The main point about the extra **-e** is that it is inserted to make the word easier to say.
Strong verbs add an extra **-e** in a similar way, but there is never an extra **-e** when the stem vowel changes.
e.g. **finden**, to find
In the present tense an extra **-e** is added: du findest, er/sie/es findet, ihr findet. But in the imperfect, because of the change of stem vowel, no extra **-e** is required: du fandst, ihr fandt.
Take particular note of verbs like **halten**, to hold.
Present tense:
ich halte   wir halten
du hältst   ihr haltet
er/sie/es hält sie halten

No extra **-e** in the singular because of the vowel change, but 'ihr haltet' has the extra **-e**.

35 No 'ge-' in the past participle

Apart from inseparable verbs (see pages 38–40) there is one other group of verbs which does not have the **ge-** in the past participle. The verbs in this group are all weak and the infinitive ends in **-ieren**, e.g. **studieren**, to study; **rasieren**, to shave.
Er hatte studiert. *He had studied.*
Ich habe mich rasiert. *I have shaved.*

36 Mixed conjugation verbs

There is a group of nine verbs which are basically weak, but which change the vowel in the imperfect and the past participle. They have weak verb endings but a change of stem vowel, hence the name 'mixed conjugation'.

Infinitive	Meaning	Present	Imperfect	Perfect
brennen	*to burn*	brennt	brannte	hat gebrannt
bringen	*to bring*	bringt	brachte	hat gebracht
denken	*to think*	denkt	dachte	hat gedacht
*kennen	*to know*	kennt	kannte	hat gekannt
nennen	*to name*	nennt	nannte	hat genannt
rennen	*to run*	rennt	rannte	ist gerannt
senden	*to send*	sendet	sandte	hat gesandt
wenden	*to turn*	wendet	wandte	hat gewandt
†wissen	*to know*	weiß	wußte	hat gewußt

NB Compounds of these verbs follow the same pattern, e.g. **erkennen**, to recognize: ich erkannte; **verbringen**, to spend (of time): er verbrachte.

37 Modal verbs

There are six modal verbs which, like **haben, sein** and **werden**, are auxiliaries. For their use, see pages 44–5. The six verbs are:

dürfen, to be allowed to **müssen**, to have to
können, to be able to **sollen**, to be supposed to
mögen, to like to **wollen**, to wish/want to

The present indicative of each verb is slightly irregular, as follows:

ich	darf	kann	mag	muß	soll	will
du	darfst	kannst	magst	mußt	sollst	willst
er/sie/es	darf	kann	mag	muß	soll	will
wir	dürfen	können	mögen	müssen	sollen	wollen
ihr	dürft	könnt	mögt	müßt	sollt	wollt
sie	dürfen	können	mögen	müssen	sollen	wollen

The imperfect indicative endings are the weak verb forms **-te**, etc., i.e. ich durfte, konnte, mochte, mußte, sollte, wollte.

In the perfect tense, all six modal verbs use **haben** as the auxiliary, but the past participle is hardly ever used. The reason for this is that these verbs are usually accompanied by a **dependent infinitive.** When this happens the past participle of the modal verb is replaced by the infinitive in the perfect tenses.

e.g. Er hat nicht gehen können *He has not been able to go.*

For a fuller explanation of this and other details regarding modal verbs, see pages 44–5.

38 Reflexive verbs

These are the verbs which require a reflexive pronoun. The reflexive pronoun is usually in the accusative, though there are a few verbs where the reflexive pronoun is in the dative. The action is 'reflected on oneself' in a reflexive verb, as in this example.

sich waschen, to wash oneself
ich wasche mich	*I wash myself*
du wäschst dich	*you wash yourself*
er/sie/es wäscht sich	*he/she/it washes himself/herself/itself*
wir waschen uns	*we wash ourselves*
ihr wascht euch	*you wash yourselves*
sie waschen sich	*they wash themselves*
Sie waschen sich	*you wash yourself (yourselves)*

Waschen is a strong verb. Reflexive verbs can be weak or strong, separable or inseparable. What makes them reflexive is the use of the reflexive pronouns. For the position of pronouns see page 49.

* **Kennen** means 'to be acquainted with', and is normally used of people and places.
† **Wissen** means 'to know', of facts. It is also irregular in the present tense: ich weiß, du weißt, er/sie,es weiß, wir wissen, ihr wißt, sie wissen, (Sie wissen).

sich vorstellen, to imagine

This verb has the reflexive pronouns in the dative. It is a weak verb and has a separable prefix **vor**.

ich stelle mir vor	*I imagine*
du stellst dir vor	*you imagine*
er/sie/es stellt sich vor	*he/she/it imagines*
wir stellen uns vor	*we imagine*
ihr stellt euch vor	*you imagine*
sie stellen sich vor	*they imagine*

The commonest reflexive verbs are:

WEAK VERBS

sich ängstigen	*to become anxious*
sich ängstigen (um+**acc.**)	*to worry (about)*
sich anstrengen (**sep.**)	*to make an effort*
sich ärgern (über+**acc.**)	*to get annoyed (about)*
sich aufregen (**sep.**) (über+**acc.**)	*to get excited (about)*
sich ausruhen (**sep.**)	*to have a rest*
sich beeilen (**insep.**)	*to hurry*
sich bemühen (**insep.**)	*to take the trouble*
sich beschäftigen (**insep.**)	*to busy oneself*
sich entschuldigen (**insep.**)	*to apologize*
sich entwickeln (**insep.**)	*to develop*
sich erholen (**insep.**)	*to recover*
sich erinnern (**insep.**) (an+**acc.**)	*to remember*
sich erkälten (**insep.**)	*to catch cold*
sich freuen (über+**acc.**)	*to be pleased (about)*
sich freuen (auf+**acc.**)	*to look forward (to)*
sich hinlegen (**sep.**)	*to lie down*
sich interessieren (für+**acc.**)	*to be interested (in)*
sich (**dat.**) das Haar kämmen	*to comb one's hair*
sich kleiden	*to get dressed*
sich melden (zu+**dat.**)	*to report/present oneself (to)*
sich nähern (+**dat.**)	*to approach*
sich öffnen	*to open (as in 'The door opens')*
sich rasieren	*to have a shave*
sich setzen	*to sit down*
sich umkleiden (**sep.**)	*to get changed*
sich vorstellen (**sep.**)	*to introduce oneself*
sich (**dat.**) vorstellen (**sep.**)	*to imagine*
sich wohl fühlen	*to feel well/at home*
sich wundern (über+**acc.**)	*to be surprised (at)*

STRONG VERBS

(For details of principal parts see list on pages 52–4.)

sich anziehen (**sep.**)	*to get dressed*
sich ausziehen (**sep.**)	*to get undressed*
sich befinden (**insep.**)	*to be situated*
sich entscheiden (für+**acc.**) (**insep.**)	*to decide*
sich entschließen (**insep.**)	*to decide*
sich umsehen (**sep.**)	*to look around*
sich umziehen (**sep.**)	*to get changed*
sich unterhalten (**insep.**)	*to converse*
sich verfahren (**insep.**)	*to lose one's way (in a car, etc.)*
sich verlassen (auf+**acc.**) (**insep.**)	*to rely (on)*

The abbreviations used in the list above are as follows:

acc. = accusative; **dat.** = dative; **sep.** = separable; **insep.** = inseparable.

39 Separable and inseparable verbs

These are verbs which begin with a prefix (often a preposition), which, as its name suggests, is fixed on to the front of a basic verb. In every other respect the verbs are conjugated normally, depending on whether they are strong or weak.

There are three kinds of prefix:
(1) always inseparable; (2) always separable; (3) sometimes separable and sometimes inseparable.

There is only one way of remembering which is which and that is to learn them in groups. An aid to remembering which group a verb belongs to is that an inseparable prefix is not stressed in pronunciation – the emphasis falls on the stem of the basic verb.
  e.g. **beginnen** is inseparable; the stress is on **-ginn-**.
When the prefix is separable the accent falls on the prefix.
  e.g. **ankommen**, to arrive; the stress is on **an-**.

GROUP 1: ALWAYS INSEPARABLE

There are eight inseparable prefixes:

be-, ge-, er-, ver-, zer-, emp-, ent-, miß-

The only difference between an inseparable verb beginning with one of these prefixes and the basic verb from which it comes is that the inseparable verbs do not have a **ge-** in the past participle:

Er hat begonnen. *He has begun.*
Die Bombe hatte das Haus zerstört. *The bomb had destroyed the house.*

GROUP 2: ALWAYS SEPARABLE

Most of these prefixes are prepositions or adverbs. The reason why they are called separable is that they can be separated from the verb in the ways shown below.

Look at the following examples carefully. Note the position of the separable prefix.

Example: **ankommen**, to arrive
Main clause/statement:
  Er kam um acht Uhr **an**. *He arrived at eight o'clock.*
Subordinate clause when the verb is also at the end of the clause:
  Als er in Stuttgart **an**kam, regnete es. *When he arrived in Stuttgart it was raining.*
Compound tense with a past participle:
  Er ist noch nicht **an**gekommen. *He has not yet arrived.*
Infinitive construction with **zu**:
  Er mußte früh aufstehen, um pünktlich in der Schule **an**zukommen.
  He had to get up early, in order to arrive punctually at school.
Infinitive construction without **zu**:
  Er wollte um neun Uhr in Köln **an**kommen. *He wanted to arrive in Cologne at nine o'clock.*
See page 48 for the rules governing the position of separable prefixes.

The commonest separable prefixes plus an example of a verb are given in the following list:

Prefix	Infinitive	Meaning
ab-	abfahren	*to depart/leave/drive off*
an-	ankommen	*to arrive*
auf-	aufhören	*to stop/cease*
aus-	ausgehen	*to go out*
bei-	beibringen	*to teach*
dar-	darstellen	*to represent*
davon-	davonlaufen	*to run away*
ein-	einsteigen	*to get into*
entgegen-	entgegenkommen	*to approach*
fern-	fernsehen	*to watch television*
fest-	festhalten	*to hold on to*
fort-	fortsetzen	*to continue*
heim-	heimgehen	*to go home*
her-	herstellen	*to produce*
hin-	hingeben	*to give up*
los-	losgehen	*to set out*
mit-	mitteilen	*to inform*
nach-	nachdenken	*to consider*
nieder-	niedersinken	*to sink down*
statt-	stattfinden	*to take place*
teil-	teilnehmen	*to take part*
vor-	vorhaben	*to have in mind*
weiter-	weiterkommen	*to progress*
zu-	zugeben	*to concede, to admit*
zurück-	zurückgehen	*to go back*
zusammen-	zusammenstoßen	*to collide*

NB **hin-**, **her-** and **vor-** are often used with another preposition to form a few other separable prefixes, e.g. **hinausgehen**, to go out; **vorbeifahren**, to go/drive past.

GROUP 3

The only way to tell whether verbs with these prefixes are separable or inseparable is pronunciation. When they are inseparable the prefix is unaccented in pronunciation.
The prefixes concerned in this group are:

durch-, hinter-, über-, um-, unter-, voll-, wider- and **wieder-.**

In general, they are used separably when the verb has its literal meaning. The mark ′ indicates where the stress is laid in the examples below:

wiéderholen (**sep.**), *to fetch back*
wiederhólen (**insep.**), *to repeat*

Apart from **wiederhólen**, to repeat, **wieder-** is always a separable prefix.

Hinter-, voll-, wider-
These three are nearly always inseparable.

Voll- is only used separably when the verb is used quite literally.

e.g. Ich habe den Koffer vollgepackt. *I have packed the suitcase full.*

Durch- and **-um-**
Both of these are used either way quite frequently.
Durch- is always separable in the following:
dúrchfallen, *to fall through*   dúrchführen, *to carry through*
dúrchhelfen, *to help through*   dúrchlassen, *to let through*

It is always inseparable in:

durchlöchern, *to perforate*   durchkréuzen, *to cross*

A small number of verbs change their meaning according to whether **durch-** is separable or inseparable:

	Separable	**Inseparable**
durchblicken	*to look through* (*literal*)	*to see through*
durchbrechen	*to break . . . through*	*to break through*
durchsetzen	*to carry through*	*to mix, intersperse*

Er brach den Stock durch. *He broke the stick through.*
Sie durchbrachen die Linie. *They broke through the line*

Um- when used separably has three meanings:
(a) 'afresh' or 'over again'
umsteigen, to change (trains)
Sie stiegen in Köln um. *They changed in Cologne.*
(b) 'down'
umwerfen, to overturn
Der Wagen wurde umgeworfen. *The car was overturned.*
(c) 'in a reverse sense'
umkehren, to retrace
Er kehrte auf demselben Wege um. *He retraced his steps.*

Umbringen, to kill, and **umkommen,** to perish, are separable verbs.

Um- used inseparably generally means 'round' or 'round about'. Note these common examples:
umarmen, to embrace   **umgeben,** to surround

Über- and **unter-**
Both of these prefixes are usually inseparable, unless the verb has a literal meaning in a physical sense, i.e. broadly 'over' or 'under' – **hin** and **her** are frequently used in conjuction with these two.

Separable

untergehen, to set
Die Sonne ging gestern um zehn Uhr unter. *The sun set yesterday at ten o'clock.*
(hin)übersetzen, to take across
Der Mann setzte mich über den Fluß (hin)über. *The man took me across the river.*

Inseparable

überreden, to persuade   **unterbrechen,** to interrupt
Er konnte mich nicht überreden. *He could not persuade me.*
Sie unterbrach mich. *She interrupted me.*

40 Impersonal verbs

All impersonal verbs are used only in the third person singular with the subject **es**. They can be classified as follows:

(a) Those describing the weather:

es blitzt, *there is lightning*   es hagelt, *it is hailing*
es donnert, *it is thundering*   es regnet, *it is raining*
es friert, *it is freezing*   es schneit, *it is snowing*

(b) Those taking the dative:

es tut mir leid, *I am sorry*   es gefällt mir, *I like it*
es tut ihm weh, *it hurts him*   es gelingt mir, *I succeed*
es tut mir wohl, *it does me good*   es fällt mir ein, *it occurs to me*

(c) Those used reflexively:

es handelt sich (um + **acc.**), *it is a question (of)*
es lohnt sich, *it is worthwhile*

41 Uses of the infinitive

(a) The infinitive can be used as a noun. These nouns are always neuter.
Das Betreten des Rasens ist verboten. *Walking on the grass is forbidden.*
Beim Lesen des Briefes lächelte er. *On reading the letter he smiled.*

(b) The infinitive without **zu**:
(i) Infinitives dependent on modal verbs do not require **zu**:
Er kann nicht kommen. *He cannot come.*
(ii) Infinitives depending on **sehen** and **hören** also have no **zu**:
Ich sah ihn kommen. *I saw him coming.*
Er hörte sie kommen. *He heard her coming.*

(c) The infinitive with **zu**:
Generally infinitives are preceded by **zu** in German, except in the constructions explained above. Here are some examples showing the normal use of infinitives. Remember to place the infinitive at the end of the clause/sentence in which it is used.
(i) Ich habe nichts zu tun. *I have nothing to do.* (Main statement.)
(ii) Er hatte keine Lust, ins Kino zu gehen. *He did not want to go to the cinema.*
(When the infinitive construction includes another word, it must be separated from the rest of the sentence by a comma, as in this example.)
(iii) Ich freue mich darauf, ihn wieder zu sehen. *I am pleased to see him again.*
(As **(ii)**; and note the use of **darauf**.)
(iv) Obgleich das nicht leicht zu verstehen ist, muß er nach Hause gehen.
Although that is not easy to understand, he has to go home.
(This example shows the position of the infinitive in a subordinate clause, and an infinitive dependent on a modal verb.)

(d) The **um ... zu** construction.
This infinitive construction is separated from the rest of the sentence by a comma.
Er setzte sich hin, um die Zeitung zu lesen. *He sat down (in order) to read the newspaper.*

(e) Ohne ... zu (as **(d)**)
Er ging, ohne ein Wort zu sagen. *He went without saying a word.*

42 The present and past participles

Both the present and the past participles can be used as nouns. As nouns they are written with a capital letter and declined like an adjective:

der Reisende, *the traveller*   ein Reisender, *a traveller*
der Gefangene, *the prisoner*   ein Gefangener, *a prisoner*

They can also be used as adjectives, again with the appropriate endings:

ein lachendes Kind, *a laughing child*
der aufgeregte Junge, *the excited boy*

Note these two uses which are idiomatic to German:
Ein über dem Sofa hängendes Bild. *A picture hanging above the sofa.*
Er kam ins Zimmer gelaufen. *He came running into the room.*

The present participle is used much more frequently in English than it is in German. You must therefore take great care *not* to use the German present participle except in the kind of constructions described above. There are a number of different ways of expressing the English present participle, in which the German present participle must be avoided.

(a) You can use a clause beginning with **als**, **indem**, **nachdem**:
Als er zum Bahnhof ging, sah er seinen alten Freund, Fritz.
Going to the station, he saw his old friend Fritz.
Indem ich am Tisch saß, schrieb ich einen Brief. *Sitting at the table, I was writing a letter.*
Nachdem sie sich gesetzt hatte, begann sie zu weinen. *Having sat down, she began to cry.*
These three are all time clauses.

(b) You can use a clause beginning with **da** indicating a reason for doing something:
Da ich wußte, daß es dunkel wurde, machten wir uns auf den Weg nach Hause.
Knowing that it was getting dark, we set off for home.

(c) You can use a relative clause:
Ein Mann, der eine Zeitung las, saß ihm gegenüber.
A man reading a newspaper sat opposite him.

(d) You can make the present participle phrase into another main clause:
Er legte das Buch auf den Tisch und begann zu lächeln.
Putting the book on the table, he began to smile.

43 The passive voice

The passive is formed with the tenses of **werden** (one of the three main auxiliary verbs) plus the past participle of the verb which is in the passive. (In English we use the tenses of the verb 'to be' plus the past participle to form the passive.)
Look at these examples:

Tennis wird gespielt.	*Tennis is played.* (Present)
Tennis wurde gespielt.	*Tennis was played.* (Imperfect)
Tennis wird gespielt werden.	*Tennis will be played.* (Future)
Tennis würde gespielt werden.	*Tennis would be played.* (Conditional)
Tennis ist gespielt worden.	*Tennis has been played.* (Perfect)
Tennis war gespielt worden.	*Tennis had been played.* (Pluperfect)
Tennis wird gespielt worden sein.	*Tennis will have been played.* (Future perfect)
Tennis würde gespielt worden sein.	*Tennis would have been played.* (Conditional perfect)

Note that in the perfect tenses of the passive the **ge-** of **geworden** is omitted.

A passive construction can only be used if the verb is transitive, i.e. takes a direct object in the accusative. The person by whom the action is done is called the *agent* in the passive, whereas the thing by which the action is completed is known as the *means* through which the action is done.

We mainly write sentences in the active voice. To make an active sentence passive, the direct object has to become the subject. The tense of the passive is the same as that of the active. **Von** (+dat.) translates 'by' with an agent (person). **Durch** (+acc.) translates 'by' with things or the 'means'.

Active: Der Mann sah den Hund im Garten.
          The man saw the dog in the garden.
Passive: Der Hund wurde vom Mann im Garten gesehen.
          The dog was seen by the man in the garden.
Active: Die Bomben zerstörten die Stadt.
          The bombs destroyed the town.
Passive: Die Stadt wurde durch Bomben zerstört.
          The town was destroyed by bombs.

The passive can be avoided simply by turning the sentence into the active.
The lawn was mown by my mother.
Der Rasen wurde von meiner Mutter gemäht. (Passive)
Mein Mutter mähte den Rasen. (Active) *My mother mowed the lawn.*
Here the agent – **meine Mutter** – is used as the subject of the active sentence.

Where there is no agent the word **man** can be supplied. **Man** means 'one', 'they', 'you' in general terms.

Tennis wird gespielt.   *Tennis is played.* (Passive)
Man spielt Tennis.   *One plays tennis.* (Active)

Be careful not to mix up true passives like the examples above with the use of a past participle with **sein**, indicating the state of things.

Die Tür wurde von mir geschlossen. *The door was shut by me.*

This is a true passive involving the action of closing the door.

Die Tür ist geschlossen. *The door is shut.*

This indicates a state of affairs. The door is closed as opposed to open and no action is carried out. Hence the verb used is **sein** and not **werden**.

Some verbs take the dative case and are therefore intransitive. To make such verbs passive an impersonal construction has to be used:

Es wurde mir geholfen. *I was helped.* (Passive)

or more simply:

Man half mir. *One helped me* (literally). This is obviously the active version.

44 The subjunctive

The formation of the subjunctive is straightforward. There are really only two forms: the present and the imperfect. All the other tenses of the subjunctive are formed with either the present or the imperfect subjunctive of the auxiliary verbs **haben, sein** and **werden**.

The present subjunctive of all verbs, strong or weak, with the exception of **sein**, has the following endings, which are added to the stem of the infinitive:

-e, **-est**, **-e**, **-en**, **-et**, **-en**.

The present subjunctive of **haben**, to have, is:

ich habe, du habest, er/sie/es habe,
wir haben, ihr habet, sie haben, (Sie haben)

No vowel changes occur in the present subjunctive of strong verbs as they do in the present indicative.

ich werde, du werdest, er/sie/es werde,
wir werden, ihr werdet, sie werden, (Sie werden)

Only **sein** has a slightly irregular present subjunctive:

ich sei, du sei(e)st, er/sie/es sei,
wir seien, ihr seiet, sie seien, (Sie seien)

The imperfect subjunctive of weak verbs is the same as the imperfect indicative.

spielen, to play

ich spielte, du spieltest, er/sie/es spielte,
wir spielten, ihr spieltet, sie spielten, (Sie spielten)

Haben has an Umlaut throughout the tense:

ich hätte, du hättest, er/sie/es hätte,
wir hätten, ihr hättet, sie hätten (Sie hätten)

The only other weak verb formations which have an Umlaut are the modal verbs. Where an Umlaut exists in the infinitive it reappears in the imperfect subjunctive:

ich dürfte, ich könnte, ich möchte, ich müßte, ich sollte, ich wollte, *etc.*

Note the irregular imperfect subjunctives of mixed conjugation verbs:

ich brennte, ich kennte, ich nennte, ich rennte, ich sendete, ich wendete

The endings of the imperfect subjunctive are **-e, -est, -e, -en, -et, -en**. In using strong verbs these endings are added to the stem of the original verb in the imperfect indicative.

If the vowel of the imperfect indicative stem is **a, o, au,** or **u**, then an Umlaut is added in the imperfect subjunctive:

ich war (imperfect indicative)→**ich wäre** (imperfect subjunctive)
ich wurde (indicative)→**ich würde** (subjunctive)

USES OF THE SUBJUNCTIVE

English students are always puzzled by the subjunctive because it rarely causes any change of meaning when translating from German into English. One of the clearest forms is in the title of the song: 'If I *were* a rich man'. 'Were' in this context is the subjunctive in English.

Perhaps the easiest way to deal with the subjunctive in German is to learn carefully the types of sentence in which it is mainly used. In general terms the subjunctive expresses doubt, uncertainty or unreality. Its principal uses are:

(a) To express a wish:

Es lebe die Königin! *Long live the Queen!*

(b) The imperfect subjunctive frequently replaces the conditional tense of strong verbs, especially **sein. Ich wäre** – 'I should be' – is much more common than **ich würde sein**. The modal verbs, with the exception of **wollen**, also use the imperfect subjunctive instead of the more clumsy conditional tense. The same is true of **haben**.

So **ich dürfte, ich könnte, ich möchte, ich müßte, ich sollte** (I ought to) and **ich hätte** are preferred to the conditional tense.

(c) The pluperfect subjunctive is normally used for all verbs in preference to the conditional perfect.

Ich hätte gespielt. *I should have played.*
Ich wäre gekommen. *I should have come.*

(d) The subjunctive has to be used in reported speech in German:

Er sagte, daß er nicht angekommen wäre. *He said he had not arrived.*
Er fragte, ob er nach Hause gehen könnte (or könne). *He asked whether he could go home.*

Care is sometimes needed in deciding which tense of the subjective to use in reported speech. The general rule is that the tense of the subjunctive should be the same as the tense used when the words are *actually said* (as opposed to reported). This rule holds true for the present subjunctive as long as it differs from the present indicative. Where it does *not*, the imperfect subjunctive should replace it. This rule tends to be neglected in modern usage.

(e) After **als ob**, as if. This is a straightforward construction, a conjunction requiring the subjunctive.

Er sprach, als ob er krank wäre. *He spoke as if he was ill.*

Note the change of word order if the **ob** is omitted:

Er sprach, als wäre er krank.

(f) Conditional clauses with **wenn** meaning 'if'.
The indicative is used in the present and future but the subjunctive must be used in the past tenses.

Indicative: Wenn er kommt, (so) werde ich ihn sehen.
              If he comes, I shall see him. (Present/Future)
Subjunctive: Wenn er käme, | (so) würde ich ihn sehen.
                            | (so) sähe ich ihn.
              If he came, I should see him. (Past/Conditional)
              Wenn er gekommen wäre, (so) hätte ich ihn gesehen.
              If he had come, I would have seen him. (Pluperfect/Conditional perfect)

These are typical conditional sentences and should be learnt by heart. Do not forget that they can be streamlined a little by the omission of **wenn**, but watch the word order, which is very different, and remember that the **so** in the main clause becomes compulsory if **wenn** is omitted.

Here are the three examples without **wenn**:

Kommt er, so werde ich ihn sehen.
Käme er, so sähe ich ihn.
Wäre er gekommen, so hätte ich ihn gesehen.

45 The uses of modal verbs

The main use of modal verbs is with a dependent infinitive. Remember there is no **zu** before the infinitive after a modal verb and the infinitive must stand at the end of the clause or sentence in which it is used.

Er darf nicht ausgehen. *He is not allowed to go out.*
Wir können noch nicht nach Hause gehen. *We cannot go home yet.*

When a modal verb is used in the perfect tenses with a dependent infinitive, the infinitive of the modal verb replaces the past participle.

Er hat es tun müssen. *He has had to do it.*
Wir hatten es tun wollen. *We had wanted to do it.*

Note that, like the past participle which this replaces, the infinitive of the modal verb comes last of all.

The conditional perfect, usually written as the pluperfect subjunctive, is worth taking special note of, as in these examples.

Ich hätte es tun dürfen. *I should have been allowed to do it.*
Ich hätte es tun mögen. *I should have liked to do it.*
Ich hätte es tun müssen. *I should have had to do it.*
Ich hätte es tun wollen. *I should have wanted to do it.*
Ich hätte es tun können. *I could have done it.*
Ich hätte es tun sollen. *I ought to have done it.*

The last two examples have a slightly different construction in English, as can be seen from the meaning.

These two infinitives coming together at the end of a clause/sentence as in the examples given remain at the end when the construction is used in a subordinate clause. The finite verb precedes the two infinitives at the end of the clause. With modal verbs this can happen in the perfect tenses, the future and the conditional tenses.

Ich weiß nicht, ob ich den Brief **werde** schreiben müssen.
I do not know whether I shall have to write the letter.
Obgleich er gestern **hätte** kommen sollen, ist er noch nicht angekommen.
Although he ought to have come yesterday, he has still not arrived.

DÜRFEN

Denotes permission to do something – in the negative it is a prohibition.
Darf ich ins Kino gehen? *May I go to the cinema?*
Das durfte er tun. *He was allowed to do that.*
Wir dürfen nicht hier Fußball spielen. *We must not play football here.*

KÖNNEN

Denotes possibility, ability or knowledge.
Das könnte sein. *That could be.*
Er kann sehr schnell laufen. *He can run very fast.*
Sie kann Deutsch. *She can speak German.*

MÖGEN

Denotes possibility, inclination or liking.
Das mag sein. *That may be.*
Ich möchte gerne in die Schweiz fahren. *I should like to go to Switzerland.*

MÜSSEN

Denotes compulsion, or being obliged to.
Das muß schwer sein. *That must be difficult.*
Er muß in die Schule gehen. *He has to go to school.*
Wir mußten lachen. *We had to laugh. (We could not help laughing.)*
Note the difference between:
Er muß einen Bleistift kaufen. *He has to buy a pencil.*
and Er hat ein Haus zu verkaufen. *He has a house to sell.*

Remember – 'must not' usually means 'is not allowed to' and is therefore **dürfen nicht** in German.

SOLLEN

Means 'to be to', 'to be supposed to', 'shall', 'should'.
Er soll nach Italien fahren. *He is to go to Italy.*
Der Prinz soll sehr reich sein. *The prince is supposed to be very rich.*
Er sollte später eine Reise machen. *He was to go on a journey later.*
Er sollte das nicht tun, weil es gefährlich ist. *He should not do that because it is dangerous.*
Er sollte nächste Woche abfahren. *He ought to leave next week.*

WOLLEN

Denotes wish, willingness, intention.
Wollen Sie mitkommen? *Will you come with (me)?*
Er will alles sehen. *He wants to see everything.*
Wir wollen eben ausgehen. *We are on the point of going out.*
Die Sonne wollte eben aufgehen. *The sun was about to rise.*

LASSEN

Though not a modal verb, **lassen** is used in a similar way to the modal verbs. It means 'to let', 'to allow', 'to leave', 'to have (something done)', or 'to make'.
Laß mich kommen! *Let me come!*
Er ließ sie nicht zur Diskothek gehen. *He did not allow her to go to the disco.*
Ich habe das Buch auf dem Tisch liegen lassen. *I have left the book lying on the table.*
Ich habe mir die Haare schneiden lassen. *I have had my hair cut.*
Er hat mich warten lassen. *He made me wait.*

46 The uses of tenses

The **present tense** is generally used in German as it is in English. Note the use of the present tense in German with **seit** (+dat.) to indicate an action which is still going on at the time of writing or speaking, even though in English the perfect tense is used.

Er wohnt seit vier Jahren in Köln. *He has been living in Cologne for four years.*

The present tense also translates the immediate future in German:

Ich schreibe dir bald. *I shall soon be writing to you.*

The **imperfect tense** is the main past tense, used for telling a story:

Ich stand auf, ging ins Badezimmer, wusch mich schnell, ging die Treppe hinunter, setzte mich an den Tisch und begann, die Zeitung zu lesen.

I got up, went to the bathroom, washed myself quickly, went downstairs, sat down at the table and began to read the newspaper.

The imperfect is used for 'would' in the sense of 'used to' (i.e. a repeated/habitual action in the past).

Er las jeden Tag die Zeitung. *He would (used to) read the paper every day.*

The imperfect with **seit** (+dat.) expresses what had been going on and still was going on, even though in English the pluperfect is used:

Er arbeitete schon seit vier Stunden. *He had already been working for four hours.*

The **perfect tense** is used for isolated acts in the recent past where English often uses the simple past tense.

Er hat heute angerufen. *He rang up today.*

47 Cases after verbs

After intransitive verbs the complement is in the nominative case:
Es war ein schöner Tag. *It was a fine day.*

The **accusative** case is used for the direct object of a transitive verb:
Der Polizist sah den Straßenunfall. *The policeman saw the road accident.*

Some verbs have two accusatives:
Er lehrte mich Erdkunde. *He taught me geography.*

The following verbs govern the *dative* (not the accusative):

begegnen, to meet	**gefallen**, to please	**glauben**, to believe
danken, to thank	**gehorchen**, to obey	**helfen**, to help
folgen, to follow	**gelingen**, to succeed	**(sich) nähern**, to approach

Er folgte mir ins Kino. *He followed me to the cinema.*
Wir müssen ihm gehorchen. *We must obey him.*
Er hat dem jungen Mann geholfen. *He has helped the young man.*
Niemand wollte ihm glauben. *No one wanted to believe him.*

48 Conjunctions

These are usually small words used to join clauses together to make longer, often more complex sentences. There are basically two types: **(a)** 'co-ordinating' and **(b)** 'subordinating' conjunctions.

(a) Co-ordinating conjunctions link clauses without affecting the word order. They are:

und, and   **aber**, but
oder, or   **sondern**, but (after a negative, contradicting)
denn, for

Er kann heute nicht kommen, denn er ist viel zu krank.
He cannot come today, for (because) he is much too ill.
Heinrich wollte nicht arbeiten, sondern er wollte spielen.
Heinrich did not want to work, but he wanted to play.

Und, oder and **sondern** can also link nouns, pronouns, adjectives, etc. with one another; **aber** can be used to link adjectives.

du und ich, *you and I*
meine Schwester oder mein Vater, *my sister or my father*
Sie ist nicht schön, sondern häßlich. *She is not beautiful, but ugly.*
Er ist klug, aber faul. *He is clever, but lazy.*

(b) Subordinating conjunctions introduce subordinate clauses in which the finite verb is placed at the end of the clause. The difference between a main clause and a subordinate clause is that a **main clause** can stand on its own. It is independent of any other part of a sentence. Frequently it is a sentence itself.

'Paul helps his father in the garden', is a main clause/statement/sentence. But 'If he finishes his work . . .' is a **subordinate clause** which demands a follow-on statement to complete the sense.

The most common of the subordinating conjunctions are:

als,	when, as	**seitdem,**	since
als ob,	as if	**sobald,**	as soon as
als wenn,	as if	**sowie,**	as soon as
auch wenn,	even if	**solange,**	as long as
bis,	until	**so daß,**	so that
bevor,	before	**sooft,**	as, often as
ehe,	before	**während,**	while
da,	as, since	**wenn,**	when, if
daß,	that	**wenn auch,**	
damit,	in order that	**selbst wenn,**	}even if
falls,	in case that	**auch wenn,**	
indem,	while	**wann,**	when (*indirect question*)
nachdem,	after	**weil,**	because
ob,	whether, if	**wie,**	how, as
obgleich			
obschon	}although		
obwohl			

Bevor er zu Bett ging, trank er ein Glas Milch.
Before he went to bed, he drank a glass of milk.
Er konnte nicht ausgehen, weil er so krank war.
He could not go out, because he was so ill.

49 Word order

The rules concerning word order in German are very important. They are formal and rarely alter. Unlike English, German does not depend on the order of the words to convey the sense. Reverse the positions of the subject and the direct object of a verb in English and you change the meaning completely:

(a) The girl saw the man in the town.

(b) The man saw the girl in the town.

Now look at these two German sentences:

(a) Das Mädchen sah den Mann in der Stadt.

(b) Den Mann sah das Mädchen in der Stadt.

In German both sentences mean the same, even though the word order has changed. The reason for this is that we know which is the subject (nominative case) and which is the direct object (accusative case) because of the case ending. Therefore in **(b) den Mann** is accusative (direct object); the subject of the verb is **das Mädchen**.

RULES GOVERNING WORD ORDER

Rule 1

(a) Main clauses (statements)
In a main clause the finite verb must be the second idea. Frequently the subject of the verb will be the first idea:

Der junge Mann **stand** vor dem Rathaus.
The young man was standing in front of the town hall.

If the subject of the verb in a main clause is not the first idea, then the subject must follow the verb in what is known as inverted word order, or *inversion*. The verb remains the second idea.

Gestern **stand** der junge Mann vor dem Rathaus.
Yesterday the young man was standing in front of the town hall.

(b) Main clauses (questions)
Inverted word order is also used in direct questions where the verb is placed first:

Geht sie bald nach Hause? *Is she going home soon?*

This word order is also used in questions which begin with an interrogative:

Was sieht er unter dem Tisch? *What does he see under the table?*

Rule 2

Separable prefixes, past participles and infinitives must be placed at the end of the main clause in which they occur.

Er fuhr schnell am Rathaus vorbei. *He drove quickly past the town hall.*

Du mußtest zu Hause bleiben. *You had to stay at home.*

Letzte Woche ist die Sonne am Mittwoch um halb zehn untergegangen.
Last week the sun set at half past nine on Wednesday.

Rule 3

Transposed word order. This means that in subordinate clauses the finite verb is placed at the end:

(a) Als der Mann durch den Park **ging**, sah er seinen Freund.
 When the man walked through the park, he saw his friend.

(b) Obgleich er sehr müde **war**, wollte er nicht zu Bett gehen.
 Although he was very tired, he did not want to go to bed.

(c) Er kam früh in der Schule an, weil der Wecker ihn um halb sieben aufgeweckt **hatte**.
 He arrived at school early, because the alarm clock had woken him at half past six.

(d) Da er endlich ins Zimmer kommen **mußte**, war er sehr böse.
 As he finally had to come into the room, he was very angry.

  Note the position of separable prefixes, past participles and infinitives in subordinate clauses, which these examples illustrate:

(c) aufgeweckt is a past participle of a separable weak verb placed in a subordinate clause immediately before the finite verb **hatte**.

(d) kommen is an infinitive placed in a subordinate clause immediately before the finite verb **mußte**.

  Note also the examples of complex sentences containing a main clause and a subordinate clause. When this kind of sentence begins with the subordinate clause ending with a verb, the verb of the main clause will be the next word, so we have 'verb, verb'! **(a) (b)** and **(d)** above illustrate this clearly.

  Watch out for these other points, all concerned with word order in subordinate clauses:

(a) Where there are two infinitives in a subordinate clause the finite verb comes before them:
Der Arzt, der sie **wird** untersuchen wollen, ist sehr gut.
The doctor, who will want to examine her, is very good.

(b) Direct speech: The finite verb comes in the second position in the speech:
Er sagte: „Ich **gehe** jetzt ins Kino." *He said: 'I am going to the cinema now'.*

(c) Indirect speech without **daß**:
Er sagte, er sei krank. *He said he was ill.*

(d) When **wenn** is omitted in conditional clauses the finite verb comes first:
Wäre er gestern gekommen, so hätten wir ihn gesehen.
If he had come yesterday, we would have seen him.

(e) Similarly when **ob** is omitted in **als ob** the finite verb follows **als**:
Er sah aus, als **hätte** er nichts gegessen. *He looked as if he had eaten nothing.*

WORD ORDER WITHIN THE CLAUSE

Direct and indirect objects

There are three things to remember:

(a) If both objects are nouns, then the dative precedes the accusative (**Nouns Dative Accusative**).

Er gab dem Mann das Buch. (NDA) *He gave the man the book.*

(b) If both are pronouns, the cases are reversed, and the accusative precedes the dative (**Pronouns Accusative Dative**).

Er gab es ihm. *He gave him it.* (PAD)

(c) If one object is a pronoun and the other a noun, the pronoun will always come first and the case will be irrelevant.

Er gab **es** dem Mann.   ⎫
He gave it to the man.   ⎬ Pronoun first
Er gab **ihm** das Buch.   ⎬
He gave him the book.   ⎭

Reflexive and personal pronoun objects

In a main clause, the reflexive or personal pronoun object immediately follows the finite verb in normal word order, i.e. subject, verb, object:

Er hat **sich** gewaschen.

When there is inverted word order, then the reflexive or personal pronoun object will follow the subject if it is a pronoun, or precede the subject if it is a noun:

Dann setzte er **sich**, *but:* Dann setzte **sich** Mutti.
Dann gab er **ihm** ein Buch, *but:* Dann gab **ihm** mein Bruder ein Buch.

In subordinate clauses it is better German to place the reflexive pronoun or the personal pronoun object before a noun subject:

Da sich meine Schwester erkältet hat, . . . *As my sister has caught a cold, . . .*

If the subject is a pronoun, then the reflexive or personal pronoun object will immediately follow it:

Weil er mir das Buch gegeben hat, . . . *Because he has given me the book, . . .*

The position of nicht

Examine these examples carefully. In main clauses:

Wir haben ihn **nicht** gesehen. *We have not seen him.*
Heute abend kannst du **nicht** ausgehen. *You cannot go out this evening.*
Stehen Sie bitte jetzt **nicht** auf! *Please do not get up now!*
Gestern war es **nicht** kalt. *Yesterday it was not cold.*
Sie ist **nicht** meine Frau. *She is not my wife.*
Gestern ist er **nicht** in die Schule gegangen. *Yesterday he did not go to school.*
Er mag mich **nicht** sehr. *He does not like me very much.*

In these examples **nicht** is placed immediately before a past participle, an infinitive, a separable prefix, an adjective used predicatively, a noun, an adverbial phrase and an adverb. If none of these words occurs in a main clause, then **nicht** is placed last.

Wir sehen ihn **nicht**. *We do not see him.*
Vergiß mich **nicht**! *Don't forget me!*

In subordinate clauses **nicht** is placed before the finite verb. If there is a past participle, one or more infinitives, a predicative adjective or noun, or an adverb or adverbial phrase in the clause, **nicht** will precede these:

Wenn er es **nicht** sieht, . . . *If he does not see it . . .*
Wenn er es **nicht** gesehen hätte, . . . *If he had not seen it . . .*
Wenn er **nicht** hätte kommen können, . . . *If he had not been able to come . . .*
Da es **nicht** so kalt ist, . . . *As it is not so cold . . .*
Weil sie **nicht** meine Tochter ist, . . . *Because she is not my daughter . . .*
Obgleich er **nicht** schnell läuft, . . . *Although he does not run quickly . . .*
Obgleich er **nicht** in die Schule geht, . . . *Although he is not going to school . . .*
Obgleich er **nicht** in die Schule gegangen ist, . . . *Although he has not gone to school . . .*

Adverbial phrases

The order of adverbial phrases in main or subordinate clauses is: time **(1)**, manner **(2)**, place **(3)**.

Er kam um neun Uhr mit dem Zug in Berlin an.
         (1)   **(2)**   **(3)**

Very often the time phrase is put at the beginning, followed by inverted word order. This tends to balance the sentence more:

Um neun Uhr kam er mit dem Zug in Berlin an.
He arrived in Berlin by train at nine o'clock.

Note that the word order of these phrases in English is the reverse of the German word order.

50 Numerals, measurements, expressions of time

CARDINAL NUMERALS

1	eins	21	einundzwanzig
2	zwei	22	zweiundzwanzig
3	drei	30	dreißig
4	vier	40	vierzig
5	fünf	50	fünfzig
6	sechs	60	sechzig
7	sieben	70	siebzig
8	acht	80	achtzig
9	neun	90	neunzig
10	zehn	100	hundert
11	elf	101	hunderteins/hundertundeins
12	zwölf	120	hundertzwanzig
13	dreizehn	221	zweihunderteinundzwanzig
14	vierzehn	1,000	tausend
15	fünfzehn	1,101	tausendeinhundert(und)eins
16	sechzehn	1,000,000	eine Million
17	siebzehn	2,000,000	zwei Millionen
18	achtzehn		
19	neunzehn		
20	zwanzig		

Note the slight irregularities in 16, 17, 30, 60 and 70.

Tausend is not usually used in dates:
Im Jahre neunzehnhundertzweiundachtzig.

Eins is used in counting. When a noun is used or implied, **ein** must be declined, just like the indefinite article.
Wieviele Koffer hat er? Er hat nur einen. *How many suitcases has he got? He has only one.*

Hundert and **tausend** can be used as neuter nouns:
Da waren Hunderte/Tausende von Kindern. *There were hundreds/thousands of children there.*

FRACTIONS, DECIMALS

Fractions are formed as neuter nouns by adding **-tel** to the cardinals 4–19 and **-stel** from 20 onwards:
drei und zwei Fünftel, *three and two fifths*
vier Zwanzigstel, *four twentieths*
die Hälfte, *the half*
das Drittel, *the third*
anderthalb, *one and a half*

Halb is an adjective meaning 'half'.
eine halbe Stunde, *half an hour*
The decimal point is a comma in German:
5,9 = 5·9
fünf Komma neun, *five point nine*

ORDINAL NUMERALS

To form the ordinals simply add **-t** to the cardinal number as far as 19th. From 20th you add **-st** plus the appropriate case ending after **der**, i.e. weak declension endings. 1st, 3rd, 8th are slightly irregular.

1st **der erste**
3rd **der dritte**
4th **der vierte**
5th **der fünfte**
8th **der achte**
20th **der zwanzigste**

The ordinals are always inflected. To write ordinals as figures in German, write the cardinal number and add a full stop.
am 1. Januar, *on the first of January*

Mal is used for the word 'time' after an ordinal number.
das erstemal, *the first time*
zum drittenmal, *for the third time*

Note also:
einmal, once
zweimal, twice
dreimal, three times
viermal, four times
'Firstly', 'secondly', 'thirdly', (etc.) are as follows:
erstens, zweitens, drittens

EXPRESSIONS OF TIME

Wieviel Uhr ist es? *What time is it?*
Wie spät ist es? *What time is it?*
Es ist ein/zwei/drei Uhr   *It is one/two/three o'clock.*
um vier Uhr, *at four o'clock*
gegen acht Uhr, *about eight o'clock*
(der) Mittag, (die) Mitternacht, *midday, midnight*
eine halbe Stunde, *half an hour*
eine Viertelstunde, *a quarter of an hour*
Es ist Viertel nach drei. *It is a quarter past three.*
Es ist Viertel fünf. *It is a quarter past four.*
Es ist halb eins. *It is half past twelve.*
Es ist Viertel vor drei. *It is a quarter to three.*
Es ist dreiviertel drei. *It is a quarter to three.*
Es ist zehn (Minuten) nach fünf. *It is ten past five.*
Es ist zwanzig (Minuten) vor sieben. *It is twenty (minutes) to seven.*
morgens, nachmittags, abends, nachts, *in the morning, afternoon, evening, at night*
heute morgen/früh, heute nachmittag, heute abend, heute nacht, *this morning, this afternoon, this evening, tonight (i.e. during the coming night)*
Guten Morgen. *Good morning.*   Guten Tag. *Good day/afternoon.*
Guten Abend. *Good evening.*   Gute Nacht. *Good night.*
Definite time is expressed by the accusative:
jeden Abend, *every night*
nächsten Montag, *next Monday*
den ganzen Tag, *all day, the whole day*
Einen Augenblick bitte! *A moment please!*
Indefinite time is expressed by the genitive:
eines Tages, *one day*
Other phrases:
heute vor acht Tagen, *a week ago today*
heute in acht Tagen, *today week*
während der Ferien, *during the holidays*
Er arbeitete drei Wochen lang. *He worked for three weeks.*
Er fährt auf vier Wochen nach Köln. *He is going to Cologne for four weeks.*

'WHEN' IN GERMAN

Wann asks a question:
Wann fährt der Zug ab? *When does the train leave?*

Als refers to a single occasion in the past:
Als er nach Hause kam, spielte er Fußball. *When he came home he played football.*

Wenn is used for 'When' in sentences referring to present or future time or repeated occasions in the past, where it has the alternative meaning 'whenever':
Wenn er krank ist, muß er zu Hause bleiben. *When he is ill, he has to stay at home.*
Wenn er zum Bahnhof ging, pflegte er eine Zeitung zu kaufen.
When(ever) he went to the station, he used to buy a newspaper.

THE DATE

Days of the week are all masculine:
Sonntag, Montag, Dienstag, Mittwoch, Donnerstag, Freitag, Samstag (Sonnabend).
Months of the year are all masculine:
Januar, Februar, März, April, Mai, Juni, Juli, August, September, Oktober, November, Dezember.
The date on a letter heading is in the accusative:
den 5. März im Jahre 1983
Der wievielte ist es heute?
Den wievielten haben wir heute? } *What is the date today?*

AGE

Wie alt bist du? }
Wie alt sind Sie? } *How old are you?*
Ich bin sechzehn Jahre alt. *I am 16 years old.*

51 Punctuation

(a) The comma is used in German between all clauses, and before an infinitive construction, **um ... zu ...** (etc.)

(b) Inverted commas are used as in English but they are written differently:
„Er kann nicht kommen", sagte meine Mutter. *'He cannot come,' my mother said.*

(c) The colon is used to introduce direct speech.
Er fragte: „Wie geht es dir?" *He asked, 'How are you?'*

(d) The exclamation mark must be used after an imperative:
Steh auf! *Get up!*
It may also be used at the start of a letter:
Lieber Fritz! *or* Liebe Uschi! *Dear Fritz, or Dear Uschi,*

(e) Full stops, semi-colons, question marks, dashes and brackets are all used in the same way as in English.

52 The 'ß'

The **ß** is used in certain cases to replace **ss**. Most of the Examination Boards will accept **ss** instead of the **ß**, but state that if you use it at all, you must keep using it. You will not be penalized for not using it, but you will lose marks if you use it incorrectly.

The rule about its use is as follows:
-ss- is used between two vowels when the first vowel is short, e.g. **müssen, Flüsse.**
ß is used in all other cases, i.e. after a long vowel, at the end of a word and before a 't',
e.g. **er muß, der Fluß, draußen, ihr müßt.**

53 Strong verbs

This list gives the third person singular (**er/sie/es** form) of all the common strong verbs in German. Candidates for GCSE at the Higher Levels would be expected to know or be able to recognize all of these. Although there are some verbs where the pattern of the vowel changes in the principal parts is similar (e.g. **fallen**, to fall: **fällt, fiel, ist gefallen**, and **schlafen**, to sleep: **schläft, schlief, hat geschlafen**), it is probably easiest to learn these verbs individually as you meet them in your work. Use this list for reference when revising. Rember that compounds of a verb have the same vowel changes as the basic verb (e.g. **durchfallen**, to fall through, to fail, is like **fallen**, to fall). The auxiliary verbs **sein** and **werden** have been omitted from this list (see pages 31–2).

Infinitive	Meaning	Present	Imperfect	Perfect
backen	*to bake*	bäckt	backte	hat gebacken
befehlen	*to command*	befiehlt	befahl	hat befohlen
beginnen	*to begin*	beginnt	begann	hat begonnen
beißen	*to bite*	beißt	biß	hat gebissen
bekommen	*to get, obtain*	bekommt	bekam	hat bekommen
bersten	*to burst*	birst	barst	ist geborsten
bewegen	*to induce*	bewegt	bewog	hat bewogen
biegen	*to bend*	biegt	bog	hat gebogen
bieten	*to offer*	bietet	bot	hat geboten
binden	*to bind, tie*	bindet	band	hat gebunden
bitten	*to ask, beg*	bittet	bat	hat gebeten
blasen	*to blow*	bläst	blies	hat geblasen
bleiben	*to remain*	bleibt	blieb	ist geblieben
brechen	*to break*	bricht	brach	hat gebrochen
dringen	*to pierce, penetrate*	dringt	drang	ist gedrungen
einladen	*to invite*	lädt ein	lud ein	hat eingeladen
empfehlen	*to recommend*	empfiehlt	empfahl	hat empfohlen
erlöschen	*to die down, go out (of fire, light)*	erlischt	erlosch	ist erloschen

Infinitive	Meaning	Present	Imperfect	Perfect
erschrecken	*to be frightened*	erschrickt	erschrak	ist erschrocken
essen	*to eat*	ißt	aß	hat gegessen
fahren	*to drive, ride*	fährt	fuhr	ist gefahren
fallen	*to fall*	fällt	fiel	ist gefallen
fangen	*to catch*	fängt	fing	hat gefangen
finden	*to find*	findet	fand	hat gefunden
fliegen	*to fly*	fliegt	flog	ist geflogen
fliehen	*to flee*	flieht	floh	ist geflohen
fließen	*to flow*	fließt	floß	ist geflossen
fressen	*to eat* (of animals)	frißt	fraß	hat gefressen
frieren	*to freeze*	friert	fror	hat gefroren
geben	*to give*	gibt	gab	hat gegeben
gehen	*to go*	geht	ging	ist gegangen
gelingen	*to succeed*	gelingt	gelang	ist gelungen
genießen	*to enjoy*	genießt	genoß	hat genossen
geschehen	*to happen*	geschieht	geschah	ist geschehen
gewinnen	*to gain, win*	gewinnt	gewann	hat gewonnen
gießen	*to pour*	gießt	goß	hat gegossen
gleichen	*to resemble*	gleicht	glich	hat geglichen
gleiten	*to glide*	gleitet	glitt	ist geglitten
graben	*to dig*	gräbt	grub	hat gegraben
greifen	*to seize*	greift	griff	hat gegriffen
halten	*to hold, stop*	hält	hielt	hat gehalten
hängen	*to hang, be suspended*	hängt	hing	hat gehangen
heben	*to lift*	hebt	hob	hat gehoben
heißen	*to be called*	heißt	hieß	hat geheißen
helfen	*to help*	hilft	half	hat geholfen
klingen	*to sound*	klingt	klang	hat geklungen
kommen	*to come*	kommt	kam	ist gekommen
kriechen	*to creep*	kriecht	kroch	ist gekrochen
laden	*to load*	lädt	lud	hat geladen
lassen	*to let*	läßt	ließ	hat gelassen
laufen	*to run*	läuft	lief	ist gelaufen
leiden	*to suffer*	leidet	litt	hat gelitten
leihen	*to lend*	leiht	lieh	hat geliehen
lesen	*to read*	liest	las	hat gelesen
liegen	*to lie*	liegt	lag	hat gelegen
lügen	*to tell lies*	lügt	log	hat gelogen
meiden	*to avoid*	meidet	mied	hat gemieden
messen	*to measure*	mißt	maß	hat gemessen
nehmen	*to take*	nimmt	nahm	hat genommen
pfeifen	*to whistle*	pfeift	pfiff	hat gepfiffen
preisen	*to praise*	preist	pries	hat gepriesen
raten	*to advise, guess*	rät	riet	hat geraten
reiben	*to rub*	reibt	rieb	hat gerieben
reißen	*to tear*	reißt	riß	hat gerissen
reiten	*to ride*	reitet	ritt	hat geritten
riechen	*to smell*	riecht	roch	hat gerochen
rufen	*to call*	ruft	rief	hat gerufen
scheiden	*to part*	scheidet	schied	ist geschieden
scheinen	*to appear, shine*	scheint	schien	hat geschienen
schieben	*to shove, push*	schiebt	schob	hat geschoben
schießen	*to shoot*	schießt	schoß	hat geschossen
schlafen	*to sleep*	schläft	schlief	hat geschlafen
schlagen	*to strike, hit*	schlägt	schlug	hat geschlagen
schleichen	*to creep*	schleicht	schlich	ist geschlichen
schließen	*to shut*	schließt	schloß	hat geschlossen
schmelzen	*to melt*	schmilzt	schmolz	ist geschmolzen
schneiden	*to cut*	schneidet	schnitt	hat geschnitten
schreiben	*to write*	schreibt	schrieb	hat geschrieben
schreien	*to cry out, shout*	schreit	schrie	hat geschrie(e)n
schreiten	*to stride*	schreitet	schritt	ist geschritten
schweigen	*to be silent*	schweigt	schwieg	hat geschwiegen
schwellen	*to swell*	schwillt	schwoll	ist geschwollen
schwimmen	*to swim*	schwimmt	schwamm	ist geschwommen
schwingen	*to swing*	schwingt	schwang	hat geschwungen
schwören	*to swear*	schwört	schwor	hat geschworen

Infinitive	Meaning	Present	Imperfect	Perfect
sehen	*to see*	sieht	sah	hat gesehen
singen	*to sing*	singt	sang	hat gesungen
sinken	*to sink*	sinkt	sank	ist gesunken
sitzen	*to sit*	sitzt	saß	hat gesessen
spinnen	*to spin*	spinnt	spann	hat gesponnen
sprechen	*to speak*	spricht	sprach	hat gesprochen
springen	*to spring, jump*	springt	sprang	ist gesprungen
stechen	*to prick, sting*	sticht	stach	hat gestochen
stehen	*to stand*	steht	stand	hat gestanden
stehlen	*to steal*	stiehlt	stahl	hat gestohlen
steigen	*to ascend*	steigt	stieg	ist gestiegen
sterben	*to die*	stirbt	starb	ist gestorben
stoßen	*to push, knock, bump*	stößt	stieß	hat gestoßen
streichen	*to paint, spread*	streicht	strich	hat gestrichen
streiten	*to argue, fight*	streitet	stritt	hat gestritten
tragen	*to carry, wear*	trägt	trug	hat getragen
treffen	*to hit, meet*	trifft	traf	hat getroffen
treiben	*to drive*	treibt	trieb	hat getrieben
treten	*to step, kick (football)*	tritt	trat	hat getreten
trinken	*to drink*	trinkt	trank	hat getrunken
tun	*to do*	tut	tat	hat getan
verbieten	*to forbid*	verbietet	verbot	hat verboten
verderben	*to spoil*	verdirbt	verdarb	hat verdorben
vergessen	*to forget*	vergißt	vergaß	hat vergessen
verlieren	*to lose*	verliert	verlor	hat verloren
verschwinden	*to disappear*	verschwindet	verschwand	ist verschwunden
verzeihen	*to pardon*	verzeiht	verzieh	hat verziehen
wachsen	*to grow*	wächst	wuchs	ist gewachsen
waschen	*to wash*	wäscht	wusch	hat gewaschen
weisen	*to show*	weist	wies	hat gewiesen
werfen	*to throw*	wirft	warf	hat geworfen
wiegen	*to weigh*	wiegt	wog	hat gewogen
winden	*to wind*	windet	wand	hat gewunden
ziehen	*to draw, pull*	zieht	zog	hat gezogen
zwingen	*to force*	zwingt	zwang	hat gezwungen

There are two kinds of vocabulary, which all students of foreign languages need to develop. These are *passive* vocabulary and *active* vocabulary. The Examining Groups for GCSE refer to them as *receptive* and *productive*. They have also issued lists of vocabulary in topic areas describing the use of vocabulary in a series of tasks. The tasks for each topic area are as far as possible to be authentic and relevant to the needs of candidates in coping successfully in *real* situations on visits to German-speaking countries and in encounters with German-speaking people.

The Examining Groups lay great stress on productive oral and writing skills but the receptive skills of reading and listening are taken into account in the lists of vocabulary which the Examining Groups have made available to examination centres. The tasks set are given for both Basic and Higher Levels of the examination and students should realize that if they are attempting the higher-level papers of GCSE German it is assumed that they know the vocabulary for Basic Level as well. Individual students should obtain the vocabulary list or syllabus content booklet for their particular Examining Group.

In this section every effort has been made to include all the vocabulary listed by all the Examining Groups at both levels of the examination. The knowledge of vocabulary can be improved in a number of different ways. Systematic learning on a daily or weekly basis is one. A programme of revision as detailed on pages xiii–xiv which involves working systematically through the lists of vocabulary given here is a good way of acquiring a wide-ranging active vocabulary. Do not try to learn too many words at a time and always ensure that you test yourself in writing when you think you have learned the list properly.

Other strategies that you can employ to improve your knowledge of vocabulary include listening to German radio, especially news programmes which often contain the same news items as our own programmes on a particular day; reading German short stories, newspapers or magazines; and arranging an exchange with a German-speaking family so that you can go and stay in the foreign country for a short period, living as a member of that family. Remember that German is spoken in Austria and Switzerland as well as in Germany itself. If you cannot visit a foreign country on an exchange, you can easily have a German-speaking penfriend to whom you should write in German on a regular basis. This will not only help your knowledge of vocabulary, but it will also be useful for the productive writing you may have to do if you enter for the writing elements of the GCSE.

Any or all of these strategies are of little use in expanding your vocabulary unless you work at it. When reading or listening to German you need to note words you do not recognize, write them down, then look them up in a reasonably large dictionary and finally commit them to memory.

It is perhaps worth noting at this point that the structure of German vocabulary is much more formalized than that of English, for example. German vocabulary consists of relatively few basic words and many compounds, which are derived from those basic words. It is possible to learn words in German by studying the derivative groups. Here is an example:

suchen	to look for, to seek
die Suche (-n)	the search
besuchen	to visit
der Besuch (-e)	the visit
versuchen	to try, to attempt
der Versuch (-e)	the attempt
die Versuchung (-en)	the temptation
untersuchen	to investigate
die Untersuchung (-en)	the investigation
aufsuchen	to look up
aussuchen	to seek out
durchsuchen	to search, to frisk
nachsuchen	to look and see

This group of words, all based on **suchen**, shows how words are interconnected in German, how nouns are formed from verbs and how the meanings are linked with the basic idea and what effect the prefixes have. This approach of looking for connections between words can help to make an educated guess at the meaning of a complicated compound word that you have never seen or heard before, particularly in the receptive areas of the examination, when your passive vocabulary becomes important.

Undoubtedly the best way of learning vocabulary is to learn it in context. On the next few pages there are a number of pictures illustrating the main topic areas out of those listed by the GCSE Examining Groups. The Examining Groups indicate what vocabulary they expect the candidate to know. Vocabulary suitable for Higher Level is printed in colour. The lists contain words which are related to the topic area and useful phrases in the context of the topic area.

1 Personal identification and family relationships

PERSONAL IDENTIFICATION

der **Name** (-n)	name
der **Nachname/Familienname** (-n)	nick-/surname
der **Vorname** (-n)	Christian name
heißen	to be called
nennen	to call
in Ordnung	in order
Herr, Frau, Fräulein	Mr, Mrs, Miss
(*e.g.* **Herr Schmidt**)	(Mr Smith)
(unter) schreiben	to write (to sign)
die **Unterschrift** (-en)	signature
der **Ausweis** (-e)	identity card
der **Paß** (-ässe)	passport
die **Adresse/Anschrift** (-n/-en)	address
der **Wohnort** (-e)	home
wohnen	to live
die **Straße (Str.)** (-n)	street (St.)
die **(Haus) Nummer (Nr.)** (-n)	(house) number
der **Staat** (-en)	state
die **Postleitzahl** (-en)	post code
England/Deutschland/BRD/	England/Germany/FRG/
DDR/Österreich	GDR/Austria
die **Schweiz/Bundesrepublik**	Switzerland/Federal Republic
die **Telefon (nummer)**	telephone number
geboren am . . .	born on . . .
(*e.g.* **am dritten Mai**)	(on the 3rd of May)
geboren in . . .	born in . . .
der **Geburtstag** (-e)	birthday
das **Geburtsdatum** (daten)	date of birth
der **Geburtsort** (-e)	place of birth
das **Alter** (-)	age
das **Jahr** (-e)	year
der **Monat** (-e)	month
das **Kind** (-er)	child
Erwachsene(r)	adult
jung	young
der **Mann**(-er)	man/husband
Herren (H)	gentlemen
der **Junge** (-n)	boy
die **Dame** (-n)	lady
Damen(D)	ladies
das **Mädchen** (-)	girl
die **Staatsangehörigkeit**	nationality
der/die **Engländer/in**	Englishman/woman
englisch (*adj*)	English
eine/ein **Deutsche/r**	a German woman/man
deutsch (*adj*)	German
von wo	from where
das **Land** (-er)	country, state
was für (ein) . . . ?	what sort of . . . ?
wie . . . ?	what . . . like?
(*e.g.* **Wie ist dein Chef?**)	(What is your boss like?)

freundlich	friendly/kind
unfreundlich	unfriendly/unkind
lustig	merry
faul	lazy
fleißig	hard working
intelligent	intelligent
dumm	stupid
aussehen	to appear, to look like
dick	fat
schlank	slim
der **Schnurrbart** (¨e)	moustache
die **Brille** (-n)	glasses/spectacles

der **Bart** (¨e)	beard
ähnlich	similar
reich	rich
arm	poor
die **Vorwahlnummer** (-n)	code number
der **Gottesdienst** (-e)	church service
allein	alone
böse	angry
glücklich	happy
lachen	to laugh
die **Angst** (¨e)	fear, anxiety
erkennen	to recognize

der **Mädchenname** (-n)	maiden name
geb.	né(e)/born
buchstabieren	to spell
der **Weg** (-e)	road, way
Jugendliche(r)	girl (boy)
das **Geschlecht** (-er)	sex
männlich	male/masculine
weiblich	female/feminine
verlobt	engaged
verheiratet	married
ledig	single
geschieden	divorced
Verlobte(r)	fiancé(e)
die/ der **Witwe**(r)	widow (widower)
Österreicher	Austrian
österreichisch (*adj*)	Austrian
Schweizer	Swiss
der **Ausländer** (-)	foreigner
die **Heimat** (-en)	home, native country
sympathisch	sympathetic
ehrlich	honest, honourable
nervös	nervous
gut/schlecht gelaunt	good/bad humoured
neugierig	curious
blöd	stupid
doof	stupid, simple
dünn	thin
(sich) erinnern	to remember
lebhaft	lively
frech	cheeky, bold
schüchtern	shy
leiden können	to like/to be able to put up with

sich vertragen	to get on well together
die **Religion** (-en)	religion
katholisch	catholic
evangelisch	evangelical

FAMILY RELATIONSHIPS

der/ein **Älteste/r**(-n)	eldest
das **Baby** (-s)	baby
der **Bruder** (·)	brother ·
das **(Einzel) Kind**(-er)	(only) child
die **Eltern** (no sing.)	parents
der/die **Enkel/in** (-/-innen)	grandson/daughter
die **Familie** (-n)	family
die **Frau/Hausfrau** (-en)	woman, wife, housewife
der/die **Freund/in** (-e/-innen)	friend (*m* and *f*)
die **Großeltern**	grandparents
die **Großmutter** (·)	grandmother
der **Großvater** (·)	grandfather
heiraten	to marry
das **Mädchen** (-)	girl
der **Mann** (·er)	man, husband
die **Mutter** (·)/**Mutti**	mother/mum
der **Neffe** (-n)	nephew
die **Nichte** (-n)	niece
die **Oma**	granny
der **Onkel** (-)	uncle
der **Opa**	grandad
die **Schwester** (-n)	sister
der **Sohn** (·e)	son
die **Tante** (-n)	aunt
die **Tochter** (·)	daughter
der **Vater/Vati** (·)/(-s)	father/dad
der/ein **Verwandte/r** (-n)	relation
der **Vetter** (-n)	cousin (*m*)
der/die **Cousin/-e** (-s/-n)	cousin (*m* and *f*)
die **Ehefrau** (-en)	married woman, wife
der **Ehemann** (·er)	married man, husband
das **Ehepaar** (-e)	married couple
die **Kusine** (-n)	cousin (*f*)
der/die **Schwager/·in** (·/-innen)	brother/sister-in-law
Schwieger-	. . .-in-law
der **Schwiegersohn** (·e)	son-in-law (*etc*)

DESCRIBING ONESELF

aussehen	to look like
blaß	pale
blau	blue
blond	blond
braun	brown
dunkel	dark
erkennen	to recognize
grau	grey
groß	tall
grün	green
das **Haar**(-e)	hair
häßlich	ugly
hell	light (*of colour*)
hübsch	pretty
kurz	short
lang	long
mager	thin, lean
mittelgroß	medium sized
rund	round
schlank	slim
schön	beautiful
schwach	weak
schwarz	black
stark	strong
was für (ein) . . . ?	what sort of . . . ?
weiß	white
wie ist . . . ?	what is . . . like?

Angst (haben)/(machen)	to be afraid, make afraid
böse	angry
denken	to think
faul	lazy
fleißig	hard working
gern mögen	to like
glücklich	happy
gut	good
hoffen	to hope
intelligent	intelligent
komisch	funny
lächeln	to smile
lachen	to laugh
nett	nice
ruhig	calm
schlimm	bad
traurig	sad
überraschen	to surprise
die **Überraschung** (-en)	surprise
wollen	to want
enttäuschen	to disappoint
die **Enttäuschung** (-en)	disappointment
gut/schlecht gelaunt	good/bad tempered
höflich	polite
neugierig	curious
raten	to advise, guess
sich schämen	to be ashamed
sympathisch	likeable
(un)recht haben	to be right (wrong)

BODY AND HEALTH

der **Arm**(-e)	arm
das **Auge**(-n)	eye
das **Bad** (¨er)	bath
baden	to bathe
das **Bein** (-e)	leg
die **Blutprobe** (-n)	blood test
der **Durchfall**	diarrhoea
Durst haben	to be thirsty
durstig	thirsty
erkältet sein	to have a chill
Fieber haben	to have a temperature
der **Finger** (-)	finger
der **Fuß**(¨e)	foot
das **Gesicht**(-er)	face
gesund	healthy
die **Grippe** (-n)	flu
das **(Haar) Shampoo**	shampoo
das **Haarwaschmittel** (-)	shampoo
der **Hals** (¨e)	neck
die **Hand** (¨e)	hand
das **Handtuch** (¨er)	hand towel
Heimweh haben	to be homesick
Hunger haben	to be hungry
hungrig	hungry
der **Kopf** (¨e)	head
krank	ill
der **Magen/Bauch** (-/¨e)	stomach
die **Magenverstimmung** (-en)	stomach upset
mir ist heiß/kalt	I feel hot/cold
mir ist übel/schlecht/	I feel unwell/bad/
schwindlig	dizzy
müde	tired
der **Mund** (¨er)	mouth
die **Nase** (-n)	nose
das **Ohr** (-en)	ear

der **Rücken** (-)	back
satt	full, well fed
sauber	clean
schlafen	to sleep
-schmerzen	. . . aches
schmutzig	dirty
seekrank	seasick
die **Seekrankheit** (-en)	seasickness
die **Seife** (-n)	soap
sich ausruhen	to have a rest
sich waschen	to wash oneself
die **Spritze** (-n)	injection
(un)fit	(un)fit
was fehlt . . . ?	what is wrong?
was ist . . . los?	what is the matter?
-weh	. . . ache
weh tun	to hurt
der **Zahn** (¨e)	tooth

blind	blind
bluten	to bleed
die **Brust** (¨e)	breast, chest
der **Daumen** (-)	thumb
dreckig	muddy, dirty
die **Erkältung**	chill, cold
genesen	to recover, to get better
das **Herz** (-en)	heart
das **Knie** (-)	knee
der **Körper** (-)	body
der **Schnupfen** (-)	cold in the head
die **Schulter** (-n)	shoulder
sich bürsten	to brush
sich die Zähne bürsten/putzen	to brush/clean one's teeth
sich erholen	to recover
sich hinlegen	to lie down
sich kämmen	to comb
sich rasieren	to shave
sich (wohl) fühlen	to feel (well)
stumm	dumb
taub	deaf
verstopft	constipated
die **Verstopfung** (-en)	constipation
die **Zehe** (-n)	toe
die **Zunge** (-n)	tongue

Useful phrases (both levels)

zu Fuß	on foot
auf Zehenspitzen gehen	to walk on tiptoe
den Kopf schütteln	to shake one's head
mit dem Kopf nicken	to nod one's head
sich (dat) die Hände schütteln	to shake hands
mit der Hand winken	to wave one's hand
auf etwas zeigen	to point to something
sich die Nase putzen/ sich schneuzen	to blow one's nose
mit lauter/leiser Stimme	in a loud/quiet voice
sich (dat) die Haare schneiden lassen	to have one's hair cut
Kopfweh haben	to have a headache
Zahnschmerzen haben	to have toothache
mit den Achseln/ Schultern zucken	to shrug one's shoulders

2 House and home

alt	old
(an)bauen	to build (on)
der **Bauernhof** (¨e)	farm
der **Block** (¨e)	block
der **Bungalow** (-s)	bungalow
das **Doppelhaus** (¨er)	semi-detached house
das **Einfamilienhaus** (¨er)	detached house
die **Etage** (-n)	floor (*of a building*)
der **Garten** (¨)	garden
das **Gebäude** (-)	building
groß	big, large
das **Haus** (¨er)	house
die **(Haus) Tür** (-en)	(front) door
der **Hof** (¨e)	yard
kaufen/verkaufen	to buy, to sell
der **Keller** (-)	cellar
klein	small
klingeln	to ring
klopfen	to knock
die **Mauer** (-n)	wall (*outside*)
mieten	to hire, rent, lease
modern	modern
nett	nice
neu	new
oben	above, upstairs
das **Reihenhaus** (¨er)	terrace house
die **Scheune** (-n)	barn
der **Schlüssel** (-)	key
schön	beautiful
das **Stockwerk** (-e)	storey
unten	below/downstairs
wechseln	to change
wohnen	to live, dwell
die **Wohnung** (-en)	flat
das **Badezimmer** (-)	bathroom
bequem	comfortable
das **Eßzimmer** (-)	dining room
der **Fahrstuhl** (¨e)	lift
das **Fenster** (-)	window
der **Flur** (-e)	hall
der **(Fuß) Boden** (¨)	floor
die **Garage** (-n)	garage
die **Küche** (-n)	kitchen
der **Lift** (-e) or (-s)	lift
das **Möbel** (-)	furniture
der **Platz** (¨e)	seat, place
der **Raum** (¨e)	room, space
das **Schlafzimmer** (-)	bedroom
die **Toilette**/das **Klo(sett)** (-n/-e)	toilet

die **Treppe** (-n)	stairs
die **Wand** (ⁱe)	wall
das **Wohnzimmer** (-)	living room
das **Zimmer** (-)	room
die **Aussicht** (-en)	view
das **Dach** (ⁱer)	roof
das **Erdgeschoß** (-sse)	ground floor
heizen	to heat
die **Lage** (-n)	situation
das **Hochhaus** (ⁱer)	skyscraper, tall block
das **Obergeschoß** (-sse)	upper storey
umziehen	to move, browse
die **(Zentral) Heizung** (-en)	(central) heating
(an)streichen	to paint (*house*)
der **Dachboden** (ⁱ)	loft, attic
die **Decke** (-n)	ceiling
der **Gang** (ⁱe)	passage, corridor
gemütlich	cosy, snug
möbliert	furnished
tapezieren	to paper (*walls*)
die **Terrasse** (-n)	terrace, patio

DAS SCHLAFZIMMER

das **Schlafzimmer** (-)	bedroom
das **Bett** (-en)	bed
das **Bettzeug** (-e)	bedding, bed clothes
eigen	own
die **Kleiderbürste** (-n)	clothes brush
der **Kleiderschrank** (ⁱe)	cupboard
die **Kommode**	chest
die **Lampe** (-n)	lamp
der **Sessel** (-)	armchair
der **Stuhl** (ⁱe)	chair
teilen	to share
der **Wecker** (-)	alarm clock
die **(Bett) Decke** (-n)	blanket (bedspread)
das **Bettlaken** (-)	sheet
das **Bettuch** (ⁱer)	sheet
die **Bettwäsche** (-n)	bed linen/clothes
das **Federbett** (-en)	feather eiderdown
die **Gardine** (-n)	curtain (*net*)
das **Kopfkissen** (-)	pillow
der **Nachttisch** (-e)	bedside table
der **Spiegel** (-)	mirror
die **Steppdecke** (-n)	quilt
der **Teppich** (-e)	carpet
der **Vorhang** (ⁱe)	curtain

DIE KÜCHE

die **Küche** (-n)	kitchen
anmachen	to turn on
der **Apparat** (-e)	appliance
ausmachen	to turn off
die **Gabel** (-n)	fork
das **Glas** (ⁱer)	glass
der **Herd** (-e)	stove, cooker
die **Kaffeekanne** (-n)	coffee pot
der **Knopf** (ⁱe) **(drücken)**	button (to press)
der **Kühlschrank** (ⁱe)	fridge
das **Licht** (-er)	light
der **Löffel** (-)	spoon
das **Messer** (-)	knife
die **Teekanne** (-n)	teapot
der **Teller** (-)	plate
der **Tisch** (-e)	table
die **Waschmaschine** (-n)	washing machine

der **(Wasser)Hahn** (-e)	tap
ziehen	to pull
der **(Abfall)Eimer** (-)	bucket (waste bin)
an sein (Das Licht ist an)	to be on (the light is on)
ausschalten	to switch off
einschalten	to switch on
elektrisch	electric
Elektro-	electric (in compounds)
das **Geschirr** (-e)	dishes
der **(Koch)Topf** (-e)	saucepan
die **Schale** (-n)	basin, dish, bowl
die **Schüssel** (-n)	dish, basin, bowl
die **Spülmaschine** (-n)	washing-up machine
das **Spülmittel** (-)	washing-up liquid
der **Staubsauger** (-)	vacuum cleaner
die **Tiefkühltruhe** (-n)	deep freezer
das **Waschpulver** (-)	washing powder
wegwerfen	to throw away

DAS BADEZIMMER

das **Badezimmer** (-)	bathroom
das **Bad** (-er)	bath
die **Badewanne** (-n)	bath (tub)
die **Dusche** (-n)	shower
das **(Haar)Shampoo**	shampoo
das **Toilettenpapier** (-e)	toilet paper
die **Zahnbürste** (-n)	toothbrush
die **Zahnpasta**	toothpaste
das **Handtuch** (-er)	hand towel
der **Rasierapparat** (-e)	shaver
das **Waschbecken** (-)	wash basin
der **(Wasch)Lappen** (-)	face cloth

DAS EßZIMMER/DAS WOHNZIMMER

das **Bild** (-er)	picture
das **Eßzimmer** (-)	dining room
der **Fernsehapparat** (-e)	TV set
der **Fernseher** (-)	TV set
das **Foto** (-s)	photo
die **Pflanze** (-n)	plant
das **Sofa** (-s)	settee, sofa
die **Stereo(anlage)** (-n)	stereo (unit)
der **Tisch** (-e)	table
die **Uhr** (-en)	clock
das **Wohnzimmer** (-)	living room
das **Kissen** (-)	cushion
das **Regal** (-e)	bookshelf
das **Tablett** (-e)	tray
die **Tischdecke** (-n)	tablecloth

SERVICES

die **Elektrizität**	electricity
das **Gas** (-e)	gas
das **Holz** (-er)	wood
der **Knopf** (-e)	knob
das **Öl** (-e)	oil
die **Steckdose** (-n)	wall socket
das **Wasser** (-)	water
anschließen	to connect
die **Birne** (-n)	light bulb
die **Kerze** (-n)	candle
die **Kohle** (-n)	coal
der **Ofen** (-)	stove
der **Schalter** (-)	switch
der **Stecker** (-)	plug
der **Strom** (-e)	electric current

DAILY ROUTINE

das **Abendbrot** (*no pl.*)	supper
das **Abendessen** (-)	supper, evening meal
abräumen	to clear up/away
anhaben	to have on
auf die Toilette gehen	to go to the toilet
aufmachen	to open
aufräumen	to tidy up
aufstehen	to get up
aufwachen	to wake up
bringen	to bring
decken	to lay (the table)
duschen	to shower
essen	to eat
fernsehen	to watch TV
frühstücken	to have breakfast
kochen	to boil/cook
lassen	to let/leave
machen	to make
das **Mittagessen** (-)	lunch
nähen	to sew
nehmen	to take
öffnen	to open
Platz nehmen	to take a seat
sauber machen	to clean
schlafen	to sleep
schließen	to close
sich (hin)setzen	to sit down
(sich) waschen	to wash (oneself)
sitzen	to sit
sprechen	to speak
stehen	to stand
tun	to do
tragen	to carry, wear
trinken	to drink
verlassen	to leave
vorbereiten	to prepare
zu Abend/Mittag essen	to have supper/lunch
zumachen	to close, shut
abspülen	to wash up
(ab)trocknen	to dry
abwaschen	to wash up
benutzen	to use
betreten	to enter
bügeln	to iron
einschlafen	to fall asleep
erwachen	to wake up
fallen (lassen)	to fall (drop)
füllen	to fill
leeren	to empty
plaudern	to chat
putzen	to clean
reden	to talk
(sich) anziehen	to get dressed
(sich) ausziehen	to get undressed
(sich) bewegen	to move
sich umziehen	to change (one's clothes)
stricken	to knit
die **Wäsche** (-n)	washing
wecken	to wake

GARDEN

die **Blume** (-n)	flower
die **Gartenarbeit** (-en)	work in garden
das **Gemüse** (-)	vegetables

das **Gras** (¨er)	grass
der **(Obst) Baum** (¨e)	fruit tree
die **Pflanze** (-n)	plant
begießen	to water
die **Gartengeräte** (pl.)	garden equipment
mähen	to mow
der **Rasen** (-)	lawn
wachsen	to grow

ANIMALS AND PETS

der **(Gold)Fisch** (-e)	(gold) fish
der **Hamster** (-)	hamster
das **(Haus)Tier** (-e)	animal (pet)
der **Hund** (-e)	dog
das **Insekt** (-en)	insect
das **Kaninchen** (-)	rabbit
die **Katze** (-n)	cat
die **Kuh** (¨e)	cow
die **Maus** (¨e)	mouse
das **Meerschweinchen** (-)	guinea pig
das **Pferd** (-e)	horse
das **Schaf** (-e)	sheep
die **Schildkröte** (-n)	tortoise
das **Schwein** (-e)	pig
der **Vogel** (¨)	bird
der **Wellensittich** (-e)	budgerigar
bellen	to bark
die **Ente** (-n)	duck
die **Fliege** (-n)	fly
fressen	to eat (*animals*)
das **Futter** (-)	food (*animals*), fodder
füttern	to feed (*animals*)
die **Gans** (¨e)	goose
das **Huhn** (¨er)	fowl, hen
die **Hütte** (-n)	hut, shed, hutch
der **Käfig** (-e)	cage
der **Stall** (¨e)	stall, sty, stable, kennel
das **Vieh**	cattle

Useful phrases (both levels)

Die Familie Braun wohnt in einem alleinstehenden Haus.	*The Braun family lives in a detached house.*
Die Tochter liegt noch im Bett und schläft.	*The daughter is still in bed asleep.*
Der Sohn geht ins Badezimmer, um sich zu waschen.	*The son goes into the bathroom to get washed.*
Er putzt sich die Zähne mit seiner Zahnbürste.	*He brushes his teeth with his toothbrush.*
Die Tochter sitzt im Wohnzimmer und sieht fern.	*The daughter sits in the lounge and watches television.*
Von Zeit zu Zeit sieht sie zum Fenster hinaus.	*From time to time she looks out of the window.*
Der Junge deckt den Tisch im Eßzimmer.	*The boy is laying the table in the dining room.*
Vater ist in der Küche. Er bereitet das Mittagessen vor.	*Father is in the kitchen. He is preparing lunch.*
Mutter gräbt im Gemüsegarten um.	*Mother is digging in the vegetable garden.*
Sie hat einen Kohlkopf ausgegraben.	*She has dug up a cabbage.*
Die Eltern sorgen für die Kinder.	*The parents look after the children.*

im ersten Stock wohnen	*to live on the first floor*
im Erdgeschoß	*on the ground floor*
in ein Zimmer eintreten	*to go into a room*
in eine andere Stadt ziehen	*to move to another town*
umziehen	*to move house*
einziehen	*to move in*
an die Tür klopfen	*to knock at the door*
Jemand hat geklingelt	*Someone rang the doorbell*
die Hausarbeit machen	*to do the housework*
das Geschirr spülen	*to wash the dishes*
das Geschirr abtrocknen	*to dry the dishes*
abwaschen	*to do the washing-up*
waschen	*to do the washing*
bügeln	*to do the ironing*
fegen	*to sweep*
putzen	*to clean, do the cleaning*
seine Sachen aufräumen	*to tidy up one's things*
ein Bad nehmen	*to have a bath*
Blumen pflanzen	*to plant flowers*
Die Blumen wachsen	*The flowers grow*
den Rasen mähen	*to mow the lawn*
die Hecke schneiden	*to cut the hedge*
die Blumen gießen	*to water the flowers*
den Garten jäten	*to weed the garden*
bequem	*comfortable*
unbequem	*uncomfortable*
geräumig	*roomy*
eng	*cramped*
die Vorhänge aufmachen	*to open the curtains*
die Vorhänge zumachen	*to close the curtains*
im Fernsehen	*on television*

3 Town, countryside and beach

die **Altstadt** (¨e)	old town
die **Ampel** (-n)	traffic lights
angenehm	pleasant
auf dem Lande	in the country
die **Autobahn** (-en)	motorway
der **Bahnhof** (¨e)	station
die **Bank** (-en)	bank
die **Baustelle** (-n)	building site
der **Berg** (-e)	mountain
bei	at, near
die **Brücke** (-n)	bridge
die **Bundesstraße** (-n)	trunk road
die **Burg** (-en)	castle
der **Bürgersteig** (-e)	footpath, pavement

das **Büro** (-s)	office
die **Bushaltestelle** (-n)	bus stop
der **Dom** (-e)	cathedral
das **Dorf** (¨er)	village
das **Feld** (-er)	field
der **Fernsprecher** (-)	telephone
fließen	to flow
der **Flughafen** (¨)	airport
der **Fluß** (¨sse)	river
das **Freibad** (¨er)	open air pool
der (die) **Fußgänger (zone)** (-) (-n)	pedestrian (zone)
die **Gefahr** (-en)	danger
gefährlich	dangerous
gegenüber	opposite
das **Hallenbad** (¨er)	swimming pool (indoor)
die **Hauptstadt** (¨e)	capital
hoch	high
der **Hügel** (-)	hill
in der Nähe (von)	near
die **Industrie** (-n)	industry
die **Insel** (-n)	island
das **Kino** (-s)	cinema
die **Klinik** (-en)	clinic, hospital
die **Kirche** (-n)	church
das **Krankenhaus** (¨er)	hospital
die **Kreuzung** (-en)	crossroads
das **Land** (¨er)	country
die **Landstraße** (-n)	main road
der **Lärm** (*no pl.*)	noise
links	on the left
der **Marktplatz** (¨e)	market place
das **Meer** (-e)	sea
das **Museum** (-een)	museum
die **Natur** (-en)	nature
nett	nice
die **Neustadt** (¨e)	new town
die **Parkanlage** (-n)	public gardens
der **Parkplatz** (¨e)	car park
das **Parkhaus** (¨er)	multi-storey carpark
die **Polizei**	police
die **Polizeiwache** (-n)	police station
die (das) **Post (amt)** (-en) (¨er)	post (office)
das **Rathaus** (¨er)	town hall
rechts	on the right
ruhig	quiet
der **Sand** (*no pl.*)	sand
sauber	clean
das **Schloß** (¨sser)	castle
schmutzig	dirty
das **Schwimmbad** (¨er)	swimming pool
der **See** (-s, -n)	lake
die **See** (-n)	sea
das **Stadion** (-en)	stadium
die **Stadt** (¨e)	town
die **Stadtmauer** (-n)	rampart
die **Stadtmitte** (-n)	town centre
das **Stadtzentrum** (-tren)	town centre
der **Stein** (-e)	stone
die **Stelle** (-n)	place
still	silent, quiet
der **Strand** (-e)	shore, beach
die **Straße** (-n)	street
das **Tal** (¨er)	valley
die **Tankstelle** (-n)	petrol station
das **Theater** (-)	theatre
die **Treppe** (-n)	steps, stairs
tief	deep
der **Turm** (¨e)	tower

(un) freundlich	(un)friendly
der **Verkehr** (*no pl.*)	traffic
das **Verkehrsamt** (¨er)	tourist office
der **Wald** (¨er)	wood
die **Wiese** (-n)	meadow
der **Bach** (¨e)	stream
der **Bahnübergang** (¨e)	level crossing
der **Bezirk** (-e)	district
die **Bibliothek** (-en)	library
der **Briefkasten** (-)	pillar box
bummeln	to stroll
der **Einwohner** (-)	inhabitant
flach	flat
der **Forst** (-e)	forest
frisch gestrichen	freshly painted
das **Gebiet** (-e)	district
das **Gebirge** (-)	range of mountains
die **Gegend** (-en)	district
der **Gipfel** (-)	summit
irgendwo	anywhere
der **Kreis** (-e)	district
die **Küste** (-n)	coast
die **Landschaft** (-en)	scenery
der **Ort** (-e)	place
das **Reisebüro** (-s)	travel agency
die **Rolltreppe** (-n)	escalator
schützen	to protect
der **Stadtbummel** (-)	walk round town
der **Stadtteil** (-e)	area of town
steil	steep
die **Überfahrt** (-en)	crossing
das **Ufer** (-)	bank (of river)
der **Vorort** (-e)	suburb
der **Wegweiser** (-)	sign post
der **Zebrastreifen** (-)	zebra crossing

Useful phrases (both levels)

nach dem Weg fragen	*to ask the way*
Schlange stehen	*to queue*
besichtigen	*to visit (i.e. to tour the sights)*
Der Polizist regelt den Verkehr.	*The policeman controls the traffic.*
eine Stadtrundfahrt machen	*to go on a tour of the town*
Die Dame geht über die Straße.	*The lady crosses the road.*
in die Stadt fahren/gehen	*to go to town*
die Stadtmitte besichtigen	*to visit the town centre*
auf der anderen Seite der Straße	*on the other side of the street*
Er kennt sich in der Stadt aus.	*He knows his way about the town.*
Wo ist der nächste Weg zum Kino, bitte?	*Which is the nearest way to the cinema, please?*
in der Ferne	*in the distance*
sich verirren	*to get lost*
den Berg hinaufsteigen	*to climb the mountain*
auf dem Lande sein	*to be in the country*
aufs Land gehen	*to go into the country*
im Freien	*in the open air*
Die Landschaft ist flach, hügelig, waldreich.	*The countryside is flat, hilly, wooded.*
Der Mann angelt mit einer Angelrute.	*The man is fishing with a fishing rod.*
Der Junge füttert die Fische.	*The boy is feeding the fish.*
einen Ausflug machen	*to go on a trip*
einen Spaziergang machen	*to go for a walk*
ans Meer/an die See fahren	*to go to the sea*
ins Wasser tauchen	*to dive into the water*
seekrank werden	*to become seasick*
Es ist Flut.	*It is high tide.*
Es ist Ebbe.	*It is low tide.*
in der Sonne liegen	*to lie in the sun/sunbathe*

4 School

BUILDINGS

die **Gesamtschule** (-n)	comprehensive school
die **Grundschule** (-n)	primary/first school
das **Gymnasium** (-ien)	grammar school
die **Hauptschule** (-n)	secondary modern
in der Stadt	in the town
der **Kindergarten** (‥)	kindergarten
das **Klassenzimmer** (-)	classroom
das **Lehrerzimmer** (-)	staff room
die **Realschule** (-n)	technical school
die **Schule** (-n)	school
der **(Schul) Hof** (‥e)	playground
weit (von)	far from
die **Werkstatt** (‥e)	workshop
die **Aula** (-len)	school hall
die **Bibliothek** (-en)	library
das **(Sprach) Labor** (-s)	(language) laboratory
die **Turnhalle** (-n)	sports hall

SCHOOL ROUTINE

(an) sehen	to look at
die **Antwort** (-en)	answer
aufpassen	to pay attention
(be) antworten	to answer
das **Beispiel** (-e)	example
besuchen	to visit
der **Bleistift** (-e)	pencil
der **Direktor** (-en)	head
fehlen	to make a mistake
die **Ferien** (*pl.*)	holidays
die **Frage** (stellen)	to ask the question
fragen	ask
der **Füller** (-)	fountain pen
die **(Haus) Aufgabe** (-n)	(home) work, exercise
der **Hausmeister** (-)	caretaker
das **Heft** (-e)	exercise book
die **Klasse** (-n)	form, class
die **Klassenarbeit** (-en)	class work
der **Klassenlehrer** (-)	form/class teacher
der **Kugelschreiber** (-)	ball-point pen
der **Kuli** (-s)	ball-point pen
der **Lehrer** (-)	teacher
lernen	to learn
lesen	to read
die **Mappe** (-n)	file case

die **(Mittags) Pause** (-n)	(lunch) break
die **Morgenpause** (-n)	morning break
Oster-	Easter . . .
das **Papier** (-e)	paper
das **(Schul) Buch** (¨er)	(school) book
der **Schüler** (-)	school boy
der **Schulfreund** (-e)	schoolfriend
die **Schultasche** (-n)	school bag
das **Semester** (-)	term
Sommer-	summer . . .
streng	strict
studieren	to study
die **Stunde** (-n)	period
der **Stundenplan** (¨e)	timetable
vergessen	to forget
Weihnachts-	Christmas . . .
zuhören	to listen to
abschreiben	to copy
ausfallen	to fail to take place
bestrafen	to punish
das **Blatt** (¨er)	leaf, sheet of paper
erfahren	to learn, experience
der **Filzstift** (-e)	felt tip pen
hitzefrei	no school on account of heat
das **Klassenbuch** (¨er)	class book/register
der **Klassensprecher** (-)	class, spokesman
die **Kreide** (-n)	chalk
der **Lappen** (-)	duster, cloth
das **Lineal** (-e)	ruler
loben	to praise
nachsitzen	to be kept in
das **Pult** (-e)	desk
der **Radiergummi** (-s)	rubber
rechnen	to count, add up
schulfrei	no school
der **Schwamm** (¨e)	sponge
schwänzen	to truant
die **Strafarbeit** (-en)	imposition
die **Tafel** (-n)	blackboard
der **Unterricht** (*no pl.*)	instruction, tuition
versetzen	to move up (*a class*)
der **Zettel** (-)	note
das **Zeugnis** (-se)	school report

SUBJECTS, MARKS, FUTURE PLANS, EXAMS

die **Biologie**	biology
die **Chemie**	chemistry
der **Computer** (-)	computer
das **Deutsch**	German
das **Englisch**	English
die **Erdkunde**	Geography
das **Fach** (¨er)	subject
das **Französisch**	French
die **Fremdsprache** (-n)	foreign language
die **Geographie**	geography
die **Geschichte**	history
die **Handarbeit**	needlework
die **Handelswissenschaft**	commerce
die **Holzarbeit**	woodwork
die **Informatik**	information studies
das **Kochen**	cooking
die **Kunst**	art
das **Latein**	Latin
das **Maschineschreiben**	typing
die **Mathe (matik)**	Mathematics
die **Metallarbeit**	metalwork
die **Musik**	music

das **Nähen**	sewing
die **Naturwissenschaft** (-en)	natural science
die **Physik**	physics
die **Religion**	religion
das **Spanisch**	Spanish
der **Sport**	sport
Sport treiben	to go in for sport
die **Technik**	technical studies
das **technische Zeichnen**	technical drawing
das **Turnen**	gymnastics
ausgezeichnet	excellent
Eins (bis) Sechs	one (to) six
gut	good
interessant	interesting
langweilig	boring
leicht	easy
das **Lieblingsfach** (¨er)	favourite subject
mangelhaft	poor
die **Note** (-n)	mark
sehr gut	very good
ziemlich gut	fairly good
schwierig	difficult
die **(Abschluß) Prüfung** (-en)	(Leaving) exam
bestehen	to pass
durchfallen	to fail
das **Pflichtfach** (¨er)	compulsory subject
das **Wahlfach** (¨er)	optional subject
das **Abitur**	A Level equivalent
die **Leistung** (-en)	achievement
mogeln (slang)	to cheat
mündlich	oral
schriftlich	written
sitzenbleiben	to have to repeat the year
die **Berufsberatung** (-en)	careers advice
die **Fach (hoch) schule**	skill training school
der **Lehrling** (-e)	apprentice
die **Oberstufe** (-n)	sixth form
der **Student** (-en)	student
die **(technische) Hochschule** (-n)	polytechnic
die **Uni(versität)** (-en)	university

Useful phrases (both levels)

(nicht) gern lernen/studieren	*(not) to like learning/studying*
lieber lernen/studieren	*to prefer learning/studying*
am liebsten haben	*to like best*
(nicht) (besonders) gut im Sport/in Sprachen sein	*(not) to be (especially) good at sport/languages*
gut nähen können	*to be able to sew well*
Sprachen kann ich überhaupt nicht	*I am no good at languages at all*

5 Free time and entertainment

FREE TIME

anfangen	to begin
angeln	to fish
aufhören	to stop
der **Ausflug** (¨e)	excursion, trip
(aus) gehen	to go out
der **Badeanzug** (¨e)	bathing costume
die **Badehose** (-n)	bathing trunks
die **Bademütze** (-n)	bathing cap
baden	to bathe
das **Badetuch** (¨er)	bath towel
das **Badminton**	badminton
beginnen	to begin

der **Besuch** (-e)	visit
das **Boot** (-e)	boat
der **Computer**(-s)	computer
fahren	to travel
der **Federball** (¨e)	shuttlecock
fernsehen	to watch TV
fertig	ready
die **Flöte** (-n)	flute
der **(Foto) Apparat** (-e)	camera
die **Freizeit** (-en)	free time
der **Fußball** (¨e)	football
die **Geige** (-n)	violin
die **Gitarre** (-n)	guitar
gucken	to watch
der **Handball** (¨e)	handball
die **Hit (parade)** (-n)	hit parade
der **Hobby** (-s)	hobby
hören	to hear
(im) Fernsehen	(on) television
das **Instrument** (-e)	instrument
die **Interesse** (-n)	interest
joggen	to jog
das **Jogging**	jogging
die **Karten** (*pl.*)	cards
die **Kassette** (-n)	cassette
der **Kassettenrecorder** (-)	cassette recorder
klassisch	classical
das **Klavier** (-e)	piano
kleben	to stick
knipsen	to take snaps
die **(Langspiel) Platte** (-n)	(long playing) record
laufen	to walk, run
laut	loud
leise	soft
das **Magazin** (-e)	magazine
die **Mannschaft** (-en)	team
nähen	to sew
das **Orchester** (-)	orchestra
das **Picknick** (-e)	picnic
der **Plattenspieler** (-)	record player
die **(Pop) Musik**	(pop) music
das **Programm** (-e)	programme
radfahren	to cycle
reiten	to ride (horses)
der **Rucksack** (¨e)	rucksack
sammeln	to collect
die **Schallplatte** (-n)	record
schauen	to look
der **Schild** (-e)	shield, badge
der **Schlager** (-)	popular song
das **Schlagzeug** (*no pl.*)	percussion, drums
schwimmen	to swim
die **Sendung** (-en)	broadcast, programme
(sich) treffen	to meet
skifahren	to ski
der **Skilift** (-e)	ski lift
der **Ski** (-er)	ski
der **Skistock** (¨e)	skistick
spazierengehen	to go for a walk
der **Spaziergang** (¨e)	walk
spielen	to play
der **Sport (Sportarten)**	sport
der **Sportplatz** (¨e)	sportsground
springen	to jump
das **(Tisch) Tennis**	(table) tennis
das **(Transistor) Radio** (-s)	(transistor) radio
treiben	to go in for
die **Trompete** (-n)	trumpet

der **Verein** (-e)	club
der **Volleyball**	volleyball
wandern	to hike
die **Wanderung** (-en)	hike (noun)
der **Wasserball**	water polo
werfen	to throw
das **Windsurfen**	windsurfing
die **Zeitschrift** (-en)	magazine
die **Zeitung** (-en)	newspaper
der **Ansager** (-)	announcer, compere
die **Aufnahme** (-n)	photograph
basteln	to engage oneself in a hobby
die **(Blas) Kapelle** (-n)	(brass) band
das **Brett** (-er) (slang)	the boards (stage)
das **Dia** (-s)	slide (film)
fangen	to catch
fotografieren	to photograph
die **Freizeitsbeschäftigung** (-en)	holiday or spare time job
gestrichen	painted
die **Illustrierte** (-n)	illustrated magazine
im **Freien**	in the open air
kegeln	to bowl
klettern	to climb
die **Leichtathletik**	athletics
malen	to paint
die **Messe** (-n)	fair
das **Mitglied** (-er)	member
die **Nachrichten** (*no sing.*)	news
die **Nadel** (-n)	needle, pin
das **Netz** (-e)	net
der **Pfadfinder** (-)	scout
die **Reklame** (-n)	advertisement
rennen	to run, race
der **Rollschuh** (-e) **(laufen)**	(to) roller skate
der **Roman** (-e)	novel
das **Ruderboot** (-e)	rowing boat
rudern	to row
der **Rundfunk** (*no pl.*)	radio, broadcasting
die **Sammlung** (-en)	collection
das **Schach** (*no pl.*)	chess
der **Schläger** (-)	bat, racket
Schlittschuh laufen	to ice skate
das **Segelboot** (-e)	sailing boat, yacht
segeln	to sail
die **Seilbahn** (-en)	cable railway
die **Sendefolge** (-n)	broadcast, radio feature
senden	to broadcast
die **Sendereihe** (-n)	radio series
(sich) erkundigen	to inform oneself
(sich) trainieren	to train
(sich) trimmen	to slim (by exercising)
stricken	to knit
das **Taschenbuch** (-er)	pocket book, note book
tauchen	to dive
das **Tonbandgerät** (e)	tape recorder
das **Tor** (-e)	gate, goal (football, etc)
das **Training** (*no pl.*)	training
der **Trainingsanzug** (-e)	tracksuit
der **Umkleideraum** (-e)	changing room
das **Videogerät** (-e)	video recorder
der **Wegweiser** (-)	signpost

ENTERTAINMENT

die **Ausstellung** (-en)	exhibition
besichtigen	to go sightseeing
die **Burg** (-en)	castle
die **Diskothek/Disco** (-en)	discotheque

der **Dokumentarfilm** (-e)	documentary
der **Eingang** (¨e)	entrance
der **Eintritt** (-e)	admission
das **Eintrittsgeld** (-er)	admission fee
die **Eintrittskarte** (-n)	ticket (admission)
das **(End) Spiel** (-e)	game (final)
der **Fan (atiker)** (-)	fan(atic)
der **Film** (-e)	film
frei	free
gewinnen	to win
die **Gruppe** (-n)	group
der **(Jugend) Klub/Club** (-s)	(youth) club
die **Karte** (-n)	map, card, ticket
die **Kasse** (-n)	cash desk
das **Kino** (-s)	cinema
das **Konzert** (-e)	concert
der **Krimi** (-s)	thriller, detective story
das **Museum** (-een)	museum
der **(Not) Ausgang** (¨e)	(emergency) exit
der **Platz** (¨e)	seat
der **Rang** (¨e)	tier, row, circle of theatre
die **Reihe**	row
die **Rundfahrt** (-en)	round trip
der **Sänger** (-)	singer
das **Schauspiel** (-e)	play
das **Schloß** (¨sser)	castle
singen	to sing
das **Stadion** (-ien)	stadium
tanzen	to dance
das **Theater (Stück)** (-) (¨e)	theatre (play)
der **Trickfilm** (-e)	cartoon film
verlieren	to lose
die **Vorstellung** (-en)	performance
der **Wildwestfilm** (-e)	western
der **Zoo** (-s)	Zoo
zu Ende sein	to be at an end
der **Affe** (-n)	ape, monkey
die **Aufführung** (-en)	performance, production
ausverkauft	sold out
der **Balkon** (-s)	balcony
berühmt	famous
beschließen	to decide
die **Besichtigung** (-en)	sightseeing tour
besorgen	to see to (something)
die **Bühne** (-n)	stage
die **Bundesliga** (-gen)	German football league
eins zu null	one nil
der **Elefant** (-en)	elephant
das **Ergebnis** (-se)	result
die **Führung** (-en)	guided tour
die **Garderobe** (-n)	cloak-room
der **Jahrmarkt**	annual fair
das **Kirmes** (-sen)	church festival
die **Komödie** (-n)	comedy
der **Löwe** (-n)	lion
das **Parkett** (-e)	stalls (theatre)
der **Pokal** (e)	goblet, cup, trophy
der **Profi** (-s)	pro
der **Punkt** (-e)	point
der **Reiseführer** (-)	guide book
der **Reiseleiter** (-)	courier
der **Saal** (Säle)	hall
die **Saison** (-s)	season
schießen	to shoot
die **Schlange stehen**	to queue
der **Tiger** (-)	tiger

der **Treffpunkt** (-e)	meeting point
unentschieden	undecided
die **(Welt) Meisterschaft** (-en)	(world) championship
der **Zuschauer** (-)	spectator

Useful phrases

Ich möchte gern zwei Karten für . . .	*I should like two tickets for . . .*
Ich habe zwei Karten im ersten Rang (Seite/Mitte) (in der ersten Reihe) zu 12DM.	*I have two tickets in the first circle (side, middle) (in the front row) at 12DM.*
Die nehme ich.	*I will take them.*
Wann beginnt die Vorstellung?/Wann fängt die Vorstellung an?	*When does the performance/show begin?*
Was kosten die Karten?	*What do the tickets cost?*
Ich möchte eine Karte zu 10DM für heute abend./Zwei zu 10DM bitte.	*I should like one ticket at 10DM for this evening./Two at 10DM please.*
Wann ist das Konzert zu Ende?	*When does the concert end?*
Ist das Museum/Schloß auch am Sonntag geöffnet?	*Is the museum/castle also open on Sunday?*
Bis wann läuft die Ausstellung?	*Until when does the exhibition run?*
Die Vorstellung beginnt pünktlich um 21 Uhr.	*The performance starts promptly at 9 p.m.*

Some words for describing a film, play, etc.

besonders	special, especially	**langweilig**	boring
finden	to find	**Lieblings-**	favourite
furchtbar	terrible	**lustig**	funny
ganz	completely, quite	**meinen**	to think (express opinion)
gefallen	to please	**sehr**	very
(gern) mögen	to like	**spielen**	to play
gut	good	**toll**	super
interessant	interesting	**ziemlich**	rather
komisch	comic		

Wie teuer sind Plätze im Parkett/ auf dem ersten Rang/im zweiten Rang?	*How dear are seats in the stalls/ the lower circle/the upper circle?*
Gut, dann nehme ich drei Karten im Parkett.	*Good, then I will take three tickets in the stalls.*
Der Film war wirklich toll/furchtbar langweilig.	*The film was really super/terribly boring.*
Ich mag David Bowie ganz gern.	*I like David Bowie a lot.*
Er gefällt mir gut.	*I like him a lot./He pleases me well.*
Der Film hat mir gut gefallen.	*I liked the film a lot.*
der **Erfolg** (-e) leiden mögen (nicht) leiden können spannend	*success to like (not) to be able to stand exciting, thrilling*
Wie fandst du den Film?	*What did you think of the film? How did you find the film?*
Ich fand ihn nicht besonders.	*I did not find it anything special.*
Joan Collins? Die kann ich nicht leiden!	*Joan Collins? I cannot stand her*
Das Stück war ein Erfolg.	*The play was a success.*

6 Travel

FINDING ONE'S WAY

	abbiegen	to turn off
die	**Ampel** (-n)	lights
	am/zum Ende	at/to the end
	ander	other
	an (. . . vorbei)	past
	auf	up
	außer	besides
die	**Autobahn** (-en)	motorway
	bis zu . . .	as far as
	breit	wide
die	**Brücke** (-n)	bridge
die	**Bundesstraße** (-n)	trunk road
	da/dort (drüben)	there (over there)
	da (hin)/dort (hin)	thence
	dann	then, next
	dieser	this, the latter
das	**Dorf** (¨er)	village
die	**Ecke** (-n)	corner
	eng	narrow
	entlang	along
	Entschuldigen Sie bitte!	Excuse me please.
	erste/zweite/dritte usw.	first, second, third etc.
	fahren	to go
	finden	to find
der	**Fluß** (¨sse)	river
	folgen	to follow
	fremd (sein)	(to be) foreign
der	**Fußgänger** (-)	pedestrian
	gegenüber	opposite
	gehen	to walk
	geradeaus	straight ahead
	gleich	same
die	**Hauptstraße** (-n)	high street
	hier	here
	hinauf	up
	hinten (*adv.*)	behind
	hinter (*prep.*)	behind
	hinüber	over
	hinunter	down, under
	immer	every, always
	in der Nähe (von)	near
die	**Innenstadt** (¨e)	inner town
das	**Krankenhaus** (¨er)	hospital
die	**Kreuzung** (-en)	crossing
die	**Landkarte** (-n)	map
die	**Landstraße** (-n)	main road
	links	on the left
	nächst	next, nearest
	neben	next to, near
	nehmen	to take
	(nicht) weit (von)	(not) far (from)
der	**Platz** (¨e)	square
die	**Post**	post
das	**Postamt** (¨er)	post office
das	**Rathaus** (¨er)	town hall
	rechts	on the right
die	**Richtung** (-en)	direction
die	**Seite** (-n)	side
die	**Stadt** (¨e)	town
der	**Stadtplan** (¨e)	town plan
die	**Straße** (-n)	street
	suchen	to look for
die	**Toiletten** (*pl.*)	toilets
	über	over, across
	um	at, around

vor	in front of
der **Weg** (-e)	road, pathway
wie komme ich (am besten) . . . ?	What's the (best) way to . . . ?
zu	to, at
zu Fuß	on foot
das **Auto** (-s)	car
der **Bus** (-se)	bus
das **(Fahr) Rad** (-̈er)	bicycle
die **Fahrt** (-en)	journey
die **Klassenfahrt** (-en)	class outing
mitfahren	to accompany
das **Mofa** (-s)	moped (small)
der **Reisebus** (-se)	touring bus
spät (kommen)	to come (late)
der **Wagen** (-)	car
zu Fuß (gehen)	to go on foot
der **Zug** (-̈e)	train
dauern	to last
pünktlich	punctually
die **Nebenstraße** (-n)	side street
die **Querstraße** (-n)	cross road, side street
sich erkundigen	to make enquiries
sich verfahren	to lose one's way
sich verirren	to get lost
sich verlaufen	to lose one's way
der **Schülerlotse** (-n)	school traffic warden
überqueren	to cross over
das **Ufer** (-)	bank (river)
weg	away
verpassen	to miss

Useful phrases (both levels)

Entschuldigen Sie bitte, wie komme ich am besten zum Bahnhof/zur Post?	*Excuse me please, what's the best way to the station/to the post office?*
Nehmen Sie die erste Straße links, dann gehen Sie geradeaus.	*Take the first road on the left, then go straight on.*
Nehmen Sie die nächste Straße rechts.	*Take the next road on the right.*
Biegen Sie an der nächsten Ampel/ Kreuzung links ab.	*Turn left at the next traffic lights/crossroads.*
(Das) tut mir leid. Ich weiß es nicht.	*I am sorry. I do not know that.*
Da kann ich Ihnen nicht helfen. Ich bin hier (selbst) fremd.	*I can't help you there. I am a stranger here (myself).*
Ist das weit von hier?	*Is it far from here?*
Nein, das ist nicht weit. Zehn Minuten zu Fuß/Nur zehn Kilometer.	*No, it is not far. Ten minutes on foot/Only ten kilometres.*
Vielen Dank/Danke schön!	*Thank you very much!*
Bitte schön/Keine Ursache!	*Don't mention it!*

RAIL, BUS, PLANE

ab	off
(ab) fahren	to travel (depart)
die **Abfahrt** (-en)	departure
abfliegen	to take off, depart
an	at
(an) kommen	to come (arrive)
die **Ankunft** (-̈e)	arrival
der **Ausgang** (-̈e)	exit, way out
aussteigen	to get out/off
der **Ausstieg** (-e)	place where you get out

die **Bahn** (-en)	railway, track
der **Bahnsteig** (-e)	platform
buchen	to book
der **Bus** (-se)	bus
der **(Bus) Bahnhof/Bhf** (⁻e)	(bus) station
der **Dampfer** (-)	steamer
die **Deutsche Bundesbahn/DB**	German railway
direkt	direct

der **D-Zug** (⁻e)	through/fast train
der **Eilzug** (⁻e)	express train
einfach	simple, single
einmal/zweimal usw.	once/twice etc.
einsteigen	to get on/in
der **Einstieg** (-e)	place where you get on
erreichen	to reach, catch
der **Fahrer** (-)	driver
der **Fahrgast** (⁻e)	passenger
die **Fahrkarte** (-n)	ticket
der **(Fahrkarten) Schalter** (-)	booking/ticket office
der **Fahrplan** (⁻e)	timetable
der **Fahrschein** (-e)	ticket (bus)
festhalten	to hold on
der **Flughafen** (⁻)	airport

das **Flugzeug** (-e)	aeroplane
das **Gleis** (-e)	track (railway)
die **Haltestelle** (-n)	bus stop
der **Hauptbahnhof/Hbf** (⸚e)	main station
hinten	behind
hin und züruck	return (of ticket)
der **Inter-City-Zug** (⸚e)	intercity train
der **Kofferkuli** (-s)	luggage trolley
der **Krankenwagen** (-)	ambulance
kriegen	to get
landen	to land
langsam	slowly
die **Maschine** (-n)	plane, machine
mitten	in the middle
der **Nahverkehrszug** (⸚e)	local train
nehmen	to take
der **(Nicht) Raucher** (-)	(non) smoker
die **Nummer** (-n)	number
der **Passagier** (-e)	passenger
die **Reise** (-n)	journey
die **(Reise) Auskunft** (⸚e)	(journey) information
reisen	to travel
der **Reisende** (-)	traveller
reservieren	to reserve
die **Richtung** (-en)	direction
die **Rückfahrkarte** (-n)	return ticket
rufen	to call
die **S-Bahn** (-en)	tramway
das **Schiff** (-e)	ship
schnell	quick, fast
der **Schnellzug** (⸚e)	fast train
der **(Speise) Wagen** (-)	(dining) car, carriage
starten	to start
die **Station** (-en)	halt, stop
die **Straßenbahn** (-en)	tram
das **Taxi** (-s)	taxi
der **TEE-Zug** (⸚e)	trans-Europe express
die **U-Bahn** (-en)	underground
die **Überfahrt** (-en)	crossing
über (Köln)	via (Cologne)
umsteigen	to change (trains)
verlassen	to leave
vorn(e)	at/in the front
der **Warteraum** (⸚e)	waiting room
der **Wartesaal** (-säle)	waiting room
werktags	workdays
wochentags	weekdays
der **Zug** (⸚e)	train
der **Zuschlag** (⸚e)	additional charge
der **(Ab) Flug** (⸚e)	flight
das **Abteil** (-e)	compartment
an Bord	on board
anschnallen	to fasten, strap in
die **(Auto) Fähre** (-n)	(car) ferry
dauern	to last
die **Einzelkarte** (-n)	single ticket
erhältlich	obtainable
der **Fahrausweis** (-e)	travel permit
der **Fahrpreis** (-e)	fare
der **Feiertag/feiertags/**(-e)	holiday/holidays
die **Gepäckannahme** (-n)	left luggage office (luggage in)
die **Gepäckaufbewahrung** (-en)	left luggage office
die **Gepäckausgabe** (-n)	left luggage (luggage out)
das **Gepäcknetz** (-e)	luggage rack
gültig	valid
hinauslehnen	to lean out

der **Hubschrauber** (-)	helicopter
kontrollieren	to check
der **Liegewagen** (-)	couchette
die **Linie** (-n)	line
lösen	to buy (a ticket)
melden	to announce
die **Mehrfahrtenkarte** (-n)	season ticket
planmäßig	as timetabled
das **Reisebüro** (-s)	travel agency
der **Schaffner** (-)	conductor, guard
der **Schlafwagen** (-)	sleeping car
das **Schließfach** (¨er)	safe deposit box
der **Sicherheitsgurt** (-e)	safety belt
die **Stewardeß** (-essen)	air hostess
der **Treffpunkt** (-e)	rendezvous, meeting place
verkehren	to frequent
verpassen	to miss
verreisen	to go on a journey
verspätet	late, overdue
die **Verspätung** (-en)	delay
zuschlagspflichtig	subject to supplement

Useful phrases: rail (both levels)

den Zug erreichen	*to catch the train*
den Zug versäumen/verpassen	*to miss the train*
Der Zug hat fünf Minuten Verspätung.	*The train is five minutes late.*
auf dem Bahnhof	*at the station*
Der Zug fährt ein.	*The train enters the station.*
Der Zug kommt an.	*The train arrives.*
Der Zug fährt ab.	*The train departs.*
mit der Bahn fahren	*to travel by rail*
Der Reisende löst eine Fahrkarte.	*The passenger gets a ticket.*
Er fährt erster Klasse/zweiter Klasse.	*He travels first/second class.*
Er fährt über Aachen nach Köln.	*He travels to Cologne via Aachen.*
Er steigt in den Zug ein.	*He gets into the train.*
Er steigt aus dem Zug aus.	*He gets off the train.*
Er steigt in Köln nach Bonn um.	*He changes at Cologne for Bonn.*
Ich muß ihn vom Bahnhof abholen.	*I have to meet him at the station.*
nach Bonn einfach bitte	*a single to Bonn please*
nach Köln (hin) und zürück	*a return to Cologne*
Ist dieser Platz besetzt/frei?	*Is this seat taken/free?*
Ist das der Zug nach Bonn?	*Is that the train to/for Bonn?*
Ist das ein TEE-Zug/ein Schnellzug?	*Is that a trans-European express/ an express?*
Kann ich direkt fahren?/Fährt der Zug direkt (nach München)?	*Can I go direct?/ Is the train through (to Munich)?*
Muß ich umsteigen? Wo?	*Do I have to change? Where?*
Wo bekommt man Fahrkarten?	*Where does one get tickets?*
Wo ist der Fahrkartenschalter?	*Where is the ticket office?*
einmal zweite(r) Klasse (nach) Bonn und zurück bitte	*a return to Bonn, second class please*
einmal nach Bonn, hin und zurück bitte	*a return ticket to Bonn please*
einmal einfach nach Bonn bitte	*a single to Bonn please*
erste Klasse Hamburg, einfache Karte bitte	*a single to Hamburg, first class please*
Wann fährt der (nächste) Zug (nach Bonn) ab?	*When does the (next) train (to Bonn) leave/depart?*
Wann kommt der Zug in Köln an?	*When does the train arrive in Cologne?*
Von welchem Gleis fährt der Zug?	*From which platform does the train leave?*
Wie kann ich nach Hamburg kommen?	*How do I get to Hamburg?*

Useful phrases: bus (both levels)

Kann ich da mit dem Bus/der Straßenbahn fahren?	*Can I get the bus/train there?*
Fährt da der Bus hin?	*Does the bus go there?*
Wohin fährt die Nummer/Linie acht?	*Where does the number eight go to?*
Welcher Bus fährt nach Kassel?	*Which bus goes to Kassel?*

Useful phrases: plane (both levels)

eine Flugkarte lösen.	*to buy a ticket for a flight.*
Sie bucht einen Flug.	*She books a flight.*
Sie bucht einen Rückflug.	*She books a return flight.*
Schnallen Sie sich bitten an!	*Please fasten your seatbelts.*

TRAVEL BY ROAD

Achtung!	Look out!
die **Ausfahrt** (-en)	vehicular exit
das **Auto** (-s)	car
die **Batterie** (-n)	battery
die **Baustelle** (-n)	building site
das **Benzin**	petrol
besetzt	occupied
das **Diesel** (-)	diesel
die **(Einbahn) Straße** (-n)	(one way) street
die **Einfahrt** (-en)	vehicular entrance
einordnen	to classify
erlauben	to allow
das **(Fahr) Rad** (-̈er)	(bicycle) wheel
frei	free
freihalten	to keep free (no parking)
der **Führerschein** (-e)	driving licence
Gas geben	to accelerate
die **Gefahr** (-en)	danger
gefährlich	dangerous
gesperrt	closed (street)
gestattet	authorized
die **grüne (Versicherungs) Karte** (-n)	green card (insurance)
kaputt	bust, broken
der **Lkw (Lastkraftwagen)** (-)	lorry
der **Luftdruck** (-̈e)	air pressure
das **Mofa** (-s)	moped
das **Motorrad** (-̈er)	motorbike
nachsehen	to check
Normal	normal (i.e. 2 star)
der **Notruf** (-e)	emergency call
das **Öl**	oil
parken	to park
das **Parkhaus** (-̈er)	covered carpark
der **Parkplatz** (-̈e)	car park
Pkw	car
prüfen	to test
das **Rad/Hinterrad/Vorderrad** (-̈er)	wheel/rear/front
der **Radfahrer** (-)	cyclist
radfahren	to cycle
der **Rasthof** (-̈e)	
der **Rastplatz** (-̈e)	place to stop and rest
die **Raststätte** (-n)	
der **Reifen** (-)	tyre
der **Reifendruck** (-̈e)	tyre pressure
die **(Reparatur) Werkstatt** (-̈e)	repair workshops
reparieren	to repair
die **Selbstbedienung/SB**	self service
das **Selbsttanken** (-)	self-service petrol
Super	super (i.e. 4 star)
tanken	to put in petrol
die **Tankstelle** (-n)	garage (for petrol)

die **Umleitung** (-en)	diversion
verboten	forbidden
volltanken	to fill up (with petrol)
die **Vorfahrt** (-en)	the right of way
(die) **Vorsicht** (*no pl.*)	(foresight) look out!
der **Wagen** (-)	car
die **Warnung** (-en)	warning
die **Zufahrt** (-en)	driveway, approach
abschleppen	to tow away
der **Abschleppwagen** (-)	breakdown lorry
Abstand halten	to keep distance
abstellen	to turn off (engine)
anlassen	to start (engine)
das **Autobahndreieck** (-e)	motorway interchange
das **Autobahnkreuz** (-e)	motorway junction
die **Autowäsche** (-n)	car wash
die **Bremse** (-n)	brake
der **Dienst** (-e)	service
der **Durchgangsverkehr** (*no pl.*)	through traffic
das **Fahrzeug** (-e)	vehicle
der **Fehler** (-)	mistake
die **Gebühr** (-en)	tax, duty
gebührenpflichtig	liable to tax
die **(Geld) Strafe** (-n)	penalty (fine)
die **Hochgarage** (-n)	garage
die **(Höchst) Geschwindigkeit**	(maximum) speed
der **Kofferraum** (¨e)	boot
der **Lieferwagen** (-)	delivery van
der **Motor** (-n)	motor, engine
der **Parkschein** (-e)	parking ticket
die **Parkuhr** (-en)	parking meter
das **Parkverbot** (*no pl.*)	no parking
per Anhalter fahren	to hitch-hike
der **Roller** (-)	scooter
die **(Reifen) Panne** (-n)	breakdown (puncture)
der **Scheinwerfer** (-)	headlight
Schritt fahren	to go very slowly/dead slow
der **Stau** (-e)	traffic jam
das **Steuerrad** (¨er)	steering wheel
die **Tiefgarage** (-n)	underground garage
überfahren	to run over
der **Unfall** (¨e)	accident
die **Verkehrsstauung** (-en)	traffic jam
die **Versicherung** (-en)	insurance
die **Windschutzscheibe** (-n)	windscreen
der **Zusammenstoß** (¨e)	collision

Useful phrases (both levels)

bremsen	*to brake*
anhalten	*to stop*
sich auf den Weg machen, abfahren	*to set out/off*
Gute Fahrt!	*Have a good trip!*
eine Fahrt von drei Stunden	*a three-hour journey*
den Motor anschalten	*to switch on the engine*
den Motor abschalten	*to switch off the engine*
per Anhalter fahren	*to hitchhike*
Volltanken bitte	*Fill her up please!*
überholen	*to overtake*
mit dem Auto/Wagen fahren	*to go by car*
eine Reise machen	*to go on a journey*
Der Wagen hat eine Panne.	*The car has broken down.*
Der Fahrer fährt einen Radfahrer an.	*The driver runs into a cyclist.*
Ende der Geschwindigkeitsgrenze	*end of the speed limit*
Der Junge wird beinahe überfahren.	*The boy is nearly run over.*
Das Auto kommt nicht leicht ins Schleudern.	*The car does not easily skid.*

Zehn Liter Normal bitte!	*10 litres of 2-star please!*
Für 50 Mark Super bitte!	*50 marks worth of 4-star please!*
Können Sie bitte mal das Öl nachsehen?	*Can you please just check the oil?*
Können Sie mal den Reifendruck/ Luftdruck prüfen?	*Can you just check/test the tyre/ air pressure?*
Können Sie bitte auch das Wasser nachsehen?	*Can you also check the water please?*
Hab' ich noch genug Wasser?	*Have I still got enough water?*
Gibt es hier (in der Nähe) ein Parkhaus/einen Parkplatz?	*Is there here (nearby) a covered car park/a car park nearby?*
Meine Windschutzscheibe ist kaputt.	*My windscreen has broken.*
Mein Wagen hat eine Panne	*My car has broken down.*
Ich habe eine Panne.	*I have a puncture.*
Können Sie einen Abschleppwagen/ einen Mechaniker schicken?	*Can you send a breakdown lorry/ a mechanic?*
Wie lange dauert die Reparatur?	*How long will the repairs take?*
Haben Sie den Fehler gefunden?	*Have you found the fault?*
Ich glaube . . . ist nicht in Ordnung.	*I think . . . is not working.*

7 Holidays

auspacken	to unpack
der **Austausch** (-e)	exchange
der **Ausweis** (-e)	identity card
bleiben	to stay
Bodensee	Lake Constance
braun werden	to get brown
die **Broschüre** (-n)	brochure
das **Camping**	camping
der **Campingplatz** (-e)	campsite
die **Donau**	Danube
(ein) packen	to pack
Europa/EWG	Europe/EEC
fahren	to go
die **Ferien** (*pl.*)	holidays
das **Gasthaus** (-er)	guest house
der **Gasthof** (-e)	hotel
das **Hotel** (-s)	hotel
die **Jugendherberge** (-n)	youth hostel
Köln	Cologne
die **Kosten** (*pl.*)	costs
München	Munich
der **Norden**	north
die **Nordsee**	North Sea
organisieren	to organize
der **Osten**	east
die **Ostsee**	Baltic Sea
die **Papiere** (*pl.*)	papers
der **Paß** (-sse)	passport
die **Paßkontrolle** (-n)	passport check
der **Plan** (-e)	plan
planen	to plan
die **Reise** (-n)	journey
reisen	to go on a journey
der **Reisepaß** (-sse)	travel permit
Rhein	Rhine
die **Sandburg** (-en) (**bauen**)	sandcastle (to build)
der **Stadtplan** (-e)	town plan
der **Süden**	south
der **Urlaub** (-e)	vacation, leave
verbringen	to spend
das **Verkehrsamt** (-er)	tourist office
der **Westen**	west
Wien	Vienna
zelten	to camp in a tent

der **Zeltplatz** (¨e)	campsite for tents
der **Zoll**	customs
das **Zollamt** (¨er)	customs house
der **Zollbeamte** (-n)	customs official
die **Zollkontrolle** (-n)	passport inspection

der **Aufenthalt** (-e)	stay
die **Grenze** (-n)	border, frontier
der **Kanal**	English Channel
das **Mittelmeer**	Mediterranean
das **Reisebüro** (-s)	travel agency
sehenswert	worth seeing
die **Sehenswürdigkeit** (-en)	sight(s)
die **Unterkunft** (¨e)	accommodation
verzollen	to declare (customs)
vorhaben	to intend, to have in mind
vorzeigen	to show

Useful phrases (both levels)

zollfrei	*duty free*
durch den Zoll gehen	*to go through customs*
Haben Sie etwas zu verzollen?	*Have you anything to declare?*
Ich habe nichts zu verzollen.	*I have nothing to declare.*
Die Dame mußte ihren Koffer auspacken.	*The lady had to unpack her case.*
Wann findet die Gepäckkontrolle statt?	*When is the luggage examined for customs?*
Er mußte den Zoll bezahlen.	*He had to pay the customs duty.*
Der Zollbeamte wollte unsere Pässe ansehen.	*The customs official wanted to look at our passports.*

8 Communication

ON THE TELEPHONE

am Apparat	on the phone
anrufen	to telephone
besetzt	occupied
Bitte warten!	Wait please!
eine (falsche) Nummer wählen	to dial a (wrong) number
falsch wählen	to dial the wrong number
Hallo!	Hallo!
Hier bei Braun!	This is the Browns!
Hier Dieter Schmidt!	Dieter Smith here!
sprechen (mit)	to speak (with)
telefonieren	to telephone
Wer ist dort?	Who is that?
Wiederhören!/auf Wiederhören!	goodbye (on the phone)

POSTCARDS AND LETTERS

der **Abs** (ender) (-)	sender
alles Gute!	all the best
beilegen	to enclose
bekommen	to get
der **Brief** (-e)	letter
der (die) **Brieffreund(in)** (-e) (-innen)	penfriend
Grüße bestellen	to send compliments
hochachtungsvoll	yours respectfully/or faithfully
liebe Lotte!	dear Lotte,
lieber Wilhelm!	dear Wilhelm,
mit den besten Grüßen (und Wünschen)	with best greetings (and wishes)

mit freundlichem Gruß ⎫	with kind regards
mit freundlichen Grüßen ⎭	
schicken	to send
sehr geehrte Damen und	dear Ladies and Gentlemen
Herren!	
sehr geehrte/verehrte Frau!	dear Mrs/Ms . . .
sehr verehrte Dame!	dear Madam
sehr geehrter Herr!	dear Sir
sich freuen	to be pleased
(viele) herzliche Grüße	(many) sincere greetings
erhalten	to receive
es grüßt . . . herzlich	kind regards
Schluß machen	to bring to an end

MEETING PEOPLE

aber	but, however
abholen	fetch
ach (du lieber) Gott!	oh grief!
ach (so)!	oh dear!
die Ahnung (-en)	idea
also	so
auch	also
(auf) Wiedersehen!	goodbye!
ausgezeichnet	excellent
bekannt machen	to introduce
bestimmt	certainly
bis später/nachher/bald/	till later/afterwards/soon
gleich/morgen (dann)	immediately/tomorrow (then)
bitte (schön/sehr)	please (here you are/don't mention it)
danke (schön/sehr)	thank you (very much)
dann	then
denken	to think
denn	for
doch	yet
dürfen	to be allowed
eben	even
einladen	to invite
die Einladung (-en)	invitation
die Entschuldigung (-en)	excuse
es/das geht	that is all right
es ist mir egal	it is all the same to me
es kann (nicht) sein	it can/may (not) be
es macht nichts	that does not matter
es tut mir leid	I am sorry
Feuer haben	to have a light
der (die) Freund (in) (-e) (-innen)	friend
freut mich	I am glad
frohe Ostern!	Happy Easter!
frohe/fröhliche	Merry Christmas!
Weihnachten!	
frohes/glückliches Neujahr!	Happy New Year!
furchtbar	terribly
gern/lieber haben	to like/to prefer
gleichfalls	the same to you
grüß Gott!	good day! (Austrian)
gut	good
gute Besserung!	I hope you get better soon!
gute (Heim)Fahrt!	Have a good journey (home)!
gute Nacht!	good night!
gute Reise!	Have a good journey/trip!
guten Abend!	good evening!
guten Appetit!	good appetite!
(guten) Morgen!	(good) morning!
(guten) Tag!	good day/afternoon!
hat's geschmeckt?	Did it taste good?
herein!	Come in!
herzlichen Glückwunsch!	Congratulations!

	Himmel!	heavens!
	hoffen	to hope
	hoffentlich	I hope that
	ich hätte gern	I should have liked
	ich möchte gern	I should like to
die	**Idee** (-n)	idea
	ja	yes
	kennen	to know
	kennenlernen	to get to know
	klasse!	classic!
der (die)	**Kollege/Kollegin** (-n) (-innen)	colleague
	komm gut nach Hause!	safe journey home!
	leider	unfortunately
die	**Leute**	people
	Lust haben	to want to
	mach's gut!	all the best!
die	**Mahlzeit** (-en)	mealtime
	mal	just
	meinen	to think
	mein Gott!	my God!
	Mensch!	'struth!
	mitmachen	to take part in
	na	well
	nee	no (*coll.*)
	nein	no
	nicht	not
	nicht wahr?	isn't it?
die	**Party** (-s)	party
	prima	super
	probieren	to try
	Prost! prosit!	cheers!
	Quatsch!	rubbish!
	schlaf gut!	sleep well!
	schon	already
	schmecken	to taste
	schrecklich	terrible
	Servus!	greetings
	(sich) interessieren (für)	to be interested (in)
	(sich) vorstellen	to introduce (oneself)
	sollen	to be (supposed) to
	so (was) . . .	so what . . .
	Spaß haben/machen	to have fun
	stimmen	to agree
	toll	super
	träume süß!	sweet dreams
	Tschüß	cheers! cheerio!
	vielen Dank!	many thanks!
	viel Glück!	lots of luck!
	viel Spaß!	have fun!
	warten	to wait
	wie bitte?	what did you say?
	willkommen	welcome
	wunderbar	wonderful
	wünschen	to wish
	Zeit haben	to have time
	abgemacht	settled, agreed
	ablehnen	to decline
	annehmen	to accept
	(be)grüßen	to greet
	beliebt	favourite, popular
	bitten	to request, ask
der	Blödsinn	nonsense
	duzen	to use *du*
	einverstanden	understood
	empfehlen	to recommend
	genügen	to be enough
	gar nicht	not at all

gratulieren	to congratulate
(ich habe) nichts dagegen	I have nothing against it
klappen	to come off, succeed
mit (großen/größtem/dem größten) Vergnügen	with great/greatest/ the greatest pleasure
der **Namenstag** (-e)	Saints day, name day
Pech haben	to have bad luck
raten	to guess
sich **ärgern**	to be annoyed
(sich) **entschuldigen**	to apologize
(sich) **treffen**	to meet
sich **verabschieden**	to say goodbye
siezen	to use 'Sie'
überraschen	to surprise
die **Überraschung** (-en)	surprise
die **Verabredung** (-en)	appointment
Verzeihung!	Forgive me! Excuse me!
Vergnügen (finden/machen)	to find pleasure/delight in
vorschlagen	to suggest
vorziehen	to prefer
(wie) **schade!**	what a pity!
zufrieden	content
zum Wohl!	your health!

9 Shopping

SHOPS

die **Apotheke** (-n)	dispensing chemist's
der **Automat** (-en)	automatic machine
die **Bäckerei** (-en)	baker's
die **Drogerie** (-n)	chemist's (retail)
Einkäufe machen	to go shopping
einkaufen	to shop
die **Fleischerei** (-en)	butcher's shop
der **Friseur** (-e)	hairdresser
der **Gemüsehändler** (-)	greengrocer
das **Geschäft** (-e)	shop
die **Geschäftszeiten** (*pl.*)	shop hours
der **Händler** (-)	trader
die **Handlung** (-en)	shop
kaufen	to buy
das **Kaufhaus** (-er)	store
der **Kiosk** (-e)	kiosk
die **Konditorei** (-en)	cake shop
der **Laden** (-)	shop
das **Lebensmittelgeschäft** (-e)	grocer's

die **Metzgerei** (-en)	butcher's
die **Öffnungszeiten** (*pl.*)	opening times
der **(Super)Markt** (¨e)	(super) market
verkaufen	to sell
das **Warenhaus** (¨er)	department store
der **Zeitungsstand** (¨e)	newspaper stall
die **Betriebsferien** (*pl.*)	works holiday
das **Einkaufszentrum** (-tren)	shopping centre
der **Ruhetag** (-e)	closing day
das **Schaufenster** (-)	display window
die **Schreibwarenhandlung** (-en)	stationer's
der **Schreibwarenhändler** (-)	stationer
der **Süßwarenladen** (¨)	sweet shop

SHOPPING

der **Apfel** (¨)	apple
die **Apfelsine** (-n)	orange
der **Aufschnitt** (-e)	slice, cut
der **Ausgang** (¨e)	exit
die **Banane** (-n)	banana
bekommen	to get
(be)zahlen	to pay
die **Birne** (-n)	pear
der **Bonbon** (-s)	sweet
brauchen	to need
das **Brot** (Brotsorten)	bread
das **Brötchen** (-)	bread roll

die **Butter**	butter
die **Chips** (*pl.*)	crisps
das **Ding** (-e)	thing
die **Dose** (-n)	tin
der **Dosenöffner** (-)	tin opener
das **Ei** (-er)	egg
die **Ermäßigung** (-en)	reduction
fast	almost, nearly
die **Flasche** (-n)	bottle
das **Gemüse** (-)	vegetables
geöffnet	open, opened
geschlossen	shut, closed
das **Glas** (¨er)	glass, jar
der **Groschen** (-)	small coin
holen	to fetch
der **Honig** (*no pl.*)	honey
der **Käse** (Käsesorten)	cheese
der **Keks** (-)	biscuit
die **Konditorei** (-en)	cake shop
der **Kopfsalat**	cabbage or lettuce
kosten	to cost
kostenlos	without charge, free
der **Kuchen** (-)	cake
die **Lebensmittel** (*pl.*)	food, provisions
die **Liste** (-n)	list
das **(Mark)Stück** (-e)	coin
die **Marmelade** (-n)	jam
die **Milch**	milk
die **Münze** (-n)	coin
das **Obst** (-sorten)	fruit
das **Päckchen** (-)	packet
die **Packung** (-en)	packing, package
das **Paket** (-e)	parcel
der **Pfirsich** (-e)	peach
die **Pflaume** (-n)	plum
die **Praline** (-n)	chocolate
preiswert	cheap
die **Sache** (-n)	thing
die **Schachtel** (-n)	box, case
der **Schein** (-e)	bank note
die **Schokolade** (-n)	chocolate (block)
die **Seife** (-n)	soap
(sich) bedienen	to serve (oneself)
das **(Sonder)Angebot** (-e)	(special) offer
der **Sonderpreis** (-e)	special price
das **Stück** (-e)	piece
die **Tafel** (-n)	block (chocolate)
die **Tomate** (-n)	tomato
die **Torte** (-n)	gateau
die **Tube** (-n)	tube
die **Tüte** (-n)	paper bag
die **(Wein)Traube** (-n)	grape
die **Wurst** (¨e)	sausage
zeigen	to show
zusammen	together
die **Abteilung** (-en)	department
ausgeben	to spend
der **Ausverkauf** (¨e)	clearance sale
die **(Aus)Wahl** (-en)	choice
dienen	to serve
der **Einkaufskorb** (¨e)	shopping basket
der **Einkaufswagen** (-)	shopping trolley
das **Erdgeschoß** (-sse)	ground floor
die **Gebrauchsanweisung** (-en)	directions for use
günstig	favourable
die **Hälfte** (-n)	half
der **Kassenzettel** (-)	receipt

das **Pfand** (¨er)	pledge, deposit
die **Quittung** (-en)	receipt
der **Rabatt** (-e)	discount, rebate
die **Rolltreppe** (-n)	escalator
schälen	to peel, shell
die **Scheibe** (-n)	slice (of sausage)
der **Sommerschlußverkauf**	end of Summer Sale
das **Spülmittel** (-)	washing-up liquid
der **Topf** (¨e)	pot, jar
umsonst	in vain
der **Umtausch** (¨e)	exchange
umtauschen	to exchange
das **Untergeschoß** (-sse)	basement
das **Waschpulver** (-)	washing powder
wiegen	to weigh

Useful phrases (both levels)

ein (halbes) Pfund Tomaten	*(half) a pound of tomatoes*
ein Kilo Kartoffeln	*a kilo of potatoes*
eine (große/kleine) Dose Frankfurter	*a (large/small) tin of Frankfurter sausages*
ein Stück Seife	*a bar of soap*
eine Tüte Milch/ein Glas Marmelade	*a carton of milk/a jar of jam*
eine Tafel Schokolade	*a bar of chocolate*
eine Flasche Limonade	*a bottle of lemonade*
Hundert Gramm Schinken	*100 grams of ham*
Was/Wieviel kostet das?	*What/How much does that cost?*
Was macht das (zusammen)?	*What does that make (altogether)?*
Das ist alles	*That's everything*
Wo kann ich bezahlen?	*Where can I pay?*
Darf ich mit Scheck bezahlen?	*May I pay by cheque?*
Ich habe kein Kleingeld	*I have no small change*
Ich habe nur einen Hundertmarkschein, geht das?	*I only have a 100 mark note, is that alright?*
Da stimmt etwas nicht!	*There's something wrong here!*
Was kann ich für Sie tun?	*What can I do for you?*
Kann ich Ihnen helfen?	*Can I help you?*
Was wünschen Sie, bitte?	*What would you like, please?*
Was haben Sie für einen Wunsch?	*What sort of thing do you want?*
Sonst noch etwas?	*Anything else?*
Außerdem noch etwas?	*Anything more besides?*
Zahlen Sie an der Kasse!	*Pay at the cash desk!*
Fünfzig Pfennig das Stück	*50 Pfennigs each*
Haben Sie ein Zwei/Fünfmarkstück?	*Have you a two/five mark coin?*
Haben Sie es nicht kleiner?	*Have you got nothing smaller?*
Ja, ich kann wechseln.	*Yes, I can change it.*
Auf der Flasche ist (zehn Pfennig) Pfand.	*There is a (10 pfennig) deposit on the bottle.*
Mit 10% Rabbatt	*With 10% discount*
Haben Sie eine kleinere/größere Dose/Packung?	*Have you a smaller/larger tin/package?*
Ich glaube, das kann nicht ganz stimmen.	*I don't think that can be quite right.*
Sind Sie sicher, daß das stimmt?	*Are you sure that's right?*
Können Sie mir bitte diesen (Hundertmark) Schein wechseln?	*Can you please change this (100 mark) note for me?*
Darf ich einen Einkaufswagen haben?	*May I have a shopping trolley?*
Sechs Scheiben Leberwurst, bitte.	*Six slices of liver sausage please.*
Ich bekomme zwanzig Pfennig Pfand für die Flasche zurück	*I get a 20 pfennig deposit back on the bottle.*

CLOTHES

anhaben	to have on
der **Anorak** (-s)	anorak
der **Anzug** (¨e)	suit
die **(Armband) Uhr** (-en)	clock (wrist watch)
der **Artikel** (-)	article

der **Badeanzug** (-̈e)	bathing costume
die **Badehose** (-n)	bathing trunks
die **Bluse** (-n)	blouse
die **Brieftasche** (-n)	wallet
die **Farbe** (-n)	colour
die **Größe** (-n)	size
der **Gürtel** (-)	belt
die **Haarbürste** (-n)	hairbrush
der **Handschuh** (-e)	glove
die **Handtasche** (-n)	handbag
das **Hemd** (-en)	shirt
die **(Herren/Damen) Konfektion** (-en)	(gents/ladies) ready made clothing
die **(Herren)Mode** (-n)	(men's) fashion
die **Hose** (-n)	trousers
die **Jacke** (-n)	jacket
die **Jeans** (*pl.*)	jeans
das **Kleid** (-er)	dress
die **Kleider** (*pl.*)	clothes
die **Kleidung** (-en)	clothing
die **Krawatte** (-n)	tie
das **Paar** (-e)	pair
das **(Papier)Taschentuch** (-̈er)	(paper) handkerchief
die **Plastik**	plastic
das **Portemonnaie**	purse
der **Pulli** (-s)	pullover
der **Pullover** (-)	pullover
die **Qualität** (-en)	quality
der **(Regen)Mantel** (-̈)	(rain)coat
der **Rock** (-̈e)	coat, skirt
die **Sandale** (-n)	sandal
der **Schlafanzug** (-̈e)	pyjamas
der **Schlips** (-e)	tie
der **Schuh** (-e)	shoe
die **Socke** (-n)	sock
die **(Sonnen)Brille** (-n)	(sun) glasses
die **(Sonnen)Creme**	(sun) cream
die **Sonnenmilch**	sun milk
das **Sonnenöl** (-e)	sun oil
der (die) **Strumpf(hose)** (-̈e) (-n)	stocking (tights)
das **T-Shirt** (-s)	T-Shirt
wählen	to choose
der **Wecker** (-)	alarm clock
die **Zahnbürste** (-n)	toothbrush
die **Zahnpasta** (-en)	toothpaste
anprobieren	to try on
die **(Baum)Wolle** (-n)	wool (cotton)
der **Büstenhalter** (-)	bra
echt	genuine
(ein)reiben	to rub (in)
das **Gummi**	rubber
der **Hut** (-̈e)	hat
der **Kamm** (-̈e)	comb
das **Kostüm** (-e)	costume
der **Kunststoff** (-e)	synthetic
die **Mütze** (-n)	cap
der **Pantoffel** (-) (-n)	slipper
der **Regenschirm** (-e)	umbrella
der **Schal** (-e)	shawl, scarf
schützen	to patent
die **Seide** (-n)	silk
der **Stiefel** (-)	boot
der **Stoff** (-e)	material
die **(Unter)Wäsche** (-n)	(under) wear
das **(Wild)Leder** (-)	leather (deerskin)

Useful phrases (both levels)

Danke, ich schaue nur.	*Thank you, I'm just looking.*
Ich möchte (gern) einen Mantel/Rock/ Pullover kaufen.	*I should like to buy a coat/ skirt/pullover.*
Was kostet der?	*What does this cost?*
Das ist zu klein/groß/teuer/billig/ hell/dunkel.	*That's too small/big/dear/cheap/ light/dark*
Der gefällt mir.	*I like that.*
Gibt es ein anderes Geschäft in der Nähe?	*Is there another shop nearby?*
Können Sie mir sagen, wo ich . . . bekommen kann?	*Can you tell me where I can get . . .?*
Ich komme als nächste(r) an der Reihe.	*I am next/next in the queue.*
Sie sind an der Reihe/dran.	*You're next.*
Im Fenster haben wir einen blauen Rock gesehen.	*We saw a blue skirt in the window.*
Das Kleid paßt (mir) gut/nicht.	*The dress suits me well/does not suit me.*
Die Krawatte paßt gut/nicht zum Hemd.	*The tie goes well/does not go with the shirt.*
Die Farbe paßt nicht zu mir.	*The colour does not suit me.*
Ich habe/trage Größe 38.	*I am/I wear size 38.*
Haben Sie eine Nummer größer/kleiner?	*Have you a larger/smaller size?*
Welche Größe ist es?	*Which size is it?*
Es ist zwei Nummern zu groß/klein.	*It is two sizes too big/small.*
Ich möchte es in Braun haben.	*I should like it in brown.*
Haben Sie dasselbe in Grün?	*Have you the same in green?*
Haben Sie etwas Besseres/Billigeres/ Anderes?	*Have you something better/cheaper/ else?*
Kann ich sie einmal anprobieren?	*Can I just try it on?*
Ich nehme den kleinen/den großen.	*I'll take the small one/the big one.*
Wie hoch kommt das?	*How high does that come?*
Darf ich die Quittung/den Kassenzettel haben?	*May I have the receipt?*
Ich möchte dieses Kleid umtauschen	*I should like to change this dress*
Ich möchte ein Kleid aus Seide/Baumwolle	*I should like a silk/cotton dress*
Werden Sie schon bedient?	*Are you being served already?*
Haben Sie etwas im Fenster gesehen, was Ihnen gefällt?	*Have you seen something you like in the window?*
Suchen Sie etwas Bestimmtes?	*Are you looking for something particular?*
Das Kleid ist aus Wolle.	*The dress is made of wool.*
Die Schuhe sind aus Leder/Wildleder.	*The shoes are leather/buckskin.*
Beim Umtausch bitte den Kassenzettel vorzeigen.	*Please show the till receipt on exchanging this garment.*

10 Food and drink

PLACES

die **Bierhalle** (-n)	beer hall
das **Café** (-s)	café
die **Erfrischungen** (*pl.*)	refreshments
das **Gasthaus** (-̈er)	hotel, restaurant
der **Gasthof** (-̈e)	hotel, inn
die **Gaststätte** (-n)	restaurant
der **Imbiß** (-sse) **Imbißstand** (-̈e)	snack bar
das **Kaffeehaus** (-̈er)	coffee house
der **Kiosk** (-e)	kiosk
die **Konditorei** (-en)	cake shop
die **Milch (Bar)** (-s)	milk bar
der **Rasthof** (-̈e)	hotel, restaurant
die **Raststätte** (-n)	restaurant
der **(Rats)Keller** (-)	cellar (Town Hall) restaurant
das **Restaurant** (-s)	restaurant
der **Schnellimbiß** (-sse)	snack bar
die **Weinprobe** (-n)	wine tasting
die **Weinstube** (-n)	wine bar, wine cellar
der **Weinkeller** (-)	wine bar, wine cellar
der **Würstchenstand** (-̈e)	sausage stall
Herr Ober!	waiter!
Fräulein!	waitress, Miss!
Hallo (Bedienung)!	Hallo (Service)!
Bedienung bitte!	Service please!
die **Kneipe** (-n)	tavern, pub
die **Schenke** (-n)	tavern, inn, pub
die **Theke** (-n)	bar (in pub or inn)
der **Stammtisch** (-e)	table reserved for regulars
die **Wirtschaft** (-en)	inn
das **Wirtshaus** (-̈er)	public house, inn

Useful phrases

Im Restaurant.	*In the restaurant.*
Der Kellner bedient die Gäste.	*The waiter serves the guests.*
Die schöne Dame ißt zuerst Suppe.	*The beautiful lady first has soup.*
Der junge Mann trinkt Wein.	*The young man is drinking wine.*
Der Mann bestellt die Mahlzeit.	*The man orders the meal.*
Sie essen nach der Karte.	*They are eating a la carte.*
Er fragt: „Ist die Bedienung inbegriffen?"	*He asks 'Is service included?'*
Herr Ober: bitte, zahlen!	*Waiter, the bill, please!*
Haben Sie einen Tisch frei?	*Do you have a table free?*
Haben Sie einen Tisch für zwei?	*Do you have a table for two?*
Haben Sie einen Tisch am Fenster/in der Ecke?	*Do you have a table by the window/ in the corner?*
Ist hier noch frei/Platz?	*Is there still room here?*
Ist dieser Tisch noch frei?	*Is this table still free?*
Ich möchte drinnen/draußen sitzen	*I should like to sit inside/outside*
Ich habe schon reserviert.	*I have already reserved (a table).*

EATING OUT

das **Abendbrot** (-e)	supper
das **Abendessen** (-)	supper
die **Bedienung** (-en)	service
beißen	to bite
das **Essen** (-)	food, meal
frisch	fresh
das **Frühstück** (-e)	breakfast
frühstücken	to have breakfast
die **Gabel** (-n)	fork
geben	to give
das **Glas** (-̈er)	glass
grillen	to grill
kauen	to chew
der (die) **Kellner(in)** (-) (-innen)	waiter (waitress)

der **Kinderteller** (-)	child's portion
lecker	delicious
der **Löffel** (-)	spoon
die **Mahlzeit** (-en)	meal
die **Mehrwertsteuer/MWS** (-n)	VAT
das **Menü** (-s)	menu, table d'hôte
das **Messer** (-)	knife
mitnehmen	to take (away) with you
das **Mittagessen** (-)	lunch
das **Öl** (-e)	oil
die **Portion** (-en)	portion, helping
der **Preis** (-e)	price
reichen	to hand across, reach
riechen	to smell
sauer	sour
scharf	sharp
schlucken	to swallow
schneiden	to cut
der **(Schnell)Imbiß** (-sse)	snack (quick)
die **Speisekarte** (-n)	menu
süß	sweet
die **Tageskarte** (-n)	menu of the day
der **Teller** (-)	plate
die **(Unter)Tasse** (-n)	cup (saucer)
die **Weinliste/Weinkarte** (-n)	wine list
der **Zucker** (-)	sugar
zum Mitnehmen	for taking away
(an)bieten	to offer
einschenken	to pour out/in
einschließlich/einschl.	inclusive
gebacken	baked
gebraten	roasted
gemischt/gem.	mixed
das **Gericht** (-e)	dish, course
die **Getränkenkarte** (-n)	drinks menu
der **Getränkekellner** (-)	drinks waiter
inbegriffen/inbegr.	inclusive
paniert	dressed, garnished
der **Pfeffer** (-)	pepper
probieren	to try
das **Salz** (-e)	salt
die **Schale** (-n)	peel, rind, shell
die **Schüssel** (-n)	dish, course
der **Senf**	mustard
der **Strohhalm** (-e)	straw
das **Tablett** (-e)	tray
der **Weinkellner** (-)	wine waiter

Soup and hors d'oeuvres

die **Gulaschsuppe** (-n)	goulash soup
die **Suppe** (-n)	soup
die **Tomatensuppe** (-n)	tomato soup
die **Hühnerbrühe** (-n)	chicken soup
die **Ochsenschwanzsuppe** (-n)	oxtail soup
die **Vorspeise** (-n)	hors d'oeuvre

Egg dishes

das **gekochte Ei** (-er)	boiled egg
das **Omelett** (-s)	omlette
das **Rührei** (-en)	scrambled egg
das **Spiegelei** (-er)	fried egg

Fish

der **Fisch** (-e)	fish
die **Forelle** (-n)	trout

Sausages and cold meat

der **Aufschnitt** (-e)	cut, slice
die **Bockwurst** (¨e)	cold sausage
die **Bratwurst** (¨e)	frying sausage
die **Currywurst** (¨e)	curry sausage
die **Leberwurst** (¨e)	liver sausage
der **Schinken** (-)	ham
die **kalte Platte**	cold meats

Meat

das **(Brat)Hähnchen** (-)	(roast) chicken
das **Curry** (-s)	curry
das **Fleisch**(-sorten)	meat
das **Gulasch**	goulash
das **Kotelett** (-s)	chop, cutlet
die **Leber** (-n)	liver
das **Rindfleisch**	beef
das **Schweinefleisch**	pork
das **Schnitzel** (-)	cutlet, escalope
das **Steak** (-s)	steak
das **Wiener Schnitzel** (-)	veal cutlet
der **Braten** (-)	roast joint
das **deutsche Beefsteak**	beef steak
der **Eintopf** (¨e)	hot pot
die **Grillplatte** (-n)	grill
das **Kalbfleisch**	veal

Vegetables and salads

die **Bratkartoffel** (-n)	roast potato
der **Kartoffelsalat** (-e)	potato salad
die **Pommes frites** (*pl.*)	chips
der **Reis**	rice
der **Salat** (-e)	salad lettuce
die **Salzkartoffel** (-n)	boiled potato
das **Sauerkraut**	pickled white cabbage
die **Tomaten** (*f. pl.*)	tomatoes
der **Wurstsalat** (-e)	sausage salad
der **Blumenkohl** (-köpfe)	cauliflower
die **Bohne** (-n)	bean
der **Champignon** (-s)	mushroom
die **Erbse** (-n)	pea
die **Gurke** (-n)	gherkin
der **Kartoffelbrei**	mashed potato
das **Kartoffelmus**	potato puree
der **Knödel** (-)	dumpling
der **Pilz** (-e)	mushroom
die **Zwiebel** (-n)	onions

Desserts

die **Creme**	cream
der **Eis(becher)** (-)	ice cream
der **Joghurt** (-)	yoghurt
der **Käse** (-)	cheese
das **Kompott**	stewed fruit
der **Obstsalat** (-e)	fruit salad
der **Pudding** (-s)	pudding
die **(Schlag)Sahne** (-n)	(whipped) cream
die **Vanille**	vanilla
die **Erdbeere** (-n)	strawberry
die **Himbeere** (-n)	raspberry
die **Kirsche** (-n)	cherry
die **Zitrone** (-n)	lemon
die **Nachspeise** (-n)	sweet
der **Nachtisch** (-e)	dessert

Drinks

der **Apfelsaft** (¨e)	apple juice
das **Bier** (-e)	beer
das **Cola** (-s)	cola
ein **kleines/großes Dunkles**	a (small/large) dark beer
ein **(kleines/großes) Helles**	a (small/large) light ale
die **Flasche** (-n)	bottle
das **Getränk** (-e)	drink
der **Kaffee** (-)	coffee
der **Kakao**	cocoa
das **Kännchen** (-)	small carafe
die **Limo(nade)** (-n)	lemonade
das **(Mineral) Wasser** (-)	(mineral) water
der **Orangensaft** (¨e)	orange juice
das **Pils** (-)	pils lager
der **Rotwein** (-e)	red wine
der **Sprudel** (-)	soda water
der **Tee**	tea
der **(Weiß)Wein** (-e)	(white) wine
der **Schnaps**	Schnaps, Gin
der **Sekt** (-e)	champagne

Bread, sandwiches, cakes

der **Apfelkuchen** (-)	apple tart
das **(belegte) Brot**	bread (sandwich)
das **Brötchen** (-)	breadroll
das **Butterbrot** (-)	slice of bread and butter
das **Graubrot** (-e)	brown bread
das **Käsebrot** (-e)	cheese sandwich
der **Kirschkuchen** (-)	cherry cake
der **Kuchen** (-)	cake
das **Schinkenbrot** (-)	ham sandwich
das **Schwarzbrot** (-e)	rye/brown bread
die **Torte** (-n)	flan, tart
das **Wurstbrot** (-e)	sausage sandwich

Useful phrases (both levels)

Die (Speise) Karte bitte!	*The menu please!*
Die Weinliste bitte!	*The wine list please!*
Wir möchten essen, bitte.	*We should like to eat please.*
Ich möchte bestellen.	*I should like to order.*
Ich nehme Menü eins.	*I'll have menu one.*
Zweimal Menü zwei.	*Menu two twice.*
Einmal Brathähnchen mit Pommes frites.	*One chicken and chips.*
Darf ich etwas Wasser/Zucker haben?	*May I have some water/sugar?*
Können Sie mir bitte den Zucker reichen?	*Can you pass me the sugar?*
Nur ein bißchen.	*Only a little.*
Nur eine kleine Portion.	*Only a small portion.*
Nicht so viel, bitte.	*Not so much, please.*
Danke, das reicht	*Thank you, that will do.*
Danke, das ist genug.	*Thank you, that's enough.*
Das ist zu sauer/scharf/süß	*That's too bitter/sharp/sweet.*
Das Essen ist kalt.	*The food/meal is cold.*
Das ist nicht sauber.	*That's not clean.*
Darf ich etwas Senf/Salz/Pfeffer haben?	*May I have some mustard/salt/pepper?*
Darf ich einen Strohhalm haben?	*May I have a straw?*
Bringen Sie mir ein anderes Glas!	*Bring me another glass!*
Können Sie mir einen anderen Teller bringen?	*Can you bring me another plate?*
Es fehlt ein Messer/eine Gabel usw.	*There's a knife/fork etc. missing.*
Was ist denn das–Jägerschnitzel?	*What's Jägerschnitzel then?*
Salzkartoffel–was ist das?	*What's Salzkartoffel?*
Können Sie mir bitte erklären, was das ist?	*Can you explain to me what that is?*

Warum dauert es so lange?	*Why is it taking so long?*
Müssen wir (noch) lange warten?	*Do we (still) have to wait a long time?*
Das habe ich nicht bestellt. Ich wollte . . .	*I did not order that. I wanted . . .*
Es war sehr gut.	*It was very good.*
Es war prima/ausgezeichnet.	*It was super/excellent.*
Ich hätte gern die Getränkekarte.	*I wanted the drinks menu.*
Können Sie mir bitte die Getränkekarte bringen?	*Can you please bring the drinks menu.*
Als Vorspeise/Nachspeise möchte ich . . .	*I should like for hors d'oeuvre/for sweet . . .*
(Be)zahlen, bitte!	*Pay please!*
Die Rechnung, bitte!	*The bill please!*
Ich möchte bitte zahlen	*I should like to pay please.*
Können Sie mir bitte die Rechnung bringen?	*Can you bring me the bill please?*
Alles zusammen, bitte.	*Everything together please.*
Das stimmt, so.	*That's all right like that.*
Danke, stimmt's so.	*Thank you, that's OK.*
Und das ist für Sie.	*And that's for you.*
Stimmt das mit Bedienung?	*Is that right with service?*
Nein, nein, ich (be)zahle.	*No, no I'll pay.*
Trink doch was/einen!	*Have another drink!*
Ist die Bedienung/die Mehrwertsteuer inbegriffen?	*Is the service/the VAT included?*
zusammen oder getrennt?	*together or separately?*
Haben Sie schon gewählt?	*Have you chosen yet?*
Ich empfehle Ihnen . . .	*I recommend . . . to you.*
Unser Küchenchef empfiehlt . . .	*Our chef recommends . . .*
Das wär's?	*Is that it?*
Ich kann . . . empfehlen.	*I can recommend . . .*
Darf ich Ihnen noch Wein einschenken?	*May I pour out some more wine for you?*
Möchten Sie diesen Wein/Kuchen probieren?	*Would you like to try this wine/cake?*
Die Bedienung/Der Nachtisch kommt gleich.	*You'll be served/Dessert is coming immediately.*

11 Staying away from home

HOTEL

das **Abendessen** (-)	supper, dinner
(ab) wann?	(from) when?
allein	alone

die **Anmeldung** (-)	announcement, notification
ausfüllen	to fill out, in
das **Bad** (¨er)	bath
die **Bar** (-s)	bar, night club
die **Bedienung** (-en)	service
bequem	comfortable
bleiben	to stay
das **Doppelzimmer** (-)	double room
die **Dusche** (-n)	shower
das **Einzelzimmer** (-)	single room
der **Empfang** (¨e)	reception
die **Empfangsdame** (-n)	receptionist
der **Fahrstuhl** (¨e)	lift
das **Formular** (-e)	form
frei	free
das **Frühstück** (-e)	breakfast
frühstücken	to have breakfast
das **Gästehaus** (¨er)	guest house
das **Gepäck** (-e)	luggage
das **Hotel** (-s)	hotel
der **Koffer** (-)	case
kosten	to cost
der **Lift** (-e) *or* (-s)	lift
die **Mehrwertsteuer/MWS** (-n)	VAT
mit (+ *dat.*)	with
das **(Mittag)Essen** (-)	(lunch) meal
die **Nacht** (¨e)	night
nehmen	to take
ohne (+ *acc.*)	without
parken	to park
der **Parkplatz** (¨e)	car park
die **Pension** (-en)	boarding house, board
der **Portier** (-s)	porter
der **Preis** (-e)	price
pro	for, per
der **(Reise)Scheck** (-e) *or* (-s)	traveller's cheque
die **Reisetasche** (-n)	travel bag
reservieren	to reserve
das **Schloßhotel** (-s)	castle hotel
der **Schlüssel** (-)	key
der **Speisesaal** (-säle)	dining room
der **Stock** (-werke)	storey, floor
das **Telefon** (-e)	telephone
telefonieren	to telephone
übernachten	to stay overnight
die **Übernachtung** (-en)	overnight stay
unterschreiben	to sign
das **Zimmer** (-)	room
das **Zimmermädchen** (-)	chamber maid

der **Aufenthalt** (-e)	stay
die **Aussicht** (-en)	view
der **Blick** (-e)	view
das **Erdgeschoß** (-sse)	ground floor
das **Fremdenheim** (-e)	(visitors') hostel
das **Fremdenzimmer** (-)	spare room, guest room
inbegriffen/inbegr.	included
inklusive	inclusive
mit fließendem/heißem Wasser	with running/hot water
die **(mit) (Halb)Pension** (-en)	with (half) board
die **(mit) Vollpension** (-en)	with full board
sich anmelden	to register
sich beklagen	to complain
sich beschweren	to complain
die **warme Küche** (-n)	warm food
der **Wasserhahn** (¨e)	tap
der **Zimmernachweis** (-e)	room-booking service

Useful phrases (both levels)

im Hotel	*in the hotel*
Der Mann und seine Frau melden sich an.	*The man and his wife register.*
Das Zimmer hat Blick auf den Strand.	*The room overlooks the beach.*
ein Zweibettzimmer	*a twin-bedded room*
ein Zimmer mit Bad	*a room with a bath*
ein Zimmer reservieren/bestellen	*to reserve/book a room*
Ich habe ein Einzelzimmer reserviert.	*I have reserved a single room.*
Haben Sie (ein) Zimmer frei?	*Have you (a) room(s) free?*
Ich möchte ein Doppelzimmer.	*I should like a double room.*
für eine Nacht/zwei Nächte	*for one night/two nights*
ein Zimmer mit Bad/Dusche	*A room with bath/shower*
Ist das mit Bad?	*Is that with a bath?*
Hat das Zimmer Telefon?	*Does the room have a telephone?*
Ich möchte das Zimmer sehen.	*I should like to see the room.*
Welche Zimmernummer habe ich?	*Which room number have I got?*
Nein, das ist zu teuer.	*No, that is too dear.*
Wo ist der Fahrstuhl?	*Where is the lift?*
Wann macht das Restaurant auf?	*When does the restaurant open?*
Ab wann gibt es Frühstück?	*From what time is breakfast served?*
Kann ich im Hotel Essen bekommen?	*Can I get a meal in the hotel?*
Wo können wir parken?	*Where can we park?*
Wie komme ich auf Zimmer Nummer 11?	*How do I get to room number 11?*
Ich fahre gegen Mittag ab.	*I'm leaving around midday.*
Kann ich bitte die Rechnung haben?	*Can I have the bill please?*
Wieviele Übernachtungen?	*How many nights?*
Mit Bad oder ohne?	*With bath or without?*
Das Zimmer hat Bad/Telefon.	*The room has a bath/a telephone.*
Was für ein Zimmer soll das sein?	*What sort of room is it to be?*
Das Zimmer kostet 40DM (pro Person) pro Nacht.	*The room costs 40DM (pro person) per night.*
Wir sind leider voll.	*We are full, unfortunately.*
Wir haben unseren Parkplatz hinter dem Hause.	*Our car park is behind the house.*
Unterschreiben Sie hier!	*Sign here!*
Schreiben Sie Ihren Namen . . . hier hin.	*Write your name here.*
Können Sie bitte dieses Anmeldungsformular ausfüllen?	*Can you complete this registration form please?*
Ist der Preis mit Frühstück?	*Does the price include breakfast?*
Gibt es Ermäßigung für Kinder?	*Is there a reduction for children?*
Ich möchte Halbpension/Vollpension.	*I should like half/full board.*
Ich habe Ihnen geschrieben.	*I wrote to you.*
Können Sie mir ein anderes Hotel empfehlen?	*Can you recommend another hotel to me?*
Ich möchte Frühstück um 8 Uhr auf dem Zimmer.	*I should like breakfast at 8 o'clock in my room.*
Können wir im Zimmer frühstücken?	*Can we have breakfast in our room?*
Können Sie mich um 7 Uhr wecken?	*Can you wake me at 7 a.m.?*
Bitte schicken Sie unser Gepäck hinauf!	*Please send up our luggage!*
Kann ich noch eine Decke/einen Kopfkissen haben?	*Can I have another blanket/pillow?*
Nein, es gefällt mir nicht.	*No, I do not like it.*
Ich möchte den Direktor sprechen.	*I should like to speak to the manager.*
Ich muß ein ruhiges Zimmer haben.	*I must have a quiet room.*
Es ist zu laut/dunkel/klein.	*It is too loud/dark/small.*
Ich wollte ein Zimmer mit Bad.	*I wanted a room with a bath.*
Haben Sie etwas Besseres/Billigeres?	*Have you anything better/cheaper?*
Haben Sie ein Zimmer mit guter/einer besseren Aussicht?	*Have you a room with a good/better view?*
Haben Sie ein Zimmer weiter oben/weiter unten?	*Have you a room higher up/lower down?*
Das Waschbecken ist verstopft.	*The wash basin is blocked.*
Es kommt kein warmes Wasser.	*There is no hot water.*
Dieses Zimmer ist nicht sauber.	*This room is not clean.*

Die Birne ist kaputt.	*The light bulb doesn't work.*
Die (Bett) Laken sind feucht.	*The (bed) sheets (is) are damp.*
Bringen Sie mir bitte Seife/ Handtücher/Toilettenpapier!	*Bring me some soap/hand towels/ toilet paper please!*
Sie sagten, die Zimmer kosten nur . . .	*You said the rooms only cost . . .*
Ist alles inbegriffen?	*Is everything included?*
(Ja), es war ein sehr angenehmer Aufenthalt.	*(Yes), it was a very pleasant stay.*
Ich hoffe, Sie werden einen angenehmen Aufenthalt haben.	*I hope you will have a pleasant stay.*
Jawohl, das Zimmer ist sehr ruhig.	*Yes, the room is very quiet.*
Unser Restaurant hat warme Küche bis 22 Uhr.	*Our restaurant has hot food until 10 p.m.*
Frühstück ist nicht im Preis drin.	*Breakfast is not included in the price.*
Inklusive MWS und Bedienung.	*VAT and service included.*

YOUTH HOSTEL

erlauben	to allow
die **Herbergseltern** (*pl.*)	youth hostel wardens
der **(Herbergs)Gast** (¨e)	(youth hosteller) guest
die **Herbergsmutter** (¨)	female warden
der **Herbergsvater** (¨)	male warden
die **Jugendherberge** (-n)	youth hostel
leihen	to lend, hire
die **Person** (-en)	person
der **Schlafraum** (¨e)	dormitory
der **Schlafsack** (¨e)	sleeping bag
verboten	forbidden
das **Mitglied** (-er)	member
das **schwarze Brett** (-er)	notice board

CAMPING

die **Abreise** (-n)	departure
die **Ankunft** (¨e)	arrival
die **Batterie** (-n)	battery
das **Büro** (-s)	office
das **Camping**	camping
der **Campingartikel** (-)	camping articles/goods
der **Campinggas** (-e)	camping gas
der **Campingkocher** (-)	camping stove
der **Campingplatz** (¨e)	camp site
der **Dosenöffner** (-)	tin-opener
das **Feuer**	fire
der **Laden** (¨)	shop
der **Rucksack** (¨e)	rucksack
der **Schatten** (-)	shade, shadow
der **Waschraum** (¨e)	washroom
der **Wohnwagen** (-)	caravan
das **Zelt** (-e)	tent
zelten	to sleep under canvas
der **Zeltplatz** (¨e)	campsite for tents
abbauen	to dismantle (a tent)
der **Abfall (eimer)** (¨e) (-)	litter (bin)
aufbauen	to put up (a tent)
aufschlagen	to pitch (a tent)
die **Gebühr** (-en)	fee, charge
klappbar	collapsible, folding
der **Klappstuhl** (¨e)	folding chair
der **Klapptisch** (-e)	folding table
die **Luftmatratze** (-n)	inflatable mattress, airbed
die **Spülküche** (-n)	washing-up area
der **Strom** (¨e)	electric current
tragbar	portable

Useful phrases (both levels)

Haben Sie noch Platz für zwei Zelte/für einen Wohnwagen?	*Have you still room/space for two tents/for a caravan?*
Können wir hier zelten, bitte?	*Can we camp here, please?*
Was kostet eine Nacht hier?	*What does one night here cost?*
Liegt es im Schatten?	*Is it in the shade?*
Kann man hier Lebensmittel kaufen?	*Can we buy groceries/provisions here?*
Wo ist das Büro/der Kiosk/der Laden?	*Where is the office/kiosk/shop?*
Wo kann man hier einkaufen?	*Where can one shop here?*
Wo sind die Toiletten/die WCs/die Waschräume?	*Where are the toilets/WCs/washrooms?*
Ich brauche einen Dosenöffner/eine Batterie.	*I need a tin-opener/a battery.*
Wo ist die Steckdose?	*Where is the socket?*
Wo kann man Trinkwasser bekommen?	*Where can one get drinking water?*
Wie weit ist es zum Dorf/Fluß/Meer?	*How far is it to the village/river/ the sea?*
Kann man hier einen Schlafsack leihen?	*Can one hire a sleeping bag here?*
Wo können wir das Zelt aufschlagen?	*Where can we pitch the tent?*
Darf man auf offenem Feuer kochen?	*May one cook over an open fire?*
Dürfen wir ein Feuer machen?	*May we light a fire?*
Sind Hunde erlaubt?	*Are dogs allowed?*
Gibt es ein Schwimmbad/eine Disco?	*Is there a swimming pool/a disco?*

ON AN EXCHANGE VISIT

der **Austausch** (-̈e)	exchange
austauschen	to exchange
das **Bauernhaus** (-̈er)	farm house
der **Bauernhof** (-̈e)	farm
bei (+ *dat.*)	at the house of
der (die) **Brieffreund (in)** (-e) (-innen)	penfriend
die **Ferienwohnung** (-en)	holiday flat
der **Gastgeber** (-)	host
das **Haus** (-̈er)	house
leihen	to hire
mieten	to hire, rent
das **Quadratmeter** (-)	square metre
die **Scheune** (-n)	barn

12 The Post Office

abheben	to lift off
aufgeben	to post (a letter)
das **Ausland**	abroad, foreign country
außer Betrieb	out of use/order
der **Briefkasten** (-)	letter box, pillar box
die **Briefmarke** (-n)	stamp
der **Briefträger** (-)	postman
der **(Brief)umschlag** (-̈e)	envelope
durchwählen	to dial direct
eilt!	urgent
der **Einwurf** (-̈e)	slot, opening
das **Ferngespräch** (-e)	trunk call
das **Gespräch** (-e)	conversation
der **Hörer** (-)	receiver
das **Inland**	inland
die **Leerung** (-en)	collection
die **Luftpost**	air mail
das **Ortsgespräch** (-e)	local call
die **Postanweisung** (-en)	postal order
der **Postbeamte** (-n)	postal clerk (male)
die **Postbeamtin** (-nen)	postal clerk (female)
postlagernd	poste restante, to be called for
das **Postwertzeichen** (-)	postage stamp

die **Rückgabe** (-n)	return
das **(Rück)Gespräch** (-e)	reversed-charge call
die **Telefonzelle** (-n)	telephone box
das **Telegramm** (-e)	telegram
verbinden	to connect
die **Verbindung** (-en)	connection

Useful phrases (both levels)

Der Junge gibt den Brief auf.	*The boy posts the letter.*
Der Mann in der Telefonzelle ruft seine Mutter an.	*The man in the telephone kiosk is phoning his mother.*
Die dicke Dame füllt ein Telegram aus.	*The fat lady is filling in a telegram.*
Sechs Briefmarken zu 40 Pfennig, bitte.	*Six 40-pfennig stamps please.*
Eine Frau wiegt ein Paket.	*A woman is weighing a parcel.*
Der junge Mann nimmt den Brief.	*The young man picks up the letter.*
Die Kunden stehen Schlange.	*The customers stand in a queue.*
Wo kann ich meine Post einwerfen/ aufgeben?	*Where can I post my letters?*
Ich möchte diesen Brief nach England schicken.	*I should like to send this letter to England.*
Wo ist der Briefkasten?	*Where is the post box?*
Ich möchte ein Paket aufgeben.	*I should like to post a parcel.* ·
Wie lange braucht die Post bis England?	*How long does the post take to England?*
An welchem Schalter gibt es Briefmarken?	*At which counter position are there stamps?*
Was kostet eine Postkarte nach England?	*What does a postcard cost to England?*
Drei Briefmarken zu neunzig (Pfennig) bitte.	*Three 90-pfennig stamps please.*
An welchem Schalter kann ich eine Postanweisung einlösen?	*At which counter can I cash a postal order?*
Wo ist der Schalter für postlagernde Sendungen?	*Where is the counter for post restante?*
Ist Post für mich? Ich heiße . . .	*Is there any post for me? my name is . . .*
Ich möchte ein Telegram aufgeben.	*I should like to hand in a telegram.*
Was kostet es pro Wort?	*What does it cost per word?*
Haben Sie ein Telefonbuch für Hamburg?	*Have you a telephone directory for Hamburg?*
Können Sie mir helfen, diese Nummer zu bekommen?	*Can you help me get this number?*
Kann ich durchwählen?	*Can I dial direct?*
Ich möchte ein R-Gespräch anmelden.	*I should like to make a reverse charge call.*
Was hat das Gespräch gekostet?	*What has the call cost?*

▰▰ 13 Banks and money ▰▰

	arbeiten	to work
die	**Bank** (-en)	bank
die	**Banknote** (-n)	banknote
	billig	cheap
die	**Brieftasche** (-n)	wallet
	ein wenig	a little
	Geld sparen	to save money
	Geld verdienen	to earn money
	Geld wechseln	to change money
	genug	enough
	Groschen/Schilling	(Austrian money)
	haben	to have
die	**Kasse** (-n)	cash desk, position
	kaufen	to buy
das	**Kleingeld**	change
	kosten	to cost
	kostenlos	free
	Markstück/Mark/DM/D-Mark	mark
	Pfennig/Pf.	pfennig
	Pfund Sterling	pound sterling
das	**Portemonnaie**	purse
der	**Reisescheck** (-s)	traveller's cheque
das	**Scheckbuch** (⁻er)	cheque book
die	**Scheckkarte** (-n)	cheque card
die	**Sparkasse** (-n)	savings bank
das	**Taschengeld** (-er)	pocket money
	teuer	dear, expensive
	viel	a lot
die	**Wechselstube** (-n)	exchange booth
der	**Geldwechsel** (-)	bureau de change

Useful phrases

Der Tourist geht auf die Bank.	*The tourist goes to the bank.*
Er stellt einen Scheck aus.	*He makes out a cheque.*
Er löst einen Scheck ein.	*He cashes a cheque.*
Er zahlt Geld ein.	*He pays money in.*
Er hebt es ab.	*He withdraws it.*
Er wechselt sein Geld.	*He changes his money.*
Kann ich hier Reiseschecks einlösen?	*Can I cash traveller's cheques?*
Lösen Sie Reiseschecks ein?	*Do you cash traveller's cheques?*
Ich möchte einige Pfund wechseln.	*I should like to change some pounds.*
Wie steht das Pfund?	*How does the pound stand?*
Wie ist der (Wechsel) Kurs für englisches Geld?	*What is the rate of exchange for English money.*
Wie steht der Kurs?	*What is the rate?*
Geben Sie mir vier Zehnmarkscheine und etwas Kleingeld.	*Give me four 10-mark notes and change.*
In Zwanzigmarkscheinen bitte.	*In 20-mark notes please.*
In großen/kleinen Scheinen bitte.	*In large/small notes please.*
Hier ist mein Paß.	*Here is my passport.*

14 Lost property

	beschreiben	to describe
die	**Beschreibung** (-en)	description
	dankbar	thankful
	einreichen	to hand in
	enttäuschen	to disappoint
die	**Enttäuschung** (-en)	disappointment
das	**Fundbüro** (-s)	lost property office
	gehören	to belong to
	liegenlassen	to leave behind
	Pech haben	to be unlucky
	sich bedanken	to thank
der	**Taschendieb** (-en)	pickpocket

überraschen	to surprise
die **Überraschung** (-en)	surprise
verschließen	to lock up
verschwinden	to disappear
versichern	to insure
Angst haben (um)	to be afraid (of)
aussehen	to appear, look like
böse sein	to be cross
danken	to thank
Glück haben	to be lucky
glücklich	fortunate
die **Polizeiwache** (-n)	police station
der **Polizist** (-en)	policeman
sich freuen	to be pleased
vergessen	to forget
verlieren	to lose

15 Weather

der **Blitz** (-e)	flash of lightning
blitzen	to flash (lightning)
der **Donner** (-)	thunder
donnern	to thunder
das **Eis**	ice
frieren	to freeze
das **Gewitter** (-)	thunderstorm, storm
heiß	hot
herrlich	splendid
der **Himmel** (-)	sky
kühl	cool
naß	wet
der **Regen** (-)	rain
regnen	to rain
der **Schatten**	shade, shadow
scheinen	to shine
der **Schnee**	snow
schneien	to snow
die **Sonne** (-n)	sun
der **Sonnenschein**	sunshine
sonnig	sunny
der **Sturm** (-̈e)	storm
stürmisch	stormy
das **Wetter** (-)	weather
der **Wind** (-e)	wind
windig	windy
die **Wolke** (-n)	cloud
wolkig	cloudy
hageln	to hail
mild	mild
neblig	foggy, misty
regnerisch	rainy
das **Sauwetter**	filthy/dreadful weather
schwül	sultry
trocken	dry
trüb	overcast, dull
veränderlich	changeable

WEATHER FORECASTING

die **Aufheiterung** (-en)	clearing/brightening up
die **Bewölkung** (-en)	clouding over, cloudiness
bewölkt	overcast (with cloud)
Celsius	celsius
feucht	damp
der **Grad** (-e)	degree

der **Hagel** (*no pl.*)	hail
heiter	clear, bright
die **Hitze** (*no pl.*)	heat
der **Hochdruck** (⁼e)	high pressure
die **Kälte**	cold
das **Klima** (-s)	climate
der **Mond** (-e)	moon
der **Nebel** (-)	fog
der **Niederschlag** (⁼e)	rainfall
der **Schauer** (-)	shower
der **Stern** (-e)	star
die **(Tages) (Höchst)Temperatur** (-en)	(highest) temperature (of the day)
die **(Tages) Tiefsttemperatur** (-en)	lowest temperature (of the day)
der **Tiefdruck** (-e)	depression
der **Wetterbericht** (-e)	weather report
die **Wetterlage** (-n)	weather conditions
die **Wettervorhersage** (-n)	weather forecast
wolkenlos	cloudless

16 Occupations

der **Apotheker** (-)	pharmacist
der **Arbeiter** (-)	worker
die **(Arbeits)Stelle** (-n)	job, post
der **Arzt** (⁼e)	doctor
der **Bäcker** (-)	baker
der **Bauarbeiter** (-)/**beim Bau arbeiten/auf dem Bau arbeiten**	building worker/to work in the building trade
der **Bauer** (-n)	farmer
der **Beruf** (-e)	vocation, profession
der **Briefträger** (-)	postman
das **Büro** (-s)	office
der **Chef** (-s)	chief, boss
der **Computer** (-)	computer
der **Direktor** (-en)	manager, headmaster
der **Drogist** (-en)	chemist
der **Elektriker** (-)	electrician
der **Fabrik(arbeiter)** (-)	factory (worker)
der **Fahrer/Busfahrer/Lkw-Fahrer** (-)	driver/bus driver/lorry driver
der **Fleischer** (-)	butcher
der **Friseur** (-)	hairdresser
der **Fußballspieler** (-)	football player
die **Industrie** (-n)	industry
der **Kaufmann** (⁼er, -leute)	businessman
der **Kellner** (-)	waiter
der **Koch** (⁼e)	cook
die **Konditorei** (-en)	cake shop, confectioner's
die **Krankenschwester** (-n)	nurse
der **Lehrer** (-)	teacher
der **Mechaniker** (-)	mechanic
der **Metzger** (-)	butcher
der **Musiker** (-)	musician
das **Orchester** (-)	orchestra
der **Pilot** (-en)	pilot
der **Plan** (⁼e)	plan
der **Polizist** (-en)	policeman
das **Postamt** (⁼er)	post office
der **Sekretär** (-e)	secretary
der **(Staats)Beamte** (-n)	civil servant
die **Stewardeß** (-essen)	stewardess
der **Sport** (-arten)	sport
das **Theater** (-)	theatre
das **Verkehrsamt** (⁼er)	tourist office
vielleicht	perhaps
werden	to become
der **Zahnarzt** (⁼e)	dentist
das **Zimmermädchen** (-)	chambermaid

der **Angestellte** (-n)	clerk
der **Arbeitgeber** (-)	employer
der **Arbeitnehmer** (-)	employee
das **Arbeitsamt** (¨er)	employment office
arbeitslos	unemployed
berufstätig	employed
der **Betrieb** (-e)	large business
die **Bundesbahn** (-en)	railway
bei der Bahn arbeiten	to work on the railways
der **Feuerwehrmann** (¨er) (-leute)	fireman
die **Firma** (-men)	firm
der **Gehalt** (-e)	salary
der **Geschäftsmann** (¨er, -leute)	businessman
der **Ingenieur** (-e)	engineer
der **Lohn** (¨e)	salary, wages
der **Matrose** (-n)	sailor
das **Reisebüro** (-s)	travel agency
der **Rentner** (-)	man of private means/landlord
der **Schaffner** (-)	conductor, guard
der **Schauspieler** (-)	actor
der **Schiedsrichter**	referee, umpire
selbständig	self supporting
der **Soldat** (-en)	soldier
der **Tierarzt** (¨e)	vet
der **Verkäufer** (-)	shop assistant
das **Werk** (-e)	work

NB For the feminine forms of job-holders, add **-in** (**-innen** for the plural), e.g. die **Verkäuferin** (-innen) = female shop assistant.

17 Illness/and services

ILLNESS

atemlos	breathless
behandeln	to treat
betrunken	drunk
blaß	pale
der **E111-Schein** (-e)	E111-form
erste Hilfe	first aid
fallen	to fall
der **Feuerlöscher** (-)	fire extinguisher
der **Feuerwehrwagen** (-)	fire engine
gebrochen	broken
die **(Geld)Strafe** (-n)	fine
der **Gips** (-e)	plaster of Paris
das **(Heft)Pflaster** (-)	(sticking) plaster
der **Husten** (-)	cough
husten	to cough
körperbehindert	physically handicapped
die **Krankenkasse** (-n)	health insurance
der **Krankenschein** (-e)	doctor's note, medical report
die **Kur** (-en)	treatment, cure
der **Kurort** (-e)	spa town
die **Lebensgefahr**	danger to life
löschen	to put out (fire)
das **Löschgerät** (-e)	fire extinguisher
die **Medizin** (-en)	medicine
niesen	to sneeze
der **Notausgang** (¨e)	emergency exit
der **(Not)Dienst** (-e)	(emergency) service
der **Notruf** (-e)	emergency call
die **Operation** (-en)	operation
der **Patient** (-en)	patient
die **Pille** (-n)	pill
retten	to save
das **Rezept** (-e)	prescription

schwitzen	to sweat
sich das Bein/den Arm brechen	to break one's leg/arm
sich übergeben	to be sick, to vomit
die **Sprechstunde** (-n)	consultation
die **Spritze** (-n)	injection
sterben	to die
stürzen	to rush
die **Tablette** (-n)	tablet
der **Termin** (-e)	time, term, date
das **Thermometer** (-)	thermometer
der **Tod** (-esfälle)	death
tot	dead
der **Tropfen** (-)	drop
überfahren	to run over
überfallen	to fall, overtake (as illness)
umkommen	to die
ums Leben kommen	to die
der **Unfall** (¨e)	accident
untersuchen	to examine
der **Verband** (¨e)	bandage
verletzt	wounded
verunglücken	to meet with an accident, to be killed
verwundet	injured
weinen	to weep, cry
die **Wunde** (-n)	wound, injury
der **Zeuge** (-n)	witness
der **Zusammenstoß** (¨sse)	collision

Useful phrases

Ich brauche schnell einen Arzt.	*I need a doctor quickly.*
Bitte rufen Sie sofort einen Arzt an!	*Please ring a doctor immediately!*
Ich habe Kopfschmerzen/Halsschmerzen.	*I have a headache/pains in my throat*
Haben Sie Tabletten gegen Kopfschmerzen?	*Have you any tablets for headaches?*
Wie oft am Tag muß ich sie nehmen?	*How often in the day must I take them?*
Muß ich sie (ganz) schlucken?	*Must I swallow them (whole)?*
Soll ich gleich bezahlen, oder schicken Sie mir die Rechnung?	*Should I pay immediately, or will you send me the bill?*
Dieser Zahn schmerzt.	*This tooth hurts.*
Ich möchte ihn (nicht) ziehen lassen.	*I should (not) like to have it taken out (lit. 'pulled')*
zu Hilfe!	*Help!*
Was fehlt Ihnen?	*What is wrong with you?*
Was ist mit Ihnen los?	*What is wrong with you?*
Wo haben Sie Schmerzen?	*Where do you have pains?*
Wie lange haben Sie diese Schmerzen schon?	*How long have you had these pains now?*
Haben Sie das zum ersten Mal?	*Is this the first time you've had it?*
Ziehen Sie bitte Hose und Unterwäsche aus!	*Please take off your trousers and underpants.*
Legen Sie sich bitte hierhin!	*Lie down here please!*
Machen Sie den Mund auf!	*Open your mouth!*
Husten Sie bitte!	*Cough please!*
Ich gebe Ihnen eine Spritze.	*I am giving you an injection.*
Sie müssen drei Tagen im Bett bleiben.	*You may stay in bed for three days.*
Ich schreibe Ihnen ein Rezept.	*I shall write you a prescription.*
Nehmen Sie von dieser Medizin zwei Teelöffel alle vier Stunden/vor jeder Mahlzeit!	*Take two teaspoonfuls of this medicine every four hours/before each meal!*
Nehmen Sie zwei Tabletten viermal täglich!	*Take two tablets four times a day!*
In acht Tagen möchte ich Sie wieder sehen.	*I should like to see you again in eight days.*

SERVICES

(an)nähen	to sew (on)
ausbessern	to repair
bügeln	to iron, press
eilen	to hurry
die (Münz) Wäscherei (-en)	(coin-operated) laundry
reinigen	to clean
die (Schnell)Reinigung (-en)	(quick) cleaning

Useful phrases

Können Sie diese Uhr nachsehen?	*Can you check/overhaul this clock?*
Können Sie diese Brille reparieren?	*Can you repair these spectacles?*
Ich brauche ein neues Glas.	*I need a new lens.*
Das Armband ist kaputt.	*The strap is broken.*
Ich möchte diese Kleider bügeln/ reinigen lassen.	*I should like to have these clothes pressed/cleaned.*
Können Sie diesen Knopf annähen?	*Can you sew on this button?*
Wann ist es fertig?	*When will it be ready?*
Wann soll ich es abholen?	*When shall I fetch it?*
Ich brauche es morgen/schnell.	*I need it tomorrow/quickly.*
Können Sie es bis heute abend machen?	*Can you do it by this evening?*
Ich möchte es so schnell wie möglich.	*I should like it as quickly as possible.*
Damit eilt es nicht./Es eilt nicht./ Es hat Zeit.	*There is no hurry/There's plenty of time.*
Ist meine Wäsche fertig?	*Is my washing ready?*
Es fehlt ein Stück.	*There is one piece/item missing.*
Können Sie dieses Kleid ausbessern?	*Can you repair this dress?*

Grammar

Answers to these tests are given on pages 111–12. When you have done each test, check your answers. If you are not satisfied with your performance, check the relevant Grammar Revision sections and then test yourself again.

Test 1

Give the gender, plural and meaning of the following nouns:
(a) Nacht   (f) Tochter   (k) Wald
(b) Zeitung   (g) Vogel   (l) Glas
(c) Wärter   (h) Arzt   (m) Gegend
(d) Löffel   (i) Pferd   (n) Nachbar
(e) Gebirge   (j) Schuh   (o) Schülerin

Test 2

Complete these sentences, using the appropriate case endings:
(a) London ist ein- groß- Stadt, d- an d- Themse liegt.
(b) Letzt- Jahr fuhren wir mit ein- lang- Zug in d- Schweiz.
(c) Er wusch sich d- Hände und ging in sein- klein- Schlafzimmer zurück.
(d) Nach d- Mittagessen ging er durch d- Garten, d- Straße entlang, in d- Schule zurück.
(e) Mein- klein- Schwester sah d- jung- Wärter, als sie durch d- zoologisch- Garten ging.
(f) Wir haben kein- Tisch in unser- Wohnzimmer.
(g) Er zeigte sein- Bruder d- alt- Rathaus.
(h) D- Onkel mein- alt- Freund- wohnt in Köln.
(i) Gut- Wein kostet sechs Mark - Flasche in England.
(j) Viel- klein- Kinder wollen d- hoh- Berg sehen.

Test 3

Replace the nouns underlined in these sentences with pronouns:
(a) Der Hund läuft durch den Garten, um seinen Besitzer zu lecken.
(b) Die Leute standen auf der Straße und sahen die schönen Gebäude an.
(c) Der Mann zeigt seinem Sohn ein Buch.
(d) Die Frau gab ihrer Heimatstadt ein Denkmal.
(e) Die Schwestern folgen ihren Brüdern in die Küche.

Test 4

Supply the correct form of the relative pronoun in these sentences:
(a) Der Mann, (whom) ich gestern sah, ist mein Bruder.
(b) Die Frau, (whose) Haus ich besitze, wohnt nicht mehr da.
(c) Die Eltern, mit (whom) der Lehrer spricht, sind zornig.
(d) Der Tisch, (on which) die Bücher liegen, ist sehr alt.
(e) Das Heft, (which) in meiner Schultasche ist, gehört mir nicht.

Test 5

Supply the preposition given in brackets and add the right case endings:
(a) Er kam (without) mein- klein- Bruder.
(b) (During) d- Sommerferien fuhr ich (to) Deutschland.
(c) Er fuhr (by) d- Zug (to) d- Schweiz.
(d) Er geht langsam (into) d- Stadt, um (in) ein- Konditorei ein Stück Torte zu essen.
(e) Er stand (on) d- Marktplatz (under) ein- groß- Eiche.

Test 6

Supply the verb given in brackets:
(a) Der Mann (helped) mir mit meiner Arbeit.
(b) Wir (shall be) im August an der See.
(c) Wenn er mich (had seen), hätte er meine Handtasche gesucht.
(d) Meine Freunde (worked) auf einem großen Bauernhof.
(e) Sobald die Sonne (had set), setzten wir uns ins Wohnzimmer und (drank) eine Tasse Kaffee.

Test 7

Use idiomatic German to say the following:

(a) Imagine you are Rudi talking to your Mum about your new friend. You tell your Mum she's right and that your new friend and his family have been living in that house for six years. What would you say in German?

(b) You are talking to Mr Schultz about the film he saw in town yesterday evening. You ask him what the film was called. What do you say?

(c) Your Mother is talking about Granny coming in August. She says: 'I hope Granny will be able to come in August. We always look forward to her visits.' Imagine you are your Mother, how would you say what she said in German?

(d) You are talking to your friend about Peter who is interested in football. You tell your friend: 'Peter had been interested in football for more than ten years.' How do you say that in German?

(e) You watched Liesl carry out a series of actions. Now you are making a report about this to a policeman. You tell the policeman this: 'After she had bought a newspaper Liesl sat down at an empty table in front of her favourite café, ordered a glass of wine and began to read.' What would you say in German?

(f) Hans, your brother, has been ill since Christmas and is not allowed to go to school. You tell your friend about Hans, saying: 'As he has been ill since Christmas, Hans is not allowed to go to school.' How do you say it in German?

(g) Brigitte is apologizing to her Dad about not being able to remember the Schmidts' new address. She says: 'Sorry, Dad, I can't remember their new address'. What does she say in German?

Test 8

How would you say the following in German?

(a) What time is it?
(b) A quarter of an hour.
(c) Next Friday.
(d) About half past nine.
(e) This evening.
(f) One day during the holidays.
(g) What is the date today?
(h) It is the fifth of March.
(i) Whenever he saw me, he always used to laugh.
(j) My grandmother is ninety-five years old.

Test 9

Using a modal verb, how do you say the following in German?

(a) She wants to buy a book.
(b) My friend cannot swim.
(c) I have not been able to do it.
(d) She must not go to the cinema.
(e) Because it was late, she had to go home.
(f) I should like to go to Germany.
(g) He ought to go to bed.
(h) He has to write a letter.
(i) We could not come.
(j) Although she wanted to leave school, she was too young.

Test 10

Rewrite these sentences using the conjunctions indicated:

(a) Begin with **bevor** and make these two sentences into one:
Er ging zu Bett. Er trank ein Glas Milch.
(b) Begin with **weil** and make these two sentences into one:
Er war so krank. Er konnte nicht ausgehen.
(c) Join these two sentences with **denn** in the middle:
Sie konnte nicht viel sehen. Sie hatte ihre Brille zu Hause gelassen.
(d) Begin with **wenn** and make these two sentences into one:
Er kommt. Wir werden ihn sehen.
(e) Begin with **da** and make these two sentences into one:
Es ist so kalt. Ich gehe nicht aus.

How would you say the following in German, paying special attention to the word order:

(f) Although I was not ill, I wanted to say in bed.
(g) I showed my brother the book, which he had found yesterday.
(h) We arrived home by car at three o'clock.
(i) I got up, jumped out of bed and then went into the bathroom.
(j) They drove slowly past the town-hall.

▌ Vocabulary ▌

Write down ten key words for each of the following topic areas. Remember the gender and plural of the nouns you use.

1 House and furniture	5 The railway	9 Restaurant
2 The countryside and seaside	6 Travel (not by rail)	10 School
3 The family	7 Shopping	11 Free time and entertainment
4 The town	8 Hotel	12 Occupations

To check your answers, look at the relevant sections of the vocabulary revision.

▌ Answers ▌

GRAMMAR

Test 1

(a) die Nacht (¨e), night
(b) die Zeitung (-en), newspaper
(c) der Wärter (-), keeper
(d) der Löffel (-), spoon
(e) das Gebirge (-), mountain range
(f) die Tochter (¨), daughter
(g) der Vogel (¨), bird
(h) der Arzt (¨e), doctor
(i) das Pferd (-e), horse
(j) der Schuh (-e), shoe
(k) der Wald (¨er), wood
(l) das Glas (¨er), glass
(m) die Gegend (-en), district
(n) der Nachbar (-n), neighbour
(o) die Schülerin (-nen), schoolgirl

Test 2

(a) London ist eine große Stadt, die an der Themse liegt.
(b) Letztes Jahr fuhren wir mit einem langen Zug in die Schweiz.
(c) Er wusch sich die Hände und ging in sein kleines Schlafzimmer zurück.
(d) Nach dem Mittagessen ging er durch den Garten, die Straße entlang, in die Schule zurück.
(e) Meine kleine Schwester sah den jungen Wärter, als sie durch den zoologischen Garten ging.
(f) Wir haben keinen Tisch in unserem Wohnzimmer.
(g) Er zeigte seinem Bruder das alte Rathaus.
(h) Der Onkel meines alten Freundes wohnt in Köln.
(i) Guter Wein kostet sechs Mark die Flasche in England.
(j) Viele kleine Kinder wollen den hohen Berg sehen.

Test 3

(a) Er läuft durch den Garten, um ihn zu lecken.
(b) Sie standen auf der Straße und sahen sie an.
(c) Er zeigt es ihm.
(d) Sie gab es ihr.
(e) Sie folgen ihnen in die Küche.

Test 4

(a) den (b) deren (c) denen (d) worauf (e) das

Test 5

(a) Er kam ohne meinen kleinen Bruder.
(b) Während der Sommerferien fuhr ich nach Deutschland.
(c) Er fuhr mit dem Zug in die Schweiz.
(d) Er geht langsam in die Stadt, um in einer Konditorei ein Stück Torte zu essen.
(e) Er stand auf dem Marktplatz unter einer großen Eiche.

Test 6

(a) Der Mann half mir mit meiner Arbeit.
(b) Wir werden im August an der See sein.
(c) Wenn er mich gesehen hätte, hätte er meine Handtasche gesucht.
(d) Meine Freunde arbeiteten auf einem großen Bauernhof.
(e) Sobald die Sonne untergegangen war, setzten wir uns ins Wohnzimmer und tranken eine Tasse Kaffee.

Test 7

(a) „Du hast recht, Mutti. Mein neuer Freund und seine Familie wohnen seit sechs Jahren in jenem Haus."

(b) „Wie hieß der Film, den Sie gestern abend in der Stadt gesehen haben, Herr Schultz?"

(c) „Hoffentlich wird Oma im August kommen können. Wir freuen uns immer auf ihre Besuche."

(d) „Peter interessierte sich seit mehr als zehn Jahren für Fußball."

(e) „Nachdem sie eine Zeitung gekauft hatte, setzte sich Liesl an einen leeren Tisch vor ihrem Lieblingscafé, bestellte ein Glas Wein und fing an zu lesen."

(f) „Da er seit Weihnachten krank ist, darf Hans nicht in die Schule gehen."

(g) „Es tut mir leid, Vati. Ich kann mich an ihre neue Anschrift nicht erinnern."

Test 8

(a) Wieviel Uhr ist es? *or* Wie spät ist es?

(b) Eine Viertelstunde.

(c) nächsten Freitag.

(d) Gegen halb zehn.

(e) Heute abend.

(f) Eines Tages während der Ferien.

(g) Der wievielte ist es heute? *or* Den wievielten haben wir heute?

(h) Es ist der fünfte März.

(i) Wenn er mich sah, pflegte er immer zu lachen.

(j) Mein Großmutter ist fünfundneunzig Jahre alt.

Test 9

(a) Sie will ein Buch kaufen.

(b) Mein Freund kann nicht schwimmen.

(c) Ich habe es nicht tun können.

(d) Sie darf nicht ins Kino gehen.

(e) Weil es spät war, mußte sie nach Hause gehen.

(f) Ich möchte gern nach Deutschland fahren.

(g) Er sollte zu Bett gehen.

(h) Er muß einen Brief schreiben.

(i) Wir konnten nicht kommen.

(j) Obgleich sie die Schule verlassen wollte, war sie zu jung.

Test 10

(a) Bevor er zu Bett ging, trank er ein Glas Milch.

(b) Weil er so krank war, konnte er nicht ausgehen.

(c) Sie konnte nicht viel sehen, denn sie hatte ihre Brille zu Hause gelassen.

(d) Wenn er kommt, (so) werden wir ihn sehen.

(e) Da es so kalt ist, gehe ich nicht aus.

(f) Obgleich ich nicht krank war, wollte ich im Bett bleiben.

(g) Ich zeigte meinem Bruder das Buch, das er gestern gefunden hatte.

(h) Um drei Uhr kamen wir mit dem Auto zu Hause an *or* Wir kamen um drei Uhr . . .

(i) Ich stand auf, sprang aus dem Bett, und dann ging ich ins Badezimmer.

(j) Sie fuhren langsam am Rathaus vorbei.

4 LISTENING COMPREHENSION

Listening comprehension tests are included at both Basic and Higher Levels for all the Examining Groups including those in Wales, Northern Ireland and Scotland. The material for all tests will be recorded on tape by native speakers and will be based on German which is designed to be heard. The materials will be taken from the published lists of topic areas and settings and the recordings may include some background noise. All situations will be authentic, i.e. what a candidate might reasonably be expected to meet as an active or passive participant when visiting the foreign country or receiving German-speaking visitors to this country. All questions and answers will be in English, the setting will also be given in English. No undue stress on memory will be involved and candidates will be able to make notes during the listening to the tape. Some questions will be multiple choice with individual Examining Groups.

The best kind of preparation for this sort of test is to listen to as much spoken German as you can. This means listening to German radio programmes, perhaps exchanging a cassette recording with your German penfriend or going on an exchange visit to Germany and living with a family. Your school will also have material on tape which you can listen to and perhaps record for your own use.

In GCSE you will be expected to understand spoken German and extract information from what you hear in real-life situations. At Basic Level you will hear announcements, news items, weather forecasts, instructions, requests, interviews, dialogues, telephone conversations, etc. There is a lot of overlap between the kind of material you will hear on tape and the role-play situations in the speaking tests of the various Examining Groups.

What follows includes examples of the sorts of question you might find in the GCSE basic listening tests. The tapescript is given first, followed by the questions. You will have to remember that normally you will not see the tapescript but will only hear what is being said. It would be a good idea when using this material to ask the foreign language assistant or your teacher to record the material on tape so that you can take it home and work on it on your own. Failing that, you could work with a friend who speaks German well and make a recording together which you can both use later. The questions have been grouped together by type, so that you can practise the ones appropriate to your Examining Group. The suggested answers are given on pages 174–6.

Multiple-choice questions

1 You are shopping with your mother and have just bought some things. Your mother tells you what to do with them. Where should you put them?

Steck, bitte, diese Sachen in die Tasche und nicht in den Korb!

A In the basket.
B In the bag.
C In the boot.
D In the trolley.

2 Your German penfriend and his/her family are staying with you and they are talking about their departure. When are they hoping to leave?

Morgen um halb acht hoffen wir abzufahren.

A Today at 8.30 a.m.
B Today at 7.30 a.m.
C Tomorrow at 7.30 a.m.
D Tomorrow at 8.00 a.m.

3 You are travelling on a train which arrives in Cologne, and you hear an announcement about your train. How long does your train stop in Cologne?

Der Zug nach Koblenz fährt in fünfzehn Minuten ab.

A 10 minutes.
B 5 minutes.
C 50 minutes.
D 15 minutes.

4 You are planning to go out for the day, so you listen to the weather forecast on the radio. What should you take with you?

Hier ist die Wettervorhersage bis heute abend: Wolkig, mild, aber viele Regenschauer.

A An umbrella.
B Sunglasses.
C A heavy overcoat.
D A woollen jumper.

5 You are buying some apples at the greengrocer's. The assistant tells you how much they cost. How much do you have to pay?

Vier Äpfel zu dreißig Pfennig das Stück, das kostet eine Mark zwanzig, bitte!

A 4,30 DM.
B 20 DM.

C 1,20 DM.
D 30 Pfennig.

6 You are shopping in a supermarket and you hear an announcement about today's special offer. What is it?

Sonderangebot heute – zwei Kaffeelöffel mit jedem Glas Pulverkaffee.

A Two glasses.
B A jar of instant coffee.

C Two coffee spoons.
D Custard powder.

7 You ring up the box office at the theatre and are told when the performance starts. When does it start?

Die Vorstellung beginnt um Viertel nach acht.

A 7.45.
B 8.15.

C 8.40.
D 7.40.

8 You ask your way to the airport. What are you told to do?

Sie fahren am besten mit dem Autobus Linie zwanzig.

A Go by train.
B Go by bus.

C Go by taxi.
D Go by car.

9 You are listening to the news on radio. What has happened?

Gestern abend haben zwei Männer fünfzig Kameras von einem Fotogeschäft in Mannheim gestohlen.

A Two men have gone to Mannheim.
B Two men have bought fifty cameras.

C Two men have stolen fifty cameras.
D Two men have bought a photographic shop.

10 You are in a tourist office and want to find your way to the nearest hotel. How should you get there?

Nehmen Sie die vierte Straße rechts! Es dauert nur fünf Minuten.

A Take the fourth street on the left.
B Take the third street on the left.

C Take the fourth street on the right.
D Take the fifth street on the right.

Short items

1 You are in a café in Germany. The waitress speaks to you. What does she say?

Wollen Sie bezahlen? *Are you ready to pay*

2 You are going through customs on the way into Germany. What does the customs officer say to you?

Ist dies Ihr Koffer? *Is this your suitcase.*

3 You are travelling to Munich by train. You hear an announcement. From which platform does your train leave?

Der Zug nach München fährt um 14 Uhr von Gleis 13 ab. *Platform 13.*

4 You have gone to the swimming pool with your German penfriend. Why is she annoyed?

Ach! Wie dumm! Ich habe meinen Bikini zu Hause gelassen. *She left her bikini at home*

5 You have lost your camera. What does the man at the Lost Property office ask you?

Können Sie mir Ihre Kamera beschreiben? *Can you describe your camera.*

6 You are staying with your penfriend and offer to help. What are you told you could do?

Das ist wirklich nett von dir. Könntest du mir mit dem Abspülen helfen? *Can you help me with the washing up.*

7 Your penfriend does not want to go to the football match with you. He/she explains why. What is the reason?

Seit heute morgen habe ich Zahnweh.

8 You are talking to a hotel receptionist on the telephone. What does she say?

Einen Augenblick bitte! Bleiben Sie am Apparat!

9 You are giving a policeman your name. What does he ask you?

Wollen Sie das bitte buchstabieren?

10 You have been shopping for your penfriend's mother. You have bought some carrots, potatoes and mushrooms. How much did the potatoes cost?

Also . . . ein Kilo Karotten: 2 DM, zwei Kilo Kartoffeln: 3,50 DM, 200 Gramm Champignons: 1,50 DM. Macht zusammen: 7 DM.

Longer items

Usually in these items there is more than one question set on each dialogue or statement.

1 You have just arrived at your penfriend's house. His mother is showing you round the house for the first time.

Hier ist dein Zimmer. Leider ist es nicht sehr groß, aber es hat eine schöne Aussicht über den See. Komm! . . . Es sind schöne Bäume da drüben und du kannst die Segelboote sehen . . .
   Das Badezimmer ist hier rechts neben Pauls Zimmer. Im Badezimmer sind eine Dusche und die Toilette . . .
   Wir stehen um acht Uhr auf und frühstücken eine halbe Stunde später in der Küche. Wir essen nicht oft im Eßzimmer.

(a) What does she tell you about your room? (*2 marks*)
(b) What can you see through the window? (*3 marks*)
(c) Where is the bathroom?
(d) What does she say is in the bathroom? (*2 marks*)
(e) What time does she say breakfast will be?
(f) Where does she say you will be having breakfast?

2 You have a holiday job as receptionist at a campsite in Germany and have a conversation with a customer on the telephone. Take the details down in English on the form provided. (C = Customer. R = Receptionist.)

C: Guten Tag.
R: Guten Tag.
C: Haben Sie Platz für eine Nacht?
R: Für heute?
C: Nein, für den elften August?
R: Für einen Wohnwagen?
C: Nein, für ein Zelt.
R: Ja, wieviele Personen?
C: Vier, meine Frau, die zwei Kinder und ich.
R: Gut. Wie heißen Sie?
C: Schmidt.
R: Also, S.C.H.M.I.D.T.
C: Gibt es Duschen in den Waschräumen?
R: Ja, natürlich.
C: Was kostet die eine Nacht?
R: Fünfzehn Mark fünfzig pro Nacht.
C: Kann ich mit einem Scheck zahlen?
R: Ja, das ist in Ordnung.
C: Gut, danke schön. Auf Wiederhören.
R: Auf Wiederhören.

Name ...... SCHMIDT ......

Wieviele Personen ...... 4 ......

Wohnwagen/Zelt ...... TENT ......

Datum ...... 11th August ......

Wieviele Nächte ...... 1 night ......

Preis ...... 15 50 DM ......

Geld/Scheck ...... Check ......

3 You are buying tickets at the railway station. Listen to the conversation and then answer the questions in English.

Du: Tag! Einmal nach Hamburg bitte!
Beamte: Einfach, oder hin und zurück?
Du: Einfach. Wann fährt der nächste Zug nach Hamburg?
Beamte: In zwanzig Minuten, um dreizehn Uhr dreißig. Also zwanzig Mark fünfzig bitte!
Du: Gut. Von welchem Gleis fährt der Zug ab?
Beamte: Vom Gleis fünfzehn.
Du: Danke schön! Auf Wiedersehen!

(a) What kind of ticket do you buy to where? *One way ticket to Hamburg*
(b) At what time does the next train there leave? *13.30*
(c) What platform does the train leave from? *15*
(d) How much does it cost? *20.50 DM*

4 You are talking to your friend Monika on the telephone. She is telling you all about going to the summer sales with Helga. Listen to what she says, and answer the questions in English which occur at certain points in the conversation. You will hear each section twice.

Section 1

Monika: Hallo, hier ist Monika, schön, daß du zu Hause bist. Ich wollte dir nur etwas von dem Sommerschlußverkauf erzählen, der erst heute Morgen angefangen hat. Schon um halb acht ging ich mit Helga aus dem Haus, denn wir wollten so viele passende Sachen wie möglich zu herabgesetzten Preisen kaufen.

(a) When did Monika and Helga leave home? *7.30*
(b) What did they want to buy?

Section 2

Wir fuhren zuerst mit dem Zug und dann mit der Straßenbahn in die Innenstadt. Da viele Leute vor den Türen der Kaufhäuser standen, eilten wir zum ersten Kaufhaus, das wir besuchen wollten. Pünktlich um acht Uhr öffneten sich die Türen, und wir drängten uns durch die Menge zur Damenabteilung.

(c) How did they get to town? *Train*
(d) Why did they hurry to the first store?
(e) What time did the store open?
(f) Where did they make for, once inside?

Section 3 You ask Monika what she bought.

Du: Hast du etwas gekauft?
Monica: Ja, ich kaufte mir ein kurzes rotes Kleid und ein langes blaues Kleid, während Helga sich ein grünes Kleid aussuchte. Das blaue Kleid war besonders billig, denn es war von 59 DM auf 30 DM herabgesetzt. Dann sahen wir uns Blusen, Röcke und Schuhe an, fanden aber nichts Passendes. Letztes Jahr waren wir an der Nordseeküste im Urlaub, und damals war Helgas Badeanzug zu klein. Da wir dieses Jahr an die Ostsee fahren, gingen wir in die Sportabteilung, wo Helga einen gelben Badeanzug aus Frankreich fand.

(g) What did Monkia buy? (*2 marks*)
(h) What did Helga buy?
(i) In which part of the store did they buy Helga's bathing costume?
(j) Where was it made?

Section 4 You now ask if they found anything else.

Du: Hast du sonst noch etwas gefunden?
Monika: Natürlich suchte ich auch etwas für meinen Mann, und wir kauften ihm Unterhemden und Socken. Als wir das Kaufhaus verließen, waren wir froh. Sofort rief ich meinen Mann im Büro an, um ihm zu sagen, daß er Schuhe und Anzüge zu günstigen Preisen finden würde. Vielleicht hat er heute Zeit, hinzugehen. Ich empfehle dir das auch, und viel Glück, wenn du zum Sommerschlußverkauf gehst.
Du: Ich gehe gleich nach dem Mittagessen. Auf Wiederhören!
Monika: Auf Wiederhören!

(k) What did Monika buy for her husband? *underwear & socks*
(l) How did Monika let her husband know about the sale?
(m) What did she say he would find at good prices?
(n) What did she recommend you to do?
(o) What did you say you would do and when?

Higher Level

At Higher Level the stimulus material for you to listen to is more complex and more demanding. The settings or situations will still be authentic and you will find yourself asked to listen to a conversation, a weather forecast, a news item on the radio, a telephone conversation or something similar. In some instances the whole test may be linked to one particular situation and develop from it. In all examples you have to extract information from what you hear. The following are examples of the kinds of tests the Examining Groups have provided in their specimen materials. The final question in this chapter is from an actual GCSE paper from the 1988 examinations. Remember that you would not have the tapescript to look at in the examination.

1 Weather forecast

You are planning to go out later today, so you listen to the weather forecast on the radio.

Hier ist der Wetterbericht für heute, den achten April. Allgemeine Wetterlage: Eine Hochdruckzone über Mitteleuropa bestimmt das Wetter in Deutschland. Im Norden meist sonnig aber kalt. Tageshöchsttemperaturen um acht Grad. Nächtliche Tiefswerte um zwei Grad. Im Süden stark bewölkt oder neblig mit Sprühregen. Tageshöchsttemperatur um sechs Grad. In Mitteldeutschland herrscht Nebel. Tageschöchsttemperatur fünf Grad. Wind von Nordwesten. Aussicht: Keine durchgreifende Änderung.

(a) What is the date? *8th April*
(b) In which region is the best weather going to be? *Germany*
(c) What is the lowest night temperature going to be in North Germany? *2°*
(d) In which region is it likely to drizzle? *South*
(e) What is the coldest day-time temperature mentioned? *5°*
(f) Where is it going to be coldest during the day?
(g) Where is the wind blowing from in the central region? *N-W*
(h) What is the outlook?

2 The road accident

At the scene of a road accident, you hear two people discussing what has happened. You tell your English friend, who asks you the questions, what you have heard. (H=Herr. D=Dame.)

Section A

D: Haben Sie das gesehen?

H: Was?

D: Ein Junge ist überfahren worden.

H: Ist er tot?

D: Nein, glücklicherweise ist es nicht so schlimm.

H: Was ist eigentlich passiert?

D: Der Junge kam auf seinem Fahrrad aus der Nebenstraße und bog in die Hauptstraße ein. Der Autofahrer konnte nicht anhalten. Er bremste und schleuderte, aber er konnte den Jungen nicht vermeiden. Der Junge hat sich nicht umgesehen. Der Autofahrer ist nicht Schuld daran.

(a) What accident has just happened?   *(1 mark)*
(b) Is the boy dead?   *(1 mark)*
(c) What did the boy do to cause the accident?   *(2 marks)*
(d) Who was to blame and why?   *(2 marks)*
(e) What did the car driver do?   *(2 marks)*
(f) What could the car driver not do?   *(2 marks)*

Section B

H: Ist der Fahrer noch da?

D: Nein, er ruft die Polizei und das Krankenhaus an.

H: Wie geht es dem Jungen?

D: Er scheint viele Schmerzen zu haben, weil das Auto ihm über beide Beine gefahren ist.

H: Wie schrecklich! Hier kommt ein Polizist.

D: Gut! Jetzt wird der Polizist die Menge zurückhalten. Kann ich einen Krankenwagen hören?

H: Ja, der Krankenwagen und die Polizei kommen schon. Ich kann die Sirenen hören.

D: Ich auch. Das ist aber schnell. Es ist kaum mehr als fünf Minuten, seitdem der Unfall passiert ist.

(g) Where is the driver?   (*2 marks*)
(h) Why is the boy badly hurt?   (*2 marks*)
(i) What is the policeman going to do?   (*1 mark*)
(j) How do we know that the police and the ambulance are arriving?   (*1 mark*)
(k) How long is it since the accident happened?   (*1 mark*)

Section C

Polizist: Zurücktreten, bitte! Treten Sie bitte zurück! Lassen Sie den Krankenwagen durch!
D: Der Junge sieht jetzt ein bißchen besser aus. Die Männer heben ihn in den Krankenwagen. Er wird bald im Krankenhaus sein.
H: Schade, daß der Junge so schlimm verletzt war. Er scheint so jung zu sein.
D: Nicht älter als fünf oder sechs Jahre alt, würde ich sagen.
H: Ich hörte den Krankenwagenfahrer sagen, daß beide Beine gebrochen sind. Solche Kinder sollten nicht allein bei diesem Straßenverkehr mit einem Fahrrad farhen.
D: Ja, das meine ich auch. Der Junge hatte Glück. Man bedenkt, was sonst noch hätte passieren können, besonders wenn er von einem Lastkraftwagen oder einem Bus überfahren worden wäre. Es hatte eine Sache auf Leben und Tod sein können.

(l) What is the policeman trying to do?   (*2 marks*)
(m) How old do they say the boy is?   (*1 mark*)
(n) What did the ambulance driver say about the boy?   (*1 mark*)
(o) Why is the boy lucky?   (*1 mark*)
(p) What did the man say about children and bikes in towns?   (*1 mark*)
(q) In what way does the woman say it could have been a matter of life and death?

(*2 marks*)

3 A guided tour

You are staying in Germany with your penfriend and you go on a sightseeing tour round Bremen. You have a German guide and you listen to what is said and make notes on what you have heard as you will have to tell your class about your visit when you return home to school after the holidays.

Section A

Guten Tag, meine Damen und Herren. Ich heiße Lotte, Ihre Reiseleiterin. Ich werde Sie auf dieser Kurztour durch Bremen begleiten. Die ganze Tour dauert anderthalb Stunden. Wir fangen hier am Hauptbahnhof an und beenden die Tour in dem Schnoorviertel, wo man die alten kleinen Häuser in den engen Gassen finden kann.

(a) How long does the tour last?   (*1 mark*)
(b) What are the starting and finishing points?   (*2 marks*)
(c) What are to be found in the Schnoorviertel?   (*2 marks*)

Section B

Zuerst gehen wir in die Innenstadt zum Marktplatz. Die Bremer nennen ihren Marktplatz „die gute Stube", denn hier in den Gebäuden um den Marktplatz herum kann man besonders gut essen und trinken. Seit dem Jahre 1404 ist das Denkmal Roland der Treffpunkt für Tausende von Touristen und Einwohnern.

(d) Where are there good places to eat and drink?   (*1 mark*)
(e) What is the meeting place for tourists?   (*1 mark*)
(f) Since when has this monument been there?   (*1 mark*)

Section C

Die anderen Sehenswürdigkeiten um den Marktplatz herum und in seiner Nachbarschaft sind das Rathaus mit seinem Ratskeller, der Dom, die Westseite des Platzes mit seinen alten restaurierten Gebäuden und der Blumenmarkt auf dem Kirchhof „Unser Lieben Frauen".
   Bremen ist eine Hansestadt und auch das kleinste Land der Bundesrepublik. Der Marktplaz ist in der Fußgängerzone, nur die Straßenbahn fährt hier durch.

(g) What are the first three things mentioned as being worth seeing?   (*3 marks*)
(h) What do you find on the west side of the square?   (*1 mark*)
(i) What is sold in the market in the church yard of Our Dear Lady?   (*1 mark*)
(j) What does the guide explain about Bremen?   (*2 marks*)
(k) What two other pieces of information does the guide give about the market place?

(*2 marks*)

Section D

Auf der linken Seite sehen wir das Rathaus, das in den Jahren 1405 bis 1409 errichtet wurde. Die Fassade ist nicht so alt und wurde während der Zeit der Renaissance zwei hundert Jahre später gebaut. Führungen finden Wochentage um 10,11,12 Uhr, von März bis Ende Oktober statt. Unter dem Rathaus ist der berühmte Ratskeller, der einer der ältesten Stadtweinkeller ist. Der Ratskeller wurde im Jahre 1408 gebaut.

(l) When was the town hall built?   (*1 mark*)
(m) Does the front facade date from the same period? If not, why not?   (*2 marks*)
(n) What information does the guide give about guided tours of the town hall?   (*2 marks*)
(o) What are the claims to fame of the Ratskeller?   (*2 marks*)

Section E

Jetzt gehen wir durch das Schnoorviertel, das eines der ältesten Stadtviertel Bremens ist. Die vielen, zum Teil winzigen Häuschen aus dem siebzehnten und achtzehnten Jahrhundert sind jetzt völlig restauriert. In diesen kleinen Straßen sind Sie nämlich nicht in einem Museum sondern in einem Viertel, wo Leute – Architekten, Schriftsteller, Töpfer, und Glasbläser arbeiten. Hier können Sie bummeln und schöne, preiswerte Souvenirs kaufen. Diese Tour endet hier. Auf Wiedersehen und alles Gute für Ihre Reise durch Deutschland.

(p) When was most of the Schnoor district built?   (*1 mark*)
(q) Why does your guide say that you are not in a museum?   (*1 mark*)
(r) Name two of the kinds of people who work in Schnoor.   (*2 marks*)
(s) Why is this area of Bremen a must for tourists visiting the town?   (*2 marks*)
(t) What does the guide wish everyone at the end of the tour?   (*1 mark*)

SHORTER ITEMS

1 You are waiting on the platform at the railway station to meet your friend who is arriving from Hannover. You hear an announcement over the public address system.

Achtung! Achtung! Gleis 10! Der Zug aus Hannover hat dreißig Minuten Verspätung. Passagiere für Aachen und Ostende sollten zum Gleis 8 gehen. Der Zug fährt in fünf Minuten ab.

(a) When will the train from Hannover now arrive?
(b) From which platform is the train to Aachen and Ostend about to leave?

2 You are feeling unwell, and so you go to the chemist's. Make notes on what he tells you to do.

Du: Guten Morgen. Ich habe Kopfweh und auch ein bißchen Fieber. Ich fühle mich gar nicht wohl. Können Sie mir etwas empfehlen?
Drogist: Ja, natürlich. Ich empfehle diese Tabletten. Sie sollen sie dreimal am Tag mit Wasser nehmen. Ich würde auch raten, daß Sie zu Bett gehen und zwei oder drei Tage im Bett bleiben. Sie sollten nicht viel essen, sondern viele warme Getränke trinken. Sie haben wahrscheinlich eine kleine Grippe.
Du: Was kosten die Tabletten?
Drogist: Eine Packung zu 20 kostet 8 DM.

You should make notes on the advice the chemist gives you as follows:

You should take the tablets ....

You should stay in bed ....

You should eat ....

You should drink ....

You have probably got ....

3 You are at a hotel in Germany talking to the receptionist. You ask about a room for your parents.

Du: Ich hätte gern ein Doppelzimmer mit Dusche für meine Eltern, bitte.
Empfangsdame: Moment, mal . . . ein Doppelzimmer mit Dusche? Nein, wir haben nur noch zwei Einzelzimmer frei und leider hat keines ein Bad oder eine Dusche.

What reply did you receive? (Give all the details.)

4 You are expecting a phone call from your German penfriend's mother. What information does she give you about Inge's arrival?

Hallo. Hier spricht Frau Dinkelborg, die Mutter von Inge. Willst du deiner Mutter bitte folgendes sagen? Also, Inge kommt, wie abgemacht, in zwei Wochen in York an. Sie wird um 14 Uhr auf dem Hauptbahnhof ankommen. Sie fährt mit dem D-Zug von London. Falls du sie nicht sogleich vom Farbfoto erkennst, trägt sie einen blauen Hut, einen blauen Anorak und gelbe Hose. Sie wird einen braunen Koffer und eine grüne Tasche tragen. Sie wird auch eine Zeitschrift unter ihrem linken Arm tragen. Alles klar? Vielen Dank. Auf Wiederhören.

Complete your notes on what you have heard on the telephone.

Inge will arrive in ....

She will arrive by .... at .... (*time*)

She will be wearing .... and .... and ....

She will be carrying .... and ....

Under her arm she will also be carrying ....

5 (a) You are staying at your penfriend Anni's house in Germany. You are discussing how to spend the day. Anni's mother makes the following comments and suggestion.

Na, also! Wißt ihr schon, was ihr heute macht? Bei diesem wunderbaren Wetter ist das hier am Meer eigentlich gar keine Frage. Ihr könnt ja Hans anrufen, Anni. Seine Eltern haben ein Segelboot.

(i) How does she suggest you spend the day?
(ii) How does she suggest you arrange this?

(b) You decide to do as she suggests. You listen to Anni's conversation.

Hallo, Hans! Hier spricht Anni! Hör mal, deine Eltern haben ein Segelboot nicht wahr? Wir haben Besuch aus England, und ich dachte, wir könnten den Tag auf dem Meer verbringen. Was? . . . Ihr fährt nach Holland! Für drei Wochen! Sofort? Morgen? Na, viel Spaß! Tschüß! Wiederhören.

(iii) Things do not turn out as planned. Why not?

6 While at your penfriend's house in Germany you listen to a news bulletin.
Heute morgen fand ein Zugunglück auf der Strecke zwischen Köln und Düsseldorf statt. Ein Zug fuhr mit einer Geschwindigkeit von 45 km pro Stunde in einen anderen Zug, der bei Rotlicht stillstand.
(i) What incident is the announcer describing?
(ii) How did the incident occur? Give full details.
Nach Angaben der Polizei sind 22 Leute tödlich verunglückt, darunter 5 Kinder.
(iii) What are the results of the incident?
Unser Reporter hat vor kurzem mit einem Augenzeugen gesprochen.
Herr Lemmer was haben Sie gesehen?
Es war furchtbar. Ich hörte eine schreckliche Explosion, wie eine Bombe und sah viel Rauch...Ich eilte hin, um den Leuten beim Rausklettern zu helfen. Viele mußten auf den Rettungswagen warten...Es war furchtbar...Es war zum Weinen...
(iv) What did Herr Lemmer do?
(v) What was Herr Lemmer's reaction to the incident?
Die Verletzten werden in die Krankenhäuser gebracht – es steht noch nicht fest wieviele. Die Lage ist sehr schlimm, einige werden schon operiert. Es wird dringend Blut gebraucht.
(vi) How would you describe the present situation? Give an explanation for your answer.
(vii) An appeal has gone out. What for?

LEAG German, summer 1991

5 READING COMPREHENSION

The GCSE boards realize, quite rightly, that anybody who intends going to Germany, Austria or Switzerland, or who would like to get to know people from these countries will need to be able to understand German in its written form. Of course, this does not only refer to books.

There are all kinds of ways in which written German is used in everyday life, and the GCSE examination (reading comprehension) is there to see how effectively you can understand German which you may see written down, printed, in shop windows or wherever.

At Basic Level you may well meet the following sort of thing:

1 Public signs and notices
Warnings   Traffic signs
Directions   Menus
Price lists   Advertisements   Timetables   Handouts

2 Simple brochures about
accommodation   travel   holidays

3 Guides to
towns   regions   historic buildings
churches   monuments   places of interest

4 Letters from
friends   hotels   readers of magazines to the editor

5 Imaginative writing
Descriptions   Stories   Interviews   Jokes

This list may seem varied – indeed it is – but there are certain things that each item has in common.

1 Every item is *authentic*: that is, each item is a genuine copy of something genuinely German. Sometimes a photograph of a sign or a warning will be presented to you; at other times letters in genuine German handwriting will be reproduced in full; magazine items and advertisements will sometimes have the same pictures and the same bold headlines as the original German.

2 Every item refers to a topic area defined in your Examining Group's syllabus.
A short extract from a magazine will be found to refer to travel, or holidays, or food and drink – it will deal with an area you have covered at school. Similarly any signs you will be expected to understand will all be the sort of things you will meet often and in everyday situations in Germany.

3 Every item is fairly short at Basic Level.

At Basic Level your answers to the questions set may take the form of:

(a) multiple choice (elements in English)
(b) multiple choice (elements in German)
(c) tick the box (elements in English)
(d) tick the box (elements in German)
(e) ticking yes/no (questions in English)
(f) open-ended questions.

At Higher Level you will meet more of the same, except that:

(a) The questions will be set on *longer* items.
(b) To answer the questions completely, you will need to have learned lots of vocabulary from the higher-level vocabulary list.

NB Certain Examining Groups have decided that you will be tested on different *sources* at different levels: for example, they say that newspaper items will appear at *Higher Level only*. Find out what your Examining Group's policy is.

It is still possible to have multiple-choice questions at Higher Level, but on the whole, the open-ended question is more popular at this level.

(c) Sometimes you have to get the gist–the general idea only. (Remember that *you're not expected to understand every word* you read.)

Sometimes you have to seek out information (which you *should* be able to understand) from among a mass of information in complicated German (which you *won't* be able to understand in full.)

Sometimes you will, however, be expected to *deduce* the meaning of unfamiliar words from the context–in other words, the questions and the texts will give you a broad hint as to the meaning of certain important words.

What to do before the exam

(a) Check on the topic areas your Examining Group will use in the reading examination. (Certain groups state that only certain areas will arise.) Read as much genuine German material as you can, particularly material relating to these subject areas.

(b) If you know anyone–or have a friend who knows someone–who lives in or is visiting Germany, get them to send you any tickets or brochures they may have.

(c) Get your penfriend to write in German and swap letters with your friends so that you see as much German handwriting as you can.

(d) Remember to take into the exam pens, pencils and erasers. (These last two are useful for answering multiple-choice questions you're not sure about.) Ink is final, and cannot be altered, so first pencil in your answers, *then* use ink when you are sure.

Some boards issue computerized multiple-choice answer grids for which pencil and eraser are essential.

What to do in the exam

(a) Follow the *instructions* carefully. Do not put ticks if crosses are asked for.

(b) Read the *context* of each question (the introduction in English) carefully. Often this is as important as the German text itself.

(c) Read the text carefully to get the gist.

(d) Read the task carefully, for example, are they asking you what is allowed, or what is prohibited? *Be sure before you answer*.

(e) If they ask you to tick *one* box, you can't tick two or three of them. If they ask for the name of one person or one place, don't mention two or three people or places in your answer, thinking that 'one of them must be right'. Similarly if you are asked for four pieces of information, don't put five or six.

(f) Remember it's not always necessary to write in full grammatical sentences unless you are specifically asked to.

(g) If you can't do a question, leave it till the end. If, at the end of an examination, you are still genuinely and absolutely baffled by a question, have an (intelligent!) guess. There can be no marks awarded for a blank paper.

Example questions for revision and practice

BASIC-LEVEL READING

(a) Multiple choice (elements in English)

1 Where would you see the following sign?

A on a motorway ✓
B in a supermarket
C in a doctor's waiting room
D above a restaurant

2 Where would you see the following?

> # SCHNELLRESTAURANT
> # IM
> # DRITTEN STOCK
> ## durchgehend geöffnet!

A on a tram
B in a park
C in a department store ✓
D on a ship

3 Getting on a bus, you read:

> # ES IST VERBOTEN,
> # DEN FAHRER WÄHREND
> # DER FAHRT ZU SPRECHEN

Does it mean?
A State your destination when tendering fare.
B No boarding without correct fare.
C No speaking with the driver whilst the bus is in motion. ✓
D Do not dismount while the bus is in motion.

4 Driving through a town, you see this sign:

Does it mean?
A no entry
B one-way street ✓
C cul-de-sac
D trams only

(b) Multiple choice (elements in German)

1 At a railway station, you decide to leave your suitcase for a couple of hours while you look round the town. Which sign should you look for?

A Fundbüro

B Zu den Zügen

C Gaststätte

D Gepäckaufbewahrung ✓

2 When in a German cinema, you smell smoke and a bell begins to ring. Which sign should you make for?

A Raucherabteil

B Notausgang ✓

C Kein Ausgang

D Balkon

3 You decide to fry a steak on the last night of your German holiday. Driving through a village, you see these signs above shops. Which one should you buy the steak at?

A Metzgerei ✓

B Buchhandlung

C Möbel

D Imbiß

(c) Tick the box (elements in English)

1 As your group enters the pleasure park at Brühl, near Cologne, you notice the following ticket on the ground.

PHANTASIALAND BRÜHL

N⍛ 02165

LEHRERKARTE

(unverkäuflich)

berechtigt zum einmaligen Besuch einer Aufsichtsperson und verliert beim Verlassen des Geländes ihre Gültigkeit.

Die Karte ist aufzubewahren und auf Verlangen vorzuzeigen.

Who do you think dropped it?

☐ a pupil

☐ an attendant

☑ your teacher ✓

☐ the security-officer

2 Where would you expect to see this sign?

NICHT ZUM FENSTER HINAUSLEHNEN

☑ on a train ✓

☐ at a station

☐ in a bathroom

☐ at a travel agency

3 You notice the following weather report on the back page of a newspaper:

Nach kühler Nacht mit Temperaturen um 8 Grad wird's heute heiter bis wolkig, aber trocken. Höchst temperaturen um 20 Grad.
Weitere Aussichten: Trocken und warm.

What sort of weather can you expect today?
☐ wet
☐ misty
☑ variable cloud, but dry
☐ intermittent showers

(d) Tick the box (elements in German)

1 In your hotel, you are looking for the dining room for your breakfast. You see the following written on four doors. Which one is the right one for you?
☑ Eßsaal
☐ Küche
☐ Ausschank
☐ Gaststube

2 Your 18-year-old brother tears the leg of his trousers and you go to the department store to look for a new pair. Which department do you need?
☐ Möbel
☑ Herrenmode
☐ Schreibwaren
☑ Werkzeuge

3 You have toothache and need to see a dentist. There are four signs next to four doorbells at the entrance to the address you have been given. Which bell should you ring?
☐ Augenarzt
☑ Zahnarzt
☐ Rechtsanwalt
☐ Frauenarzt

(e) Ticking yes/no (questions in English)

1 This is a price list from a town-centre snack bar.

```
        IMBISS-STUBERL

Bockwurst mit Brötchen...............2,00
Currywurst mit Brötchen u. Salat.....3,75
Paar Frankfurter mit Brötchen........2,50
Essigwurst mit Brötchen..............2,40

Beilagen nach Wahl:

Pommes Frites (pro Portion)..........1,75
Kartoffelsalat (pro Portion).........1,00
Sauerkraut (pro Portion).............0,85

Weitere Brötchen je..................0,50
```

Which of the following can you obtain at this snack bar? Judging from the list, tick yes or no as appropriate.

	YES	NO
Curried sausage	✓	
Sweet and sour sausage		✓
Bacon		
Egg		✓
Chips	✓	
Bread rolls	✓	
Grated carrot salad		✓
Potato salad	✓	

2 This is an advertisement from a German newspaper:

Tick yes or no in answer to the following questions about Hamburger & Ohlhauser:

	YES	NO
Can you buy training shoes there?	✓	
Can you buy gifts and presents there?	✓	
Can you buy furniture there?		✓
Do sports students get 21% discount?		✓

3 You are on holiday near Moers when you see the following two advertisements in the brochure issued by the tourist information office:

Café – Restaurant

BERGHOF
Das Haus der Festlichkeiten

● **KONFIRMATION** ●
● **KOMMUNION** ●
● **HOCHZEITEN** ●

Mittag-Menü
von 12 - 14 Uhr
Auf Wunsch
Senioren- und
Kinderteller

**4130 Moers 1 (Schwafheim), Waldstr. 130
Telefon (0 28 41) 3 20 02**

Answer the following questions with yes or no:

	YES	NO
Is the *Zur Linde* open on Mondays?	✓	
Does the *Berghof* do a set-price menu at lunchtime?	✓	✓
In the *Berghof* can you get children's portions at lunchtime?	✓	✓
Can you go bowling at the *Zur Linde*?	✓	✓
Can the *Zur Linde* accommodate parties of 175?	✓	
Can the *Berghof* accommodate parties of 130?		✓

(f) Open-ended questions

1 What do the following signs mean?

(i)

APOTHEKE

chemist

(1 mark)

(ii)

ABFAHRT DER ZÜGE

....

(1 mark)

(iii)

UMLEITUNG

DIVERSION

(1 mark)

(iv)

PARKVERBOT

NO PARKING

(1 mark)

2 You notice the following advertisement.

Hilfe, dringend gesucht! Rote
Mappe, m. Akt-Zeichnungen
für Prüfung verloren.
Tel. 605115

What exactly has the person lost, and why does he/she need the drawings which were in it?

....

(2 marks)

3

MARIA ALM mit Hintermoos und Hinterthal
800–2.900 m / Salzburger Land

Urlaubsfreuden in sonniger Bergwelt: Erholung – Sport – Gesel-
ligkeit – familienfreundlich. Großartiger Naturpark, 80 km Wan-
derwege, geführte Bergwanderungen, Tennis – Reiten – Minigolf.
Urlaub für Fischer – eigenes Fischwasser. Sessellift; schöner
Moorbadesee, nur 5 km entfernt. Informieren Sie sich über unser
reichhaltiges, preiswertes Urlaubsangebot.

**Auskünfte u. Prospekte: Verkehrsverein A-5761 Maria Alm 65,
Telefon 00 43 / 65 84 / 316**

Name four of the attractions of Maria Alm.

....

(4 marks)

4 You read the following in a leaflet given to hitchhikers.

Nicht zu viel Gepäck mitnehmen!

In ganz Europa ist es nicht
gestattet, auf Autobahnen und
sonstigen Schnellstraßen
zu trampen. (Es wäre nämlich
zu gefährlich, Autos hier
anzuhalten. An Tankstellen
und auf Parkplätzen ist das
Trampen sowieso sicherer)

Wenn es möglich ist, trampen
Sie nicht am Wochenende!

What three pieces of advice are given? ....

....

(3 marks)

5 You receive the information shown on page 129 from a youth hostel.

(i) Where are the bedrooms? ....*First Floor*...
      (1 mark)

(ii) Give details of the washing facilities for people sleeping in the dormitories ....

....

      (2 marks)

(iii) Name *four* rooms you will find on the ground floor ....

....

      (4 marks)
(iv) Name *four* activities you can do in the cellar ....

....

      (4 marks)

Jugendherberge Birkenkreuzhausen

Ausstattung

Die Schlafzimmer sind im ersten Stock.

Flur A: 1 Schlafzimmer mit 2 Betten; fl. w/k Wasser;
         3 Schlafräume mit je 8 Betten, ein Waschraum mit 2 Duschen
         und Toiletten.

Flur B: 1 kleines Schlafzimmer mit 1 Bett, fl. w/k Wasser;
         2 Schlafzimmer mit je 7 Betten; 1 Schlafraum mit 6
         Betten; Waschraum mit 2 Duschen und Toiletten.

Im Erdgeschoß befinden sich folgende Räume:

1 grosser Speise-und Tagesraum für ca. 80 Personen

1 Gruppenraum für max. 30 Personen mit offenem Kamin und Sesseln

1 Gruppenraum für max. 15 Personen mit Teppichboden und Sesseln

Ausserdem sind im Erdgeschoß Garderobe, Schuhraum, sanitäre
Anlagen für den Tagesbetrieb sowie Kantine, Spül-und Wirtschaftsküche.

Im Keller ist vorhanden:

Ein grosser Spielraum mit Möglichkeiten für:

    Tischtennis
    Pool
    Fernsehen
sowie ein kleiner Leseraum.

6 Your young brother finds the following cartoon in the newspaper.

„Sie sind wohl ziemlich neu in diesem
Beruf, nicht wahr, junger Mann?!"

  (i) Who is supposed to be speaking to whom? ....
      (*1 mark*)
 (ii) What is he saying to him? ....
      (*2 marks*)

7 You come across the following when looking for a new pen-friend to write to:

> Ich suche Brieffreunde. Meine
> Hobbys: Squash, Langlauf,
> Schwimmen, Lesen, Musik hören.
> Meine Lieblingssänger sind Rein-
> hard Mey, Udo Jürgens und Peter
> Hofmann. Da mein Englisch
> schwach ist, korrespondiere ich
> nur in Deutsch. Meine Brieffreun-
> de sollten im Alter von 15 Jahren
> aufwärts sein.

(i) What hobbies does the writer have? (Name three) ....

....

....

(ii) Why must she write in German? ....

(iii) What age would she like her penfriend to be? ....
(*total 5 marks*)

8 This letter is taken from a magazine's problem page.

Älterer Bruder

**LESERIN: Ich habe ein Pro-
blem. Mein Bruder ärgert
mich oft. Er nimmt oft mein
Glas, wenn ich trinken will.
Auch glaubt er, mir befehlen
zu können, nur weil er älter
ist. Weil er das macht, werde
ich immer nervös, wenn er in
der Nähe ist. Aber trotzdem
mag ich ihn. Ich würde ihn
gern bessern, aber ich weiß
nicht wie. Vielleicht mache
ich auch etwas falsch. Wissen
Sie Rat?**

(i) Who is annoying the reader?

....

(ii) Name one annoying thing he does ....

....

(iii) Why doesn't the reader do anything about it? ....

....
(*total 3 marks*)

9 Imagine you are Markus and have just received the letter shown opposite.
  (i) What did you send her from Holland?   (*1 mark*)
 (ii) What exciting event took place in Tanja's home?   (*1 mark*)
(iii) What does Tanja think about returning to school?   (*1 mark*)

Rheurdt, den 23. August

Lieber Markus,

vielen Dank für Deinen Brief aus Holland. Inzwischen bist Du ja wieder zu Hause. Du hast sicher eine Menge erlebt. Wenn wir uns das nächste Mal sehen, mußt Du mir ganz viel erzählen.

Meine Ferien waren auch sehr schön, obwohl wir nicht fortgefahren sind. Aber unser Hund, die Aika, hat Junge bekommen. Neun Stück! Aika ist ganz stolz auf ihren Nachwuchs und läßt sich von jedem bewundern. Aber die kleinen Hunde machen auch viel Arbeit. Es ist sehr lustig, wenn ich mit allen zehn Hunden spazierengehe.

Leider fängt bald die Schule wieder an. Darauf freue ich mich gar nicht. Aber ich freue mich darauf, Dich bald wiederzusehen.

Liebe Grüße!
Deine Tanja

HIGHER-LEVEL READING

(a) Multiple choice (elements in English)

1 You read this article in a youth magazine.

Sicher zur Schule in den USA

In den USA fahren täglich 21 Millionen Kinder mit dem Schulbus, dabei verunglücken 4300 Schüler jährlich. In der Bundesrepublik fahren zwei Millionen Schüler, und es verunglücken 5600. Das heißt: In den Vereinigten Staaten ist das Risiko, beim Schulbusfahren zu verunglücken, 14mal geringer als bei uns. Woran liegt das? Zunächst: Alle amerikanischen Schulbusse sind auffallend gelb gestrichen. Wenn der Bus hält, leuchten sechs Lampen am Heck des Fahrzeugs auf, zwei vorn am Dach. Das signalisiert dem nachfolgenden Verkehr: absolutes Überholverbot. Bevor die Kinder aussteigen, klappt ein rotes Stoppschild aus. Das bedeutet für beide Fahrtrichtungen: Warten, bis die Schüler die Straße überquert haben.

(i) Are German school children travelling to school by bus

A just as safe as
B safer than
C more at risk than
D more reckless than
their American counterparts?

(ii) Which of these statements is true?

In America,

A when a school bus stops, six lights come on at the rear.

B while a school bus has children aboard, six lights flash on and off

C flashing lights on a school bus mean 'overtake with great care!'

D when a school bus is about to pull out, two lights come on at the front of the roof.

(iii) Which of these statements is true?

A While the children enter the bus, a stop-sign sticks out from the bus, preventing all overtaking.

B Before the children enter the bus, a stop-sign sticks out stopping traffic in both directions.

C While the children get off, a stop-sign is displayed to prevent overtaking.

D Before the children get off, a stop-sign is displayed, stopping traffic in both directions.

2 In a brochure you find the following list of cultural attractions for the region in which you are staying.

Dienstag **16.** **März**	**„DER MANN VON LA MANCHA"** Musical von Mitch Leigh und Robert Gilbert Stadttheater St. Pölten	Abo I
Dienstag **6.** **April**	**„LIEBELEI"** Schauspiel von Arthur Schnitzler Städtebundtheater	Abo I
Mittwoch **21.** **März**	**„DIE CSARDASFÜRSTIN"** Operette von Emerich Kálmán Stadttheater St. Pölten	Abo I
Dienstag **4.** **Mai**	**„IM WEISSEN RÖSSL"** Operette von Ralph Benatzky Stadtebundtheater	Abo I
Mittwoch **19.** **Mai**	**„CLAVIGO"** Trauerspiel von Johann Wolfgang von Goethe Salzburger Landestheater	Abo II und Jugendabo
Donnerstag **10.** **Juni**	**„OSCAR"** Lustspiel von Claude Magnier Linzer Landestheater	Abo I

Beginn jeweils **pünktlich** um 19.30 Uhr.

Kartenvorverkauf: Jeweils 8 Tage im voraus an der Theater-Kino-Kasse
von 10 bis 11.30 Uhr und ab 16 Uhr.

(i) Which statement is true?

A All the shows begin at half past seven sharp.

B All the shows end between 10 and 11.30.

C All the shows begin at half past eight sharp.

D There is a matinee at 4 p.m. on Saturdays.

(ii) Which is correct? Tickets for the shows *cannot* be bought

A less than a week in advance.

B more than a week in advance.

C after 4 p.m. on the day of the performance.

D from the cash-desk in the theatre.

3 What does the following sign mean?

DAS BETRETEN DER GLEISE IST STRENGSTENS VERBOTEN

A It is forbidden to walk on to the platform.

B Passengers are permitted to board the trains.

C It is strictly prohibited to walk across the tracks.

D It is not permitted to sell ice-cream here.

(b) Ticking yes/no

1 While on holiday in Germany, you pick up a leaflet about the local swimming pools. Read it, and then answer the questions which follow it by ticking yes or no.

Bäder

Name	Straße	Telefon
Spaßbad „Pappelsee"	Bertastraße 74	81640 o. 92-389

Hallenbad
Attraktion: 63 m lange geschlossene Wasserrutschbahn
Betriebszeit: ganzjährig
Öffnungszeiten:

Montag:	6.00 bis 13.30 Uhr öffentliches Baden
	13.30 bis 15.00 Uhr Baden für ältere Bürger
	15.00 bis 16.30 Uhr Baden für Mütter mit Klein-
	kindern und Schwangere
	16.30 bis 22.00 Uhr öffentliches Baden

Dienstag:	6.00 bis 16.00 Uhr öffentliches Baden
	16.00 bis 18.00 Lintforter Schwimmclub
	18.00 bis 22.00 Uhr öffentliches Baden

Freibad
Attraktionen: 2 gegenläufige jeweils rd. 120 m lange Wasser-rutschbahnen, Spaßpilz, Wasserkanone, Wildwasserkanal u.v.m.
Betriebszeit: Sommermonate

Lehrschwimmanlage
Lehrschwimmanlage der DLRG, Franzstraße 53

Mittwoch:	6.00 bis 20.00 Uhr öffentliches Baden
	20.00 bis 22.00 Uhr Baden für Versehrtensport-
	gemeinschaft u. Versehrte

Donnerstag:	6.00 bis 16.00 Uhr öffentliches Baden
	16.00 bis 18.00 Uhr Lintforter Schwimmclub
	18.00 bis 22.00 Uhr öffentliches Baden

Freitag:	6.00 bis 22.00 Uhr öffentliches Baden
Samstag:	7.00 bis 18.00 Uhr öffentliches Baden
Sonntag:	7.00 bis 13.00 Uhr öffentliches Baden
	13.00 bis 15.00 Uhr Zelt- u. Wassersportfreunde

Die Rutsche ist während der Badezeit jeweils ab 8.00 Uhr in Betrieb

Öffnungszeiten:
täglich von 8.00 Uhr bis 20.00 Uhr (höchstens jedoch bis zum Eintritt der Dunkelheit)

	YES	NO
Is the indoor pool open all year round?	....	....
Is the outdoor pool open all year round?	....	....
Is the indoor pool open to all swimmers for the whole of Monday?	....	....
Is the outdoor pool open daily from 8.00 to 20.00 or dusk, whichever is the earlier?	....	....

2 You are sent a copy of the proposed timetable for your coming exchange visit to Germany. It includes the following:

```
Freitag 24.05    Ankunft an der Realschule ca 13.00 Uhr.
                 Abends Welcome Party.

Samstag 25.05    11.00 Uhr: Fahrt zum Flachsmarkt in Krefeld-Linn.
                 Rückkehr gegen 16.00 Uhr.


        Die Teilnahme an dieser Veranstaltung ist freiwillig


Sonntag 26.05-)  Pfingsten        zur freien Verfügung in den Familien
Montag 27.05  )  (off Feiertag)
```

Someone who doesn't understand German asks you these questions. Answer yes or no.

	YES	NO
Is the welcome party in the afternoon?	....	....
Do we go to the flax market on Sunday?	....	....
Is there an organized programme for Sunday and Monday?	....	....
Is Monday a Bank Holiday?	....	....

(c) Open-ended questions

1   **Urlauberrücktransport aus dem Ausland:**

Das kann
teuer werden!

Marion F. hatte sich so richtig auf ihren Urlaub im sonnigen Sizilien gefreut. Nach ein paar Tagen Faulenzens am Strand in der Sonne unternahm sie gemeinsam mit anderen Urlaubern eine Sight-see-ing-Tour durch Palermo. Und dabei geschah es: An einer unübersichtlichen Kreuzung wurde sie von einem Auto angefahren. Das war das Ende des Urlaubs von Marion F. Ihre inneren Verletzungen erwiesen sich bei einer ersten Untersuchung schlimmer als zunächst angenommen. Hinzu kam: Die Krankenhäuser in der Umgebung waren voll belegt. Da gab's nur einen Ausweg – mit einem Flugzeug sofort zurück nach Hause. Marion F. mußte die Rückflugkosten selbst tragen. Sie hatte nämlich keine entsprechende Zusatzversicherung abgeschlossen, obwohl ihr diese das Reisebüro bei der Buchung angeboten hatte.

(i)   What was Marion F. doing in Palermo when her accident happened, and with whom?

(2 marks)

(ii)   Why could she not get into a local hospital?   *(1 mark)*

(iii)   What exactly did she have to do, and when?   *(2 marks)*

(iv)   Who paid for her return to Germany?   *(1 mark)*

2 You read the following in a magazine for young people.

...und ich
erwiderte den
Schlag mit
meinem
Regenschirm

LESER: Unser Chemielehrer ging für kurze Zeit aus dem Klassenzimmer. Während seiner Abwesenheit tobten wir herum. Mein Freund schlug mir aus Spaß an den Kopf, und ich erwiderte den Schlag mit meinem Regenschirm. Genau in diesem Augenblick kam der Lehrer wieder herein. Er bezeichnete mich als einen, der nicht ins Gymnasium, sondern in die Sonderschule paßt. Dies sagte er mir mit einer so verachtenden Stimme, daß mir Hören und Sehen verging. Er zeigte mir richtig, wie er mich haßt. Ich bin darüber empört. Kann man einen Lehrer wegen Schülerbeleidigung anzeigen? Kann ich sonst etwas tun?

Außerdem hat er mich 100mal schreiben lassen: „Ich darf im Unterricht nicht mit dem Schirm auf Herberts Kopf schlagen." Darüber hinaus sollte meine Mutter zu ihm in die Sprechstunde, und es könnte auch sein, daß ich noch zwei Stunden zum Nachsitzen kommen muß. Unter Umständen sei er sogar gezwungen, mir eine Sechs in Chemie zu geben. Sind diese Strafen angemessen?

(i)   What lesson did the incident take place in?   *(1 mark)*
(ii)   What did the writer do when he had been struck on the head?   *(2 marks)*
(iii)   What punishment did the writer receive?   *(2 marks)*
(iv)   What punishment might he receive if the teacher tells his mother?   *(1 mark)*
(v)   Why is the writer worried about his examination grade?   *(1 mark)*

3 Danger in the Southern Seas!

Noch mal dauerte meine Reise zwei weitere Tage, bis ich endlich in Singapur vor Anker ging. Singapur ist der richtige Stopp für mich: Hier gibt es alles zu kaufen für meine nächste, die längste Etappe auf meiner Reise nach China. Irgendwie gefällt mir die Stadt nicht. Sie wirkt wie ein großes Kaufhaus auf mich: Überall Geschäfte, Kaufhäuser, Shoppingfabriken, überall diese dollargierigen Chinesen.

Neben mir liegen noch andere Fahrtenjachten. Einige kommen aus Australien, andere wollen nach Thailand. Ich bin der einzige, der nonstop von hier nach China möchte.

Nach acht Tagen habe ich mein Schiff wider fit für das nächste, große Abenteuer: das Chinesische Meer. Schon die alten arabischen Segelanweisungen warnen vor diesem Meer auf der Sindbadroute. Und auch heute noch machen einem die schnelle Wetteränderung, die gefährliche See zu schaffen. Hinzu kommt, daß es jetzt schon Ende Mai ist, also die Hurrikansaison langsam beginnt. Ich will da nichts dramatisieren, aber schon ein mittlerer Hurrikan ist so stark wie ca. 1200 Atombomben vom Typ Hiroshima!

* * *

Genau am Morgen, als ich gerade meine Segel setze, um in Richtung China zu starten, versagt meine Selbststeueranlage. Ich kann nicht losfahren, repariere den ganzen Tag. Doch dann, am nächsten Tag, stehen die weißen Tücher: Asma nimmt Kurs auf China.

Ich sitze träumend auf Deck, beobachte die weißen Gischtkämme der Wellen und bin stolz auf Asma: Sie ist die erste Einhandjacht auf diesem Globus, die China anlaufen darf.

Am Abend meldet die Wetterstation Guam den ersten Hurrikan. Doch keine Gefahr für mich: Der tobt sich 600 Meilen nördlich von mir aus! Nachts wache ich schweißgebadet auf: Fieber! Ich fühle mich schlapp, hundeelend... Ich suche mir eine kleine Insel auf der Seekarte und steuere darauf zu, obwohl der Wind langsam dreht und fast gegen mich bläst. Ich muß dort hin, um mich zu erholen.

Section 1

(i) How long did it take the writer to reach Singapore? *(1 mark)*

(ii) What would he be able to do there? *(2 marks)*

(iii) Our writer is the only sailor going non-stop to China. What details are we given about the other boats he comes across in the harbour? *(2 marks)*

(iv) How long did he remain in Singapore? *(1 mark)*

(v) It is the end of May – why is this disconcerting? *(1 mark)*

Section 2

(i) What does he have to do when the automatic helm breaks down? *(2 marks)*

(ii) Why is he so proud of his yacht? *(2 marks)*

(iii) Why does the hurricane warning from Guam not worry him? *(1 mark)*

(iv) Why does it become necessary for him to head for the nearest island? *(1 mark)*

(v) Why is progress so difficult? *(1 mark)*

4 A tennis star considers her life and her future

„Irgendwann"–das versteht sie ja schon –„werde ich nicht mehr Tennis spielen können", sagt die 20-jährige. „Ein Beruf im Fernsehen würde mich interessieren; ich glaube, ich könnte so etwas machen. Ich schreibe auch gern, obwohl es mir nicht leicht fällt. Ich finde, daß man sich quälen muß."

Sie muß vieles für den Sport vernachlässigen. „Ich bereue es aber nicht, daß ich die Schule mit nur 16 Jahren aufgegeben habe", blickt Annaliese zurück. „Mein Leben ist auch eine Lehre." Das ist aber eine Lehre, die Annaliese keine Zeit läßt, für Dinge, die die meisten jungen Frauen gerne machen. „Ach", meint Annaliese. „Ich bin zum Beispiel keine Discogängerin. Neben den wichtigen Spielen und dem Training aber habe ich Zeit, um frische Luft zu schnappen. Ich habe leider nicht Zeit genug, um all meine Wünsche zu erfüllen. Ich würde gern Gitarre spielen können, aber dazu müßte ich üben, immer üben."

(i) What important fact does Annaliese realize, although she is only 20 years old? *(1 mark)*

(ii) What career would interest her in later life? *(1 mark)*

(iii) How does she feel about writing? *(2 marks)*

(iv) What does she not regret? *(2 marks)*

(v) What is the one unfulfilled wish which she singles out, and why must it remain unfulfilled for the time being? *(2 marks)*

5

9. Folk & Fool Festival Moers 1985

7. – 8. – 9. Juni 1985

Freitag, 7.6. – 20.00 Uhr – Schloßhof

THE SUPER ICHIZA	**(Kabuki Theatre/Japan)**
TIM BAT	**(Jonglage/London)**
PIIRPAUKE	**(Ethno-Rock/Finnl. Senegal)**

Samstag, 8.6. – 14.00 Uhr – Schloßhof

GEORGO & JACK	**(Fool-Duo/USA)**
AVAILABLE JELLY	**(Folk Musik/USA)**
MARCELINE & SYLVESTRE	**(Comedy/Spanien)**
OSKORRI	**(Folklore/Baskenland)**
TEATAR MASKA	**(Maskenballet/Jugoslawien)**
TEMPS FORT THEATRE	**(Maske & Musik/Frankr.)**
TRIBUTE	**(Folk-Rock-Symphony/Schweden)**

Sonntag, 9.6. – 14.00 Uhr – Schloßhof

DR. HOT & NEON	**(Fool-Jongleure/USA)**
KALIFI DRUM & DANCE ENSEMBLE	**(Ghana)**
PHILIPPE PILLON	**(Performance/Frankr.)**
LEO BASSI	**(Fool-Solo/Italien)**
BLOO LIPS	**(Cabaret/London)**
POOKIE SNACKENBURGER	**(Fool-Musik/London)**

Spielorte: Schloßhof Moers – am Schloßmuseum und im Stadtpark gelegen, Eissporthalle Filderstraße bei Dauerregen.
Anfahrt: Autobahn über Duisburg oder Krefeld – Abfahrt Moers Zentrum oder Moers West-Stadtmitte / Königlicher Hof · Haagstraße - Kastellplatz
Anfragen: Telefonische Anfragen an die Stadtinformation: 0 28 41 - 2 22 21
Übernachtung: Möglichkeiten zur Übernachtung bestehen im Jugendzentrum Südring – Zelten im Freizeitpark – Hotelreservierung über die Stadtinformation
Vorverkauf: Die Dauerkarte kostet 25,- DM – erhältlich bei der Stadtinformation oder im Aragon-Buchladen Moers.
Vorbestellungen: Stadtinformation

Tageskarten: 8,– 15,– und 15,– DM

Veranstalter: Träger des Folk & Fool Festivals ist der Verein zur Förderung von Jugendzentren in Moers e. V., Arbeitskreis Folk & Fool mit Unterstützung des Jugend- und Kulturamtes der Stadt Moers
Programm & Kontakt: W. Schrick, Baerler Straße 60, D-4130 Moers 1, Telefon 0 28 41 - 2 36 19

Euch wird Hören & Sehen nicht vergehen . . .

(i) From which countries do the following performers come? *(2 marks)*
Tribute
Philippe Pillon

(ii) What are the dates of the festival? *(1 mark)*

(iii) State *two* ways in which the poster suggests you might spend the night. *(2 marks)*

(iv) How much does an all-day ticket for Saturday cost? *(1 mark)*

(v) Whom would you contact for further details? *(1 mark)*

6

KÖLNER DOM
Informationsblatt zur Turmbesteigung

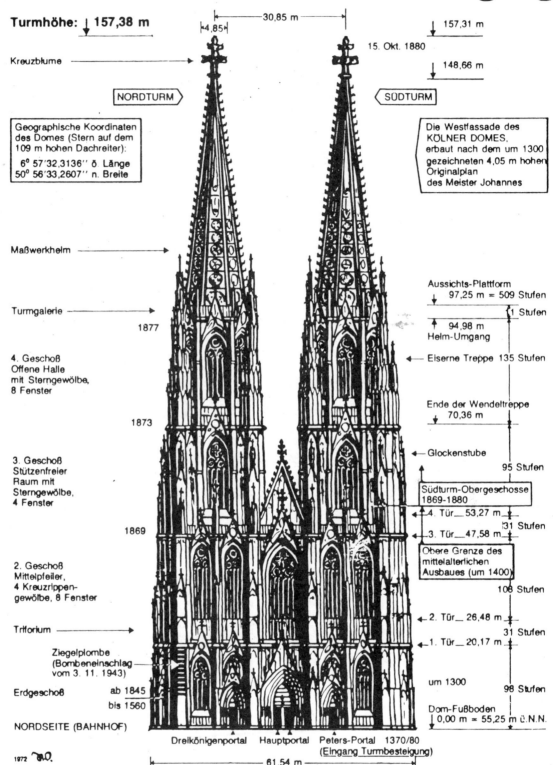

Turmhöhe: ↓ 157,38 m

├4,85┤ ├──── 30,85 m ────┤

↓ 157,31 m

15. Okt. 1880

↓ 148,66 m

Kreuzblume ──────→

[NORDTURM ⟩

⟨ SÜDTURM]

Geographische Koordinaten
des Domes (Stern auf dem
109 m hohen Dachreiter):

6° 57'32,3136'' ö. Länge
50° 56'33,2607'' n. Breite

Die Westfassade des
KÖLNER DOMES,
erbaut nach dem um 1300
gezeichneten 4,05 m hohen
Originalplan
des Meister Johannes

Maßwerkhelm ──────→

Turmgalerie ──────→

1877

Aussichts-Plattform
↓ 97,25 m = 509 Stufen

↕1 Stufen

↑ 94,98 m
Helm-Umgang

←── Eiserne Treppe 135 Stufen

4. Geschoß
Offene Halle
mit Sterngewölbe,
8 Fenster

1873

Ende der Wendeltreppe
↓ 70,36 m

3. Geschoß
Stützenfreier
Raum mit
Sterngewölbe,
4 Fenster

1869

←── Glockenstube

95 Stufen

Südturm-Obergeschosse
1869-1880

←4. Tür__53,27 m ↓↑
                    31 Stufen
←3. Tür__47,58 m ↓↑

Obere Grenze des
mittelalterlichen
Ausbaues (um 1400)

106 Stufen

2. Geschoß
Mittelpfeiler,
4 Kreuzrippen-
gewölbe, 8 Fenster

Triforium ──────→

←2. Tür__26,48 m ↓↑
                    31 Stufen
←1. Tür__20,17 m ↓↑

Ziegelplombe
(Bombeneinschlag ──
vom 3. 11. 1943)

um 1300

98 Stufen

Erdgeschoß   ab 1845

bis 1560

Dom-Fußboden
↓ 0,00 m = 55,25 m ü.N.N.

NORDSEITE (BAHNHOF)

1972 ꝑ.O.

Dreikönigenportal   Hauptportal   Peters-Portal   1370/80
(Eingang Turmbesteigung)

├──────── 61,54 m ────────┤

(i) Which side of Cologne Cathedral is represented here?

(ii) Which portal must you enter to go up the tower?

(iii) What is the height of the higher tower?

(iv) How high is the observation platform, and how many steps are there leading up to it?

(v) In which direction would you have to go to get from the Cathedral to the station: North, South, East or West?

7 You are staying with Tanja, who shows you this letter.

Katwijk, den 14. August

Liebe Tanja,

ich sende Dir herzliche Grüße von unserer Ferien-Fahrradtour nach Holland. Es ist ganz toll hier! Wir sind gestern an der Küste angekommen. Wir haben einen schönen Zeltplatz gefunden, direkt am Strand. Leider ist das Wasser sehr schmutzig, so daß ich nicht gerne darin schwimme.

Auf der Fahrt hierhin ist uns etwas Aufregendes passiert. Meine Freunde und ich haben in einem kleinen Dorf auf einer Wiese übernachtet. Als wir am Morgen aus dem Zelt kamen, waren unsere Fahrräder verschwunden. Wir haben vielleicht einen Schreck bekommen! Wir haben überall gesucht, aber wir konnten sie nicht finden. Als wir uns gerade entschlossen hatten, zur Polizei zu gehen, kam eine Frau aus dem Bauernhaus und winkte uns zu. „Ich habe Eure Räder in den Schuppen gestellt, damit niemand sie fortnehmen kann", sagte sie. „Und jetzt kommt erst mal rein, frühstücken!" Wir waren natürlich sehr froh und ließen uns die frische Milch und die warmen Brötchen schmecken. Dann setzten wir unsere Reise fort.

Bis bald!
Viele Grüße
Dein Markus

(i) What sort of holiday is Markus on? *(1 mark)*
(ii) Where exactly are they staying in Katwijk? *(1 mark)*
(iii) Why doesn't Markus fancy swimming in the sea there? *(1 mark)*
(iv) Where had the boys spent the night before they awoke to find their bicycles missing? *(1 mark)*
(v) What was the *first* thing they did on discovering the disappearance? *(1 mark)*
(vi) What happened to the bicycles? *(2 marks)*
(vii) What did they eat for breakfast? *(2 marks)*

8 You are staying with Klaus, who shows you this letter.

Rheinberg, den 24. März 1986

Lieber Klaus!

Gestern waren Petra, Gerd und ich im Krefelder Zoo. Wir haben uns fast nur am Affenfelsen mit den Pavianen aufgehalten. Es war sehr lustig. Der Affenboß wurde manchmal echt sauer, wenn ihm die Affenkinder zu toll vor der Nase herumtanzten. Nachher sind wir dann noch in die Abteilung mit den Schlangen und Krokodilen gegangen. Das war nicht so interessant, weil die blöden Viecher nur dumm rumlagen. Wir haben versucht, die Krokodile ein bißchen zu ärgern, damit sie sich endlich mal bewegten. Aber da kam ein Wärter und hat uns rausgeschmissen. Petra war stinksauer auf uns, weil wir solch einen Blödsinn gemacht hatten. Zum Glück sind wir nicht aus dem Zoo geflogen. So konnten wir uns wenigstens noch die anderen Tiere ansehen. Danach sind wir dann in eine Eisdiele gegangen und haben ein großes Eis gegessen. Es war ein toller Tag. Schade, daß Du nicht dabei warst. Hoffentlich klappt's beim nächsten Mal.

Bis bald,

Dein Jürgen

PS. Grüß Deine Schwester und gib ihr einen dicken Kuß von mir.

(i) Name two of the animals the children visited at the zoo.	*(2 marks)*
(ii) How did the *boys* behave in the reptile house?	*(1 mark)*
(iii) What did they all do after they left the reptile-house?	*(1 mark)*
(iv) What did they do after leaving the zoo?	*(1 mark)*
(v) How do you know that Jürgen is fond of Klaus's sister?	*(2 marks)*

6 THE ORAL EXAMINATION

All Examining Groups expect candidates to take an oral examination. Speaking German at the Lower or Basic Level is a compulsory element of GCSE. In Scotland the oral examination is more important than any of the other areas.

There are two main elements in the GCSE speaking tests:

role-playing situations

conversation

Most candidates for GCSE will be examined by their own teacher and the 10-15 minutes that the test usually takes will be recorded on tape. Accordingly candidates should prepare themselves by getting used to having a tape recorder running while practising for this test.

The emphasis in the speaking tests in the GCSE is very much placed on communication. The precise details of the requirements of your own particular Examining Group will be available from your teacher. The materials used in the examination itself will obviously all be based on the topic areas and settings as detailed in the syllabus and you should use this section in conjuction with Unit 2 of this book which has been set out incorporating the topic areas listed by the Examining Groups.

In the role-play section of the speaking test you should prepare yourself to play the role of an English person having to cope with an authentic real-life situation when confronted by a German-speaking person being played by the examiner. You will certainly have to be prepared to take the initiative in asking for goods or information, but you may also have to give information in return.

Conversations, whether 'guided' with set questions or 'free' with a visual stimulus of some sort, involve you in both answering questions about yourself and describing either an actual or an imaginary incident/journey, etc. in which you are one of the people taking part. You tell the story about yourself or make a report about what happened. You may be presented with a verbal stimulus, a diagram or a series of pictures which will provide you with the opportunity to speak at some length in German.

The kinds of success (and the way they are achieved) which will be tested by the speaking section of the GCSE are:

1 an ability to understand and communicate
2 the way you speak German – accent and pronunciation, including intonation
3 your ability to speak with linguistic accuracy and fluency
4 the content of what you say – i.e. breadth of vocabulary and German idiom

The mark schemes for each of the Examining Groups reflect the above areas of assessment.

Pronunciation and intonation

Speaking German demands a comprehensive knowledge of pronunciation and intonation. Remember all vowel sounds in German are pure. Each vowel can have a long and a short form as separate sounds e.g. **an** (short), **Rasen** (long). Be careful about the vowel sounds written with two letters but having only a single sound:

au – aus	**ai** – Hain
äu – Häuser	**ei** – ein
eu – treu	**ey** – Meyer

Equally the effect of adding an Umlaut to a, o, u, must be carefully learned.

Käse, cheese; **böse**, angry; **Tür**, door.

The following are the important differences in the pronunciation of consonants:

b, d, g, at the end of a word or syllable are pronounced like **p, t, k,** respectively.

-ig is pronounced like **ich**, the **ch** being pronounced in the same way as the 'h' (in English) in the word '*h*uge'.

h at the end of a syllable is *not* pronounced – sehen (to see).

j is pronounced like an English 'y' – jung (young).

l is pronounced with the tongue against the inside of the front teeth – halten (to hold).

s at the end of a syllable/word is pronounced like 'ss' in English – Gras (grass); before a vowel it is pronounced as a soft 'z' as in Gläser (glasses).

v is like the English 'f' – von (from).

140

w is like the English 'v' – **w**o (where).
z is 'ts' – **Z**immer (room).
ch is like the Scottish 'lo*ch*' after a, o or u; after all other letters it is pronounced like the 'h' of 'huge' in English. At the beginning of a word it is sometimes pronounced like a 'k' – **Ch**arakter (character).
chs is like 'x' – se**chs** (six).
dt is like 't' – Sta**dt** (town).
qu is like 'kv' – **Qu**atsch (rubbish)
sch is like 'sh' – **Sch**ule (school).
sp and **st** at the beginning of a word or syllable are pronounced 'shp' and 'sht' – **sp**rechen (to speak), auf**st**ehen (to stand up).

The glottal stop

The glottal stop in German prevents the slurring together of sounds which occur in English pronunciation. Consequently whereas in English 'an apple' would be pronounced without any break, in German 'ein Apfel' is pronounced as two separate distinct words.

Intonation

Intonation is more difficult to get right. If you listen to German on the radio or being spoken by Germans you will be able to detect the rise and fall of the sound. You should notice in general terms that at the end of each sense group the sound rises until you reach the end of a sentence, when it falls. To represent the sound pattern as a series of lines, German would look something like this:

English is totally different. In English the sound pattern is much more singsong, with the sound pattern rising and falling within each sense group, like this:

Try recording yourself on a cassette recorder reading the last two paragraphs. Play your recording back and listen to the rise and fall of the sound pattern of English. Then make a recording of the news being read on German radio. When you play this recording back again, listen to the intonation, note where the newsreader's voice rises and falls, and you will hear immediately the difference between the sound of the English and the German. To speak well you have to copy the German intonation pattern. Practise talking and recording yourself talking German. Play back this recording and compare it with your recording of the German newsreader. Another way of doing the same thing is to ask your teacher, or, if you have one in your school, the German assistant, to record some German for you onto your own tape. You can then compare your own efforts with a model which you can try to copy.

Role Playing – Basic Level

In most cases candidates are asked to choose two role-playing cards on the day of the examination, which they may then look at in the preparation time for their oral. On the role-playing cards there will be instructions in English. Here is an example of the sort of instructions you will find.

FOOD AND DRINK – CAFÉS AND RESTAURANTS

1 Imagine you are in a café in Germany. Your examiner is the waiter.
(a) Ask the waiter if he has seen an English family with two small daughters aged five and three.
(b) Order a cup of white coffee and a piece of gâteau.
(c) Tell the waiter he has forgotten to bring the sugar.

Suggested answers

(a) Haben sie eine englische Familie mit zwei Töchtern gesehen? Die Töchter sind fünf und drei Jahre alt.
(b) Eine Tasse Kaffee mit Milch und ein Stück Torte, bitte!
(c) Sie haben vergessen, den Zucker zu bringen.

This is a fairly straightforward example. Most of the role-playing situations will be similar to this. They are intended to be 'survival' situations, as realistic as possible, so that they test whether you would be able to cope linguistically in such a situation if you were in a German-speaking country. The idea is that the situations are the sort in which English people might well find themselves if they went to a German-speaking country. Within any of the topic areas it would be possible to ask for a wide variety of roles. The topic areas are those in the Vocabulary Revision section of this book.

To prepare yourself adequately for role-playing exercises of this kind involves a knowledge of the necessary basic vocabulary, much of which you will find in Unit 2. Each candidate must familiarize him- or herself with how you say in German the kinds of things which occur in everyday real-life situations.

On the examination day, do not fall into the trap of trying to translate the words on the card. This is *not* a translation exercise but a 'real-life' situation, which you have to imagine you are in. When preparing your role, try to think about what a German speaker would say in the situation which has been presented to you.

Practising role-play exercises is particularly difficult because you need another person to play the other part. Sometimes you can work together with a friend, but best of all try and persuade the German assistant to help you in your preparation, as he/she will know exactly what would be said in each situation. The use of a tape/cassette recorder to record your mini-conversations for checking back where you went wrong is a useful technique which you can employ. Do not be afraid to paraphrase the outline if you think it will make what you say more intelligible to the examiner.

Given below are some more examples of role-playing situations with some suggested answers. They are at Basic Level.

ACCOMMODATION – CAMPSITE

2 Auf dem Campingplatz
You are on a campsite in Germany. You are speaking to the warden. Tell him/her:
(a) You would like to stay for two nights.
(b) You have your own tent with you.
(c) Ask if there are showers in the washrooms.
(d) Ask if there is a camp food store.

Suggested answers

(a) Ich möchte zwei Nächte bleiben.
(b) Ich habe mein eigenes Zelt mit.
(c) Gibt es Duschen in den Waschräumen?
(d) Gibt es ein Lebensmittelgeschäft?

PUBLIC TRANSPORT

3 Auf dem Bahnhof
You are at Cologne main station and you are speaking to the man/woman in the ticket office. Ask him/her:
(a) for a single ticket for one person to Köln-Deutz.
(b) if the next train stops there.
(c) how long it takes to get there.
(d) which platform it leaves from.
(e) what time the train leaves.

Suggested answers

(a) Einmal nach Köln-Deutz bitte, einfach.
(b) Hält der nächste Zug dort?
(c) Wie lange dauert es, dorthin zu fahren?
(d) Von welchen Bahnsteig fährt der Zug ab?
(e) Um wieviel Uhr fährt der Zug ab?

HOLIDAYS

4 You are talking to a friend who has just returned from Germany.
(a) Ask where he/she stayed in Germany.
(b) Ask if he/she spoke much German.
(c) Ask if he/she is going to Germany again next year.
(d) Ask where he/she will be going in Germany.
(e) Ask how long the journey takes.

Suggested answers

(a) Wo bist du in Deutschland geblieben?
(b) Hast du viel Deutsch gesprochen?
(c) Wirst du nächstes Jahr noch einmal nach Deutschland fahren?
(d) Wohin wirst du in Deutschland fahren?
(e) Wie lange dauert die Reise?

TOURIST INFORMATION – BANKS

5 In einer Bank

You are in a bank in Germany talking to the bank clerk.

(a) Say you would like to cash a traveller's cheque for £20.
(b) Say you have your passport here.
(c) When he asks you how you would like the money, say please repeat, as you have not understood that.

Suggested answers

(a) Ich möchte einen Reisescheck zu zwanzig Pfund einlösen.
(b) Hier habe ich meinen Paß.
(c) Bitte wiederholen Sie! Ich habe das nicht verstanden.

TOURIST INFORMATION – POST OFFICE

6 Auf der Post

You are at the post office and you are talking to the person behind the counter.

(a) Ask for four 40-pfennig stamps.
(b) Say you would like to send a telegram to Hamburg.
(c) Ask if you can telephone from here.
(d) Say you wish to call a friend in Stuttgart.
(e) Ask how much the call will cost to your friend in Stuttgart.

Suggested answers

(a) Vier Briefmarken zu vierzig Pfennig bitte.
(b) Ich möchte ein Telegramm nach Hamburg schicken.
(c) Darf ich von hier telephonieren?
(d) Ich will einen Freund in Stuttgart anrufen.
(e) Wieviel kostet es, meinen Freund in Stuttgart anzurufen?

Some of the role-play situations at Basic Level are slightly more difficult because they are less structured or because you are asked to make a more complicated transaction.

TOURIST INFORMATION – IN A HOTEL

7 Im Hotel

You are at the reception desk in a hotel.

(a) Say that your father wrote and booked a single and a double room.
(b) When asked, give you name and nationality.
(c) When told which rooms you have, ask whether they both have a shower.
(d) Check that breakfast is included in the price.
(e) Ask finally how much the rooms cost per night.

Suggested answers (including the teacher/examiner's possible script)
(T/E = Teacher/Examiner.   C = Candidate.)

T/E: Sie sind an dem Empfang in einem Hotel. Ich bin der Empfangsherr/die Empfangs-dame.
Guten Abend, Mein Herr/Fräulein! Kann ich Ihnen helfen?

(a) *C:* Ja, bitte. Mein Vater hat ein Einzelzimmer und ein Doppelzimmer schriftlich bestellt.
T/E: Unter welchem Namen, bitte?

(b) *C:* Unser Name ist Davis. Wir sind Engländer.
T/E: Ja, das stimmt. Sie haben Zimmer Number 204 und 205.

(c) *C:* Haben beide Zimmer eine Dusche?
T/E: Ja, natürlich.

(d) *C:* Ist das Frühstück im Preis einbegriffen?
T/E: Ja, mein Herr/meine Dame, es ist einschließlich Frühstück.

(e) *C:* Wieviel kosten die Zimmer pro Nacht?
T/E: Sie kosten 100 DM pro Nacht zusammen.

FINDING YOUR WAY

8 You are in a town in Germany. The examiner is playing the part of a passer-by. You speak first.

(a) Stop the passer-by and ask for help.

(b) Answer the question and say you are on holiday and ask how to get to the post office.

(c) Ask how long it will take to get there on foot.

(d) Answer the examiner's question and ask whether the post office closes at lunchtime.

(e) Thank the passer-by for his/her help and say goodbye.

Suggested answers (including the teacher/examiner's possible script)

(T/E = Teacher/Examiner.   C = Candidate.)

(a) *C:* Entschuldigen Sie bitte! Können Sie mir helfen?
T/E: Ja, gern. Sind Sie hier fremd?

(b) *C:* Ja, ich bin auf Urlaub. Wie komme ich zum Postamt, bitte?
T/E: Es ist ganz in der Nähe. Gehen Sie geradeaus, dann erste Straße links.

(c) *C:* Wie lange brauche ich zu Fuß?
T/E: Fünf Minuten ungefähr. Verstanden?

(d) *C:* Ja. Ist das Postamt zu Mittag zu?
T/E: Nein, es bleibt auf.

(e) *C:* Vielen Dank für Ihre Hilfe. Auf Wiedersehen.

MAKING DOMESTIC ARRANGEMENTS – SOCIAL RELATIONSHIPS

9 On the telephone
You are in Germany, talking to your friend on the phone. You are making arrangements to meet and go to the cinema together that evening. You speak first. The examiner plays your friend.

(a) Say, hello, this is (*your name*) speaking.

(b) Say that you are going into town this evening and ask if you can meet him/her.

(c) Ask if he/she would like to go to the cinema.

(d) Ask at what time the film starts.

(e) When told, say you will meet each other at 19.30 in front of the cinema. Say goodbye.

Suggested answers (including the teacher/examiner's possible script)

(T/E = Teacher/Examiner.   C = Candidate.)

C: Hallo, hier spricht . . . (*give your name*).
T/E: Hallo, schön dich nochmal zu hören.
C: Ich fahre heute abend in die Stadt. Können wir uns treffen?
T/E: Ja sicher, ich freue mich darauf.
C: Möchtest du ins Kino gehen?
T/E: Ja, der neue James Bond Film soll sehr gut sein.
C: Um wieviel Uhr beginnt dieser Film?
T/E: Um 20 Uhr glaube ich.
C: Dann treffen wir uns um 19.30 vor dem Kino. Auf Wiederhören.
T/E: Auf Wiederhören, bis später!

DOMESTIC ARRANGEMENTS – MEETING A FRIEND AT THE AIRPORT

10 At the airport
You are meeting your German friend Hans/Inge at the airport. He/she has just arrived. The examiner is playing the part of Hans/Inge. You speak first.

(a) Say 'hello' and say how nice it is to see Hans/Inge again.

(b) Ask what the flight was like and whether he/she is tired.

(c) Ask if he/she had to open his/her luggage coming through customs.

(d) Ask how long it took to come through customs.

(e) Say that your father is waiting outside in the car.

Suggested answers (including the teacher/examiner's possible script)

(*T/E = Teacher/Examiner*   *C = Candidate.*)

(a) *C:* Hallo, wie nett dich wieder zu sehen, Hans/Inge.
T/E: Hallo, X (*this will be your name*).

(b) *C:* Wie war der Flug? Bist du müde?
T/E: Ach nein, der Flug war ganz schnell.

(c) *C:* Hast du deine Koffer beim Zoll aufmachen müssen?
T/E: Nein, sie haben nur meinen Pass angesehen.

(d) *C:* Wie lange war es denn beim Zoll?
T/E: Es dauerte nur eine kurze Zeit.

(e) Mein Vater wartet draußen im Auto.

▮▮▮ Role Playing – Higher Level ▮▮▮

Role playing at the Higher Level is more demanding. Candidates for this level should expect to be confronted with an authentic situation where you have to 'think it out' as you go along. In these kinds of situations the teacher/examiner plays a more interventionist role, for example, by presenting you with a choice if you are buying something in a shop, or by putting some kind of obstacle in your way during the role play so that you have to respond accordingly. Instead of you asking most of the questions in this kind of role-play situation, the examiner is going to ask you questions, seeking more information from you or some kind of clarification of what you want. You must be prepared to answer these questions and allow the situation to develop. Obviously this kind of role play is more complex and involves you in a less structured situation.

To prepare for this kind of test you will need to have a good command of vocabulary and idiom and an ability to use German in context. You cannot learn this kind of process off by heart. You need to be able to use the language at a reasonably high level of sophistication.

It is difficult to practise this kind of role play without working with someone who can put you under the sort of pressure that you will experience in the examination. Remember that what is paramount is communication. You are playing yourself in a given situation. The framework is there for you to see. When preparing for this test, try to imagine what might be expected of you and decide what you are going to say given those circumstances.

Here are some examples taken from the various Examining Groups' specimen materials. None of them is exactly the same as the specimen materials, but they are all similar in style and content.

TOURIST INFORMATION – IN A LOST PROPERTY OFFICE

1 You are on holiday in Germany and have lost your new Kodak camera. You go to the lost property office. The examiner is playing the part of the man/woman in the lost property office. You speak first.

(a) Say 'excuse me' and explain that you have lost your camera.

(b) Answer the examiner's question and ask if anyone has by chance handed it in.

(c) Answer the examiner's next question saying 'in the town centre' and ask how long they stay open.

(d) Answer the examiner's next question and say that you will phone tomorrow morning.

(e) Ask if they will ring you at your hotel, if someone does hand the camera in.

Suggested answers (including the teacher/examiner's possible script)

(*T/E = Teacher/Examiner.*   *C = Candidate.*)

(a) *C:* Entschuldigen Sie bitte. Ich habe meine Kamera verloren.
T/E: Können Sie Ihre Kamera beschreiben?

(b) *C:* Ja, es ist eine neue Kodak-Kamera. Hat jemand sie zufällig abgegeben?
T/E: Einen Augenblick bitte . . . Nein, leider nicht. Wo haben Sie sie verloren?

(c) *C:* In der Stadtmitte. Bis wann bleibt das Fundbüro auf?
T/E: Bis halb sechs abends. Wollen Sie die Telefonnummer aufschreiben?

(d) *C:* Nein, ich habe sie schon. Ich rufe morgen früh an.
T/E: Gut.

(e) *C:* Können Sie mich im Hotel anrufen, wenn jemand die Kamera abgibt?
T/E: Nein, leider nicht. Sie müssen uns anrufen.

SHOPPING

2 You are staying with a friend in Germany and are planning to go shopping. The examiner is playing the part of your friend. You speak first.

(a) Say that you would like to go to town at the weekend. Ask your friend if he/she would like to come with you.

(b) When asked about changing money, say yes, perhaps, because you want to buy some presents. Ask if there is a good department store.

(c) Answer you friend's question saying that you have chocolates for your mum and ask your friend if he/she can suggest anything for your father.

(d) Answer your friend's next question and say that's a good idea, your father likes drinking wine.

(e) Ask your friend at what time you will have to get up on Saturday to be ready to go to town.

Suggested answers (including the teacher/examiner's possible script)

(T/E = Teacher/Examiner.   C = Candidate.)

(a) *C:* Ich möchte am Wochenende in die Stadt fahren. Willst du mitkommen?

T/E: Ja, gerne, das können wir am Samstag machen. Willst du noch Geld wechseln?

(b) *C:* Ja, vielleicht, weil ich Geschenke kaufen will. Gibt es ein gutes Kaufhaus?

T/E: Ja, am besten gehen wir zu Horten. Du hast schon etwas für deine Mutter, nicht wahr?

(c) *C:* Ja, für Mutti habe ich Pralinen. Was kann ich für Vati kaufen?

T/E: Wie wäre es mit einer Flasche Wein? Was meinst du?

(d) *C:* Das ist eine gute Idee. Vati trinkt sehr gern Wein.

T/E: Gut.

(e) *C:* Um wieviel Uhr muß ich am Samstag aufstehen, um fertig zu sein, in die Stadt zu fahren?

T/E: Um 8 Uhr.

ARRANGING A MEETING – SOCIAL RELATIONSHIPS

3 You are on holiday in Germany, and have made a new friend. Your teacher will play the part of the new friend. You want to meet him/her tomorrow and you are free all day. Arrange a meeting.

There are three things you must do.

(a) Open the conversation by suggesting a time to meet.

(b) Respond to any suggestions your teacher puts to you.

(c) Arrange something to do, and when and where to meet.

The above are the instructions you will receive in the examination. You can see that this is far less structured than the previous examples. You have only the situation, what you are proposing to do in outline and three tasks which must be included. The rest is up to your imagination and the replies you receive from your teacher/examiner. The teacher has some instructions which tell him/her to turn down your first suggestion, saying that he/she has a prior commitment. The second suggestion which you will then make will be accepted and a time and place for the meeting is agreed. The role play might go something like this:

(T/E = Teacher/Examiner.   C = Candidate.)

C: Hallo, wie gehts?

T/E: Gut danke, und du?

C: Sehr gut, danke. Bist du frei, heute abend? Wenn das geht, können wir ins Kino gehen!

T/E: Leider nicht, ich bin am Abend mit meinen Eltern zu Freunden eingeladen.

C: Schade, aber vielleicht können wir morgen abend ins Kino gehen.

T/E: Ja, sicher, das wäre prima.

C: Wunderbar, wir werden denn uns um 7 Uhr vor dem Rathaus treffen.

T/E: Schön. Ich freue mich darauf. Bis morgen also. Tschüß!

C: Tschüß!

TRAVEL AND TRANSPORT – AT A GARAGE

4 At a service station in Germany, your father has just filled up with petrol and has sent you to pay the cashier. Your tasks are:

(a) to greet the cashier;

(b) to say you would like a litre of oil;

(c) to ask how much the oil is;

(d) to ask if they sell sweets;

(e) to say you would like to buy a map;

(f) to ask the way to the motorway to Munich.

During the course of this role play the teacher/examiner is instructed to intervene and ask you to give more information about which oil you want to buy. You will be offered three prices. You will also be asked about the sweets and the map. The conversation could therefore proceed as follows:

(*T/E = Teacher/Examiner.*   *C = Candidate.*)

C: Guten Morgen.

T/E: Guten Morgen, kann ich Ihnen helfen?

C: Ja, ich möchte ein Liter Öl, bitte.

T/E: Zu welchem Preis? 8 DM, 5,50 DM oder 5 DM?

C: Das billigste, bitte, zu 5 DM. Wieviel kostet das mit dem Benzin?

T/E: 25 DM. Sonst noch etwas?

C: Ja, verkaufen Sie Bonbons, bitte?

T/E: Ja, natürlich. Was für Bonbons möchten Sie?

C: 100 Gramm Pfefferminz, bitte und ich möchte auch eine Karte kaufen.

T/E: Sicher, welche Karte wollen Sie – von Norddeutschland oder von Süddeutschland?

C: Von Süddeutschland, da wir nach München fahren. Können Sie mir bitte zeigen, wo die Autobahn nach München liegt?

T/E: Ja, es liegt hier auf der Karte.

C: Danke schön. Das ist sehr nett von Ihnen.

MAKING AN ARRANGEMENT – SOCIAL RELATIONSHIPS

5 Arranging a holiday in England for your friend

You are speaking to your friend on the telephone. Your friend will be played by the teacher/examiner. You must answer any questions put to you by the examiner or respond to any observation. Your tasks are:

(a) To ask if he/she would like to stay with you at Christmas or at another convenient time.

(b) Tell him/her that you will fetch him/her from the airport in the car.

(c) Answer his/her question about what he/she could do during his/her stay in England.

Once again this is an open-ended topic and your teacher/examiner has instructions to counter your suggestions. He/she is not able to come at Christmas but could come at Easter. He/she will ask you what you will be doing together during the stay. At first the activity you suggest will be rejected and you will have to agree to do something different together. Here is a possible way the conversation might go:

(*T/E = Teacher/Examiner.*   *C = Candidate.*)

C: Hallo, hier ist (*say your name here*). Wie geht's, gut, hoffentlich? Möchtest du eine Woche, zu Weihnachten bei mir in Brighton verbringen?

T/E: Leider kann ich nicht, weil ich bei meinen Großeltern wohnen muß. Ich konnte aber eine Woche zu Ostern bei dir verbringen, das wäre schön, wenn es möglich wäre.

C: Schade, das du nicht zu Weihnachten kommen kannst, aber eine Woche zu Ostern wird auch schön sein. Wir werden dich vom Flughafen abholen.

T/E: Also gut, und danke sehr, ich freue mich auf die Reise mit dem Auto nach Hause vom Flughafen. Was werden wir während der Osterferien machen?

C: Wir können den Londoner Zoo besuchen oder einen Ausflug nach Cambridge machen.

T/E: Augenblick, bitte, ich habe Zoos gar nicht gern. Was könnten wir anders machen.

C: Wir könnten an die See fahren oder fischen gehen, wie du willst.

T/E: Ja, ich möchte an die See fahren. Das wäre wirklich schon, wenn das Wetter gut wäre.

C: Also gut denn, ich schreibe bald, um alles zu erklären und freue mich sehr auf die Osterferien. Bis dahin, auf Wiederhören.

T/E: Alles Gute, auf Wiederhören.

There is no doubt that these less structured role-play situations allow the candidate to show off their command of spoken German. You should therefore prepare yourself to cope with the situations presented to you and learn enough idiom and vocabulary in context to enable you to take the initiative in these kinds of extended role play.

Conversation

The second element in the speaking tests for GCSE is some form of conversation which can either be guided or more 'open ended'. The two levels of Basic and Higher are included but it is important to remember that those candidates for whom the higher test is considered appropriate will be tested on the basic-level materials as well, because Higher Level incorporates Basic Level for all the Examining Groups.

Basic-level conversation tests are usually of the 'guided' type. This varies from one Examining Group to another. For example LEAG expects a choice of three themes to be made by all candidates from a list of eleven, all of which are included in the main topic areas for the whole GCSE syllabus. One of these three themes will be tested in the examination plus unprepared questions on other themes set by the Examining Group.

The eleven themes are: your home; your family; your morning and evening routine; the town or village in which you live; your school and your school life; what you do at weekends; sports that you play or watch; your holidays; your friends; your plans for the next two or three years; a visit abroad.

The MEG syllabus indicates that there will be 16 questions on at least five topic areas from the syllabus.

For NEA there will be a short conversation using unprepared questions based on topics listed in the syllabus, but the topics will not be specified until the time of the examination.

SEG has two sections of 'guided' conversation, one based on unprepared questions on topic areas listed in the syllabus and the other based on pre-set questions on a written or visual stimulus. The material provided will include authentic details from posters, advertisements, school timetables, menus, etc.

NISEC and WJEC will be the same as NEA. The Scottish system requires special explanation. (See page 157.)

When preparing yourself for this part of the examination you will need to do a lot of work on your own as most of the questions will require individual and personal answers. One of the best ways of preparing your own answers to these types of question is to work with a friend and record the questions and your answers on tape. You can then, using the pause button, test yourself and check your answers at the same time. Once again ask a native speaker for help if you can. Certainly ask your teacher to listen to your tape and check your answers and your pronunciation.

Here are some typical questions taken from the lists of specimen material provided by the Examining Groups and grouped under topic areas. The answers given are only suggestions; you can fill in the details relevant to you. The list is not exhaustive. After the first two examples **du** is used as it seems to be preferred by the Examining Groups. Questions and answers suitable for Higher Level are printed in colour.

YOU, YOUR FAMILY AND YOUR HOME

Wie heißen Sie?	Ich heiße . .
Wie heißt du?	
Wie alt sind Sie?	Ich bin . . . Jahre alt.
Wie alt bist du?	
Wieviele Geschwister hast du?	Ich habe (zwei) Brüder und (eine) Schwester.
Wo wohnst du?	Ich wohne in . . .
Wie ist deine Adresse?	Meine Adresse ist . . .
Wohnst du in einem Haus oder in einer Wohnung?	Ich wohne in einem Haus/in einer Wohnung.
Wieviele Zimmer hat dein Haus/deine Wohnung?	Es/Sie hat (sechs) Zimmer.
Wie sieht dein Haus/deine Wohnung aus?	Es/Sie ist klein. Es/Sie hat zwei Schlafzimmer, ein Wohnzimmer, eine Küche und einen Garten.
Hast du Telefon?	Ja, wir haben Telefon.
Wie ist deine Nummer?	Sie ist . . .

Kannst du deine Mutter/deinen Vater beschreiben.

Meine Mutter/Mein Vater ist klein, hat braune Augen und blondes Haar.

Wann bist du geboren?

Ich bin im Jahre . . . geboren.

Wo bist du geboren?

Ich bin in . . . geboren.

Wie lange wohnst du schon in . . . ?

Ich wohne seit . . . Jahren hier.

Wohnst du in der Stadt oder auf dem Lande?

Ich wohne mitten in der Stadt. Ich wohne in einem Dorf auf dem Lande.

Hast du dein eigenes Zimmer?

Ja, ich habe mein eigenes Zimmer.

Beschreibe dein Schlafzimmer!

Es ist ganz groß. Es hat ein Bett, einen Nachttisch, eine Kommode und einen neuen Teppich.

Hast du einen Garten? Was hast du im Garten?

Ja, wir haben einen Garten. Im Garten haben wir einen Rasen, viele Blumen, und einige Obstbäume.

Gefällt dir dein Haus/deine Wohnung? Warum (nicht)?

Ja, es/sie gefällt mir, weil es/sie klein, bequem und gut eingerichtet ist.

Was machst du mit deinem Taschengeld?

Ich gehe ins Kino oder ich kaufe Bonbons und Schallplatten.

Was tust du, um deinen Eltern im Haushalt zu helfen?

Ich wasche das Geschirr ab und ich mähe den Rasen.

DAILY ROUTINE AND LEISURE TIME

Wann stehst du morgens auf?

Ich stehe um halb acht auf.

Wann gehst du zu Bett?

Ich gehe um halb elf zu Bett.

Was ißt du zum Frühstück/zu Mittag/zu Abend?

Ich esse ein gekochtes Ei, Toast und Marmelade zum Frühstück. Zu Mittag esse ich Fleisch und Gemüse./Zu Abend esse ich Salat und Schinken.

Was ißt du gern?

Ich esse . . . gern.

Was trinkst du gern?

Ich trinke . . . gern.

Hast du Haustiere?

Ja, wir haben einen Hund und eine Katze.

Was für Hobbys hast du?

Ich höre (Schall)platten zu./Ich spiele Fußball gern./Ich sehe fern.

Was für Musik hörst du gern?

Ich höre Popmusik gern./Ich höre klassische Musik gern.

Wieviele Platten hast du?

Ich habe . . . Platten.

Gehst du gern in einen Jugendklub?

Ja, zweimal in der Woche.

Was machst du dort?

Wir spielen Tischtennis, hören Platten zu usw.

Gehst du in eine Diskothek?

Ja, einmal in der Woche im Jugendklub.

Was für Sport treibst du?

Ich treibe Hockey/Fußball/Rugby/Netzball/ Federball/Handball usw.

Siehst du gern fern? Was ist dein Lieblingsprogramm?

Ja, es ist (*EastEnders*).

Was machst du in deiner Freizeit?

Ich besuche meine Freunde/Freundinnen. Ich spiele . . .

Was hast du letzten Samstag gemacht?

Ich bin in die Stadt gefahren, um Einkäufe zu machen.

Was hast du heute morgen getan, bevor du zur Schule gekommen bist?

Der Wecker hat mich um 7 Uhr geweckt; ich bin sofort aufgestanden, und ins Badezimmer gegangen, um mich zu waschen. Dann bin ich die Treppe hinuntergegangen. Ich habe nicht gefrühstückt.

Wann bist du gestern abend zu Bett gegangen?

Ich bin um elf Uhr gestern abend zu Bett gegangen.

Wie sieht dein Hund/deine Katze aus?

Er/sie ist schwarz und weiß.

Was macht er/sie gewöhnlich?	Er/sie schläft den ganzen Tag oft.
Welches Tier möchtest du gern haben und warum?	Ich möchte ein Pferd (*horse*) haben, weil ich es am Wochenende reiten könnte.
Was für Filme siehst du gern? Warum?	Ich sehe Kriminalfilme gern, weil ich Detektiv sein will.
Spielst du ein Instrument?	Ja, ich spiele eine Klarinette.
Wie lange spielst du es schon?	Seit fünf Jahren schon.
Wann/Wie oft übst du?	Ich übe drei Stunden in der Woche.
Spielst du im Orchester?	Ja, ich spiele im Schulorchester.
Wie hast du deinen letzten Geburtstag gefeiert?	Ich bin mit meinen Freunden/Freundinnen in eine Diskothek gegangen.

YOUR TOWN OR VILLAGE, SCHOOL LIFE AND FUTURE PLANS

Wie ist deine Stadt/dein Dorf?	Mein Dorf ist ganz klein. Wir haben ein Lebensmittelgeschäft. Es gibt auch ein Postamt und ein Wirtshaus.
Wie kommst du zur Schule?	Ich komme mit dem Bus/Fahrrad.
Was für eine Schule besuchst du?	Ich besuche eine Gesamtschule.
Wieviele Stunden hast du jeden Tag?	Ich habe acht Stunden jeden Tag.
Wie lange dauert eine Stunde?	Jede Stunde dauert (35) Minuten.
Was lernst du gern in der Schule?	Ich lerne gern Deutsch.
Was machst du in der Morgenpause/ Mittagspause?	In der Morgenpause spreche ich mit meinen Freunden/Freundinnen. In der Mittagspause gehe ich nach Hause/esse ich in der Schule.
Was hast du heute in der Schule gemacht?	Heute habe ich English, Mathematik, Turnen und Französisch gehabt.
Seit wann wohnst du in . . . ?	Seit 15 Jahren.
Seit wann besuchst du diese Schule?	Seit vier Jahren besuche ich sie.
Wieviele Studenten sind in der Schule?	Ein Tausend ungefähr.
Und weißt du wieviele Lehrer und Lehrerinnen?	Ja, sechzig ungefähr.
Wieviele Fächer hast du, was sind die Fächer, welche sind Pflichtfächer?	Ich habe 10 Fächer; sie sind Englisch, Mathematik, Deutsch, Französisch, Geographie, Biologie, Physik, Turnen, Geschichte, Religion. Pflichtfächer sind Englisch, Religion, Mathematik, Turnen.
Was ist dein Lieblingsfach, und warum?	Mein Lieblingsfach ist natürlich Deutsch, weil ich einen sehr guten Lehrer/eine sehr gute Lehrerin dafür habe.
Wieviele Fremdsprachen lernst du?	Ich lerne zwei, Deutsch und Französisch.
Was hast du heute an?	Ich habe die Schuluniform an.
Trägst du gern die Schuluniform?	Nein.
Warum nicht?	Weil ich es lieber habe, Jeans zu tragen.
Was willst du nächstes Jahr machen?	Ich will in der Schule weiter studieren.
Was willst du werden, wenn du die Schule verläßt?	Ich will . . . werden.
Möchtest du eine Arbeitsstelle haben? Warum?/Warum nicht?	Ja, weil ich die Schule verlassen will und Geld verdienen./Nein, weil ich in der Schule bleiben will, um das Abitur zu machen.

HOLIDAYS, WEATHER AND A VISIT ABROAD

Was machst du in den Sommerferien?	Ich fahre an die See/aufs Land/nach Frankreich.
Wie fährst du hin?	Ich fahre mit dem Fahrrad/mit dem Auto/ mit dem Bus/mit dem Zug/mit dem Schiff/mit dem Flugzeug.

Wie ist das Wetter heute?	Es ist schön, die Sonne scheint./Es regnet, es schneit usw.
Was machst du, wenn es heiß ist?	Ich mache nichts, ich liege in der Sonne.
Was hast du in den letzten Sommerferien gemacht?	Ich bin nach Torquay gefahren./Ich bin nach Deutschland gefahren.
Wo verbringst du deine Ferien am liebsten? Warum?	Ich verbringe meine Ferien am liebsten an der See, weil ich in der See schwimmen und fischen kann.
Wie ist das Wetter im Winter/Sommer?	Im Winter ist es oft kalt und nebelig./In Sommer scheint die Sonne und es ist warm und sonnig.
Bist du schon in Deutschland gewesen? Wie oft? Wo?	Ja, ich bin schon zweimal nach Deutschland gefahren – nach Köln.
Wann warst du zuletzt dort?	Während der letzten Sommerferien.

This particular topic, a visit to Germany (**eine Reise nach Deutschland**), could be the basis for an extended conversation, particularly at Higher Level. Other questions that could be used by the teacher/examiner might include:

(a) Wie bist du hingefahren? Bist du allein gefahren? Wie lange hat die ganze Reise gedauert?

(b) Wo hast du gewohnt? (in einem Hotel? bei einer Familie?) Beschreibe die Familie, bei der du gewohnt hast! Beschreibe das tägliche Leben bei dieser Familie!

(c) Wie hast du die Zeit verbracht? Was für Ausflüge hast du gemacht? Wie lange dauerte der Aufenthalt? Was hast du gegessen?

(d) Was kannst du mir über (*town/village*) erzählen? Was sind die Sehenswürdigkeiten dieser Stadt? Was gibt es dort zu sehen und zu machen?

The way to prepare for this kind of extended conversation on such a topic is to think about what you would want to say in answer to the sequence of questions above and prepare vocabulary and structures that you could use in the examination under subheadings. At Higher Level this conversation lasts up to seven minutes, depending on the Examining Groups concerned. Below is an outline of the sort of thing you could prepare. Whatever you do, do not try to learn it as a speech. You will be bound to forget parts of it or break down half way through under the stress of examination nerves. The outline is arranged under the same sequence as the questions above.

(a) Die Reise (The journey)

Letztes Jahr, während der Osterferien, fuhr ich mit einer Gruppe von Schulfreunden nach Münster in Westfalen.
Last year during the Easter holidays I went to Münster in Westphalia with a group of schoolfriends.

Wir fuhren um zwei Uhr nachmittags von London ab. *We left London at two o'clock in the afternoon.*

Wir fuhren mit dem Zug nach Dover. *We went by train to Dover.*

Wir fuhren mit dem Boot/Dampfer nach Ostende. *We went by boat/steamer to Ostend.*

Die Überfahrt dauerte ungefähr fünf Stunden. *The crossing lasted about five hours.*

Glücklicherweise war die See ganz ruhig und niemand war seekrank. *Fortunately the sea was completely calm and no one was seasick.*

Wir gingen durch den Zoll, aber der Zollbeamte wollte unsere Pässe nicht sehen. Ich war enttäuscht.
We went through customs but the customs official did not want to see our passports. I was disappointed.

Wir stiegen in den Kurswagen nach Münster ein. *We got into the through carriage to Münster.*
Wir hatten reservierte Plätze im Liegewagen. *We had reserved couchettes.*

Wir brauchten nicht in Köln umzusteigen. *We did not need to change in Cologne.*

Als wir in Köln ankamen, war es schon dunkel. *When we arrived in Cologne it was already dark.*

Wir konnten den berühmten Kölner Dom sehen, als wir über den Rhein fuhren. *We could see the famous Cologne Cathedral as we went over the Rhine.*

Der Dom war beleuchtet. *The cathedral was lit up.*

Endlich kamen wir in Münster an. *Finally we arrived in Münster.*

Auf dem Bahnsteig standen unsere Austauschpartner und ihre Familien. Sie warteten auf uns. *On the platform stood our exchange partners and their families. They were waiting for us.*

Es war das erste Mal, daß wir uns gesehen hatten. *It was the first time that we had seen each other.*

Wir waren alle müde und ein bißchen nervös. *We were all tired and a little nervous.*

(b) Die deutsche Familie und ihr Haus (The German family and their house)

Die Familie heißt Kittels und sie wohnen in einem schönen modernen Haus in einem Vorort von Münster.
The family is called Kittels and they live in a beautiful modern house in a suburb of Münster.

Herr Kittels ist Oberstudienrat am Gymnasium.
Mr Kittels is a senior teacher in the grammar school.

Er lehrt Englisch und Religion. *He teaches English and RE.*

Seine Frau arbeitet nicht. *His wife does not work.*

Sie hat Blumen sehr gern. *She likes flowers a lot.*

Deshalb verbringt sie viel Zeit im Garten. *So she spends a lot of time in the garden.*

In der Familie sind drei Kinder. *There are three children in the family.*

Mein Austauschpartner, Rudi, ist der älteste. *My exchange partner, Rudi, is the eldest.*

Er ist sechzehn Jahre alt. *He is sixteen years old.*

Seine Schwester, Uschi, ist dreizehn Jahre alt. *His sister, Uschi, is thirteen years old.*

Der jüngste ist Klaus, er ist erst fünf Jahre alt. *The youngest is Klaus, he is only five years old.*

Sie haben einen Hund, Fritzi, der zuviel bellt, und eine kleine schwarze Katze, Mitzi, die laut schnurrt, wenn man sie streichelt.
They have a dog, Fritzi, who barks too much, and a small black cat, Mitzi, who purrs loudly when you stroke her.

Ich schlief mit Rudi in demselben Zimmer, aber in meinem eigenen Bett.
I slept in the same room as Rudi but in my own bed.

Er spielt gerne Gitarre und Fußball.
He likes playing the guitar and football.

(c) Der Aufenthalt (The stay)

Unser Aufenthalt dauerte zwei Wochen. *Our stay lasted two weeks.*

An zwei Tagen mußten wir in die deutsche Schule gehen.
On two days we had to go into the German school.

Das war sehr interessant. *That was very interesting.*

In der Englischstunde mußte ich etwas über England und London auf Englisch sagen.
In the English lesson I had to say something about England and London in English.

Ich war erstaunt. In der Englischstunde sprach niemand Deutsch, nur Englisch wurde gesprochen.
I was surprised. In the English lesson no one spoke German, only English was spoken.

Wir machten einen Ausflug nach Wolfsburg, um die Fabrik zu besuchen, wo Volkswagen hergestellt werden.
We went on an excursion to Wolfsburg, in order to visit the factory where Volkswagen cars are manufactured.

Das war eine interessante, aber etwas lange Reise. *That was an interesting, but rather long journey.*

Wir fuhren auch nach Dortmund im Ruhrgebeit. *We also went to Dortmund in the Ruhr.*

Wir besuchten ein Stahlwerk. *We visited a steel works.*

Das Essen in Deutschland ist meistens sehr gut. *Food in Germany is mostly very good.*

Ich esse Sauerkraut night gern. *I do not like Sauerkraut.*

Westfälischer Schinken ist aber lecker. *Westphalian ham is, however, delicious.*

Die Kittels essen ihre größte Mahlzeit zu Mittag, wenn Vater von der Schule zurückkehrt. *The Kittels eat their biggest meal at midday, when father gets back from school.*

(d) Die Stadt (The town)

Münster ist eine große schöne Stadt. *Münster is a beautiful large town.*

Es hat viele große Kaufhäuser. *It has many large department stores.*

Es gibt auch viele Kirchen und kleine schöne Gärten.
There are also many churches and lovely small gardens.

Das Theater in Münster ist ein sehr modernes Gebäude.
The theatre in Münster is a very modern building.

Auf dem Aasee kann man segeln, oder man kann ein Paddelboot mieten.
On the Aa lake you can sail or hire a paddle boat.

Die Konditoreien in Münster sind sehr gut. Da kann man ein Stück Torte und eine Tasse Kaffee kaufen.
The cake shops in Münster are very good. There you can buy a piece of gâteau and a cup of coffee.

Ich mag Schwarzwaldtorte sehr gern. *I love Black Forest gâteau.*

Es gibt eine Universität, einen zoologischen Garten, mehrere Kinos, ein sehr altes, historisches Rathaus, viele Wohnhäuser, und einen alten Dom.
There is a university, a zoo, several cinemas, a very old historic town hall, lots of blocks of flats and an old cathedral.

Vor dem Dom ist ein Parkplatz. *In front of the cathedral is a car park.*

Am Mittwoch und am Samstag kann man dort nicht parken, weil der Markt auf dem Parkplatz ist.
On Wednesdays and Saturdays you cannot park there because the market is on the car park.

Ich werde nächstes Jahr nach Münster zurückgehen. *I shall go back to Münster next year.*

Mein Aufenthalt in Münster war sehr interessant. *My stay in Münster was very interesting.*

Visual material

Visual material is used in several ways in the speaking tests as detailed by the Examining Groups. There are authentic reproductions of materials such as an advertisement for a trip, a list of activities in a park, details of a department store, school timetables, details about hotels, menus, publicity handouts, television programme details or a picture or set of pictures which tell a story. There may also be diagrams, such as a street plan or a sketch map of a journey, such as the one described earlier.

At Basic Level a set of specific questions will be set on the visual material provided. At Higher Level the same questions as for Basic will be asked first but then the conversation will develop with more information being sought about the details given in the visual stimulus. Where the candidate is required to narrate a story or an incident from the visual stimulus provided, you should expect the teacher/examiner to interrupt your story and ask you to elaborate particular points.

Preparation for this kind of test demands a wide active vocabulary and a knowledge of grammar and structure, so that when you speak German you do so with fluency and confidence.

Here are some examples of the kind of visual stimulus that you might encounter in the GCSE. Remember you will not see this sort of material until the day of the examination. The following is taken from an advertising booklet of the Deutsche Bundesbahn.

4 oder 5 Tage nach

London

Sonderprogramm

Reisetermine
- vom 4.11.85 bis 28.4.86
- Ankunftstag:
  Montag.

Leistungen
Bahnfahrt 2. Klasse mit Schiffsfahrt Ostende–Dover, drei oder vier Übernachtungen mit engl. Frühstück in der Preisgruppe
K Hotel „Kennedy" (Bad oder Dusche, WC, Telefon), Cardington Street NW1 2LP.
Taxitransfer vom Bahnhof zum Hotel bei Ankunft.

Abwicklung
Sie erhalten Ihr Hotelzimmer gegen Abgabe des Arrangementgutscheines im Hotel. Dort werden Ihnen die Transferkosten erstattet.

Hinweis
Bitte beachten Sie, daß an Weihnachten und zum Jahreswechsel Schiffs- und Zugverbindungen nach London stark eingeschränkt sind.

Siehe auch London Seite 53.

Preisbeispiele (für kürzesten oder verkehrsüblichen Reiseweg) in DM

Preisgruppe	Komfort		Fahrt 1. Kl.
Anzahl der Übernachtungen	3	4	
Code	503	504	
ab			
Basel Bad Bf	474	537	+ 96
Berlin ü Helmstedt	498	562	+ 110
Bremen	440	503	+ 80
Dortmund	398	461	+ 58
Frankfurt (M)	422	485	+ 70
Hamburg	462	525	+ 90
Hannover	436	499	+ 78
Kassel	432	495	+ 76
Köln	376	439	+ 48
Mannheim	424	487	+ 72
München	494	557	+ 106
Nürnberg	462	525	+ 90
Saarbrücken	428	491	+ 74
Stuttgart	452	515	+ 86
Einzelzimmerzuschlag	+ 94	+ 127	

Anmeldeschluß
Donnerstag, 12 Uhr, 12 Tage vor der Ankunft.
Für Gruppen ab 6 Personen spätestens drei Wochen vor der Ankunft.

The questions which might be asked about this are as follows:

Basic Level

1 In welchem Hotel bleibt man in London?
2 Wieviel kostet eine Reise ab Hamburg für drei Übernachtungen?
3 Wie kommt man vom Bahnhof zum Hotel bei Ankunft?
4 Wievel mehr kostet es erste Klasse ab Stuttgart?
5 Was für ein Frühstück bekommt man in der Preisgruppe K?

Higher Level

Questions 1-5 plus other questions as follows:
6 Wie lange dauert die Reise nach London?
7 Beschreibe die Fahrt von Deutschland nach England!
8 Was für Zimmer werden im Hotel Kennedy gebucht?
9 Auf welcher anderen Seite der Broschüre kann man Auskunft über Reisen nach London finden.
10 Was ist der Zuschlag für ein Einzelzimmer, wenn man vier Nächte in London bleibt?
11 An welchem Tag kommt man in London an?
12 Kann man diese Reise im Sommer machen? Warum nicht?
13 Was erhält man gegen Abgabe des Arrangementgutscheines?
14 Wann is der Anmeldeschluß für eine Gruppe mit vier Personen?
15 Was ist die teuerste Reise und wieviel kostet sie erste Klasse für vier Nächte?

Suggested answers

1 Im Hotel Kennedy.
2 Vierhundertzweiundsechzig Mark.
3 Mit einem Taxi.
4 Sechsundachtzig Mark.
5 Ein englisches Frühstück.

6 Vier oder fünf Tage.
7 Bahnfahrt zweite Klasse von Deutschland, dann mit dem Schiff von Ostende nach Dover, dann mit dem Zug nach London.
8 Zimmer mit Bad oder Dusche, Toilette und Telefon.
9 Auf Seite 53 (dreiundfünfzig).
10 Der Zuschlag ist hundertsiebenundzwanzig Mark für vier Nächte.
11 Am Montag.
12 Nein, weil die Reisetermine von November bis April sind.
13 Man erhält sein Hotelzimmer.
14 Der Anmeldeschluß ist Donnerstag um Mittag, zwölf Tage vor der Ankunft.
15 Die teuerste Reise ist ab Berlin. Sie kostet sechshundertzweiundsiebzig Mark erste Klasse.

Another example of questions on a visual stimulus follows:

1 Wo liegt das Hotel zur Post in Bremen?
2 Was ist die Adresse?
3 Wo kann man Spezialitäten essen?
4 Wo findet man Schwimmbad, Sauna und Solarium?
5 Wie heißen die Inhaber?

6 Seit wann ist diese Familie Inhaber dieses Hotels?
7 Was ist besonders über das Tingheter Restaurant?
8 Warum ist das Hotel zur Post ideal für Konferenzen und Tagungen?
9 Wo kann man nach Mitternacht noch trinken?
10 In welchem Teil des Hotels wechseln täglich die Menues?
11 Wo wird es empfohlen, sich nach Feierabend zu treffen?
12 Wo darf man aktiv entspannen?
13 Was kann man im Fitness-Club machen?
14 Warum, meinst du, heißt ein Restaurant eigentlich „Kachelstübchen"?
15 Was macht man meistens in der Theke?
16 Wie würdest du die Theke beschreiben?
17 Wie kommt man zum Hotel?

Suggested answers

1 Das Hotel liegt am Hauptbahnhof.
2 Die Adresse ist Bahnhofsplatz 11, Bremen.
3 Im Kachelstübchen.
4 Im Fitness-Club.
5 Sie heißen Fritz Rößler und Sohn.

6 Sie ist Inhaberin seit achtzehnhundertneunundachtzig.
7 Es hat eine internationale Küche, wechselnde Menus und eine große Weinkarte.
8 Es ist das größte Haus in Bremen, es liegt am Hauptbahnhof und ist leicht zu erreichen.
9 An der Theke.
10 Im Restaurant Tingheter.
11 Im Kachelstübchen.
12 Im Fitness-Club.
13 Man kann schwimmen oder eine Massage haben, in der Sauna sitzen oder under dem Solarium liegen.
14 Es heißt Kachelstübchen, weil es dort einen antiken Kachelofen gibt.
15 Man trinkt Bier oder internationale Drinks.
16 Die Theke ist eine Bar, wo man bis spät in der Nacht trinken kann. Die Atmosphäre ist rustikal. Man trinkt Bier vom Faß nicht aus einer Flasche.
17 Man kommt mit jedem Vehrkehrsmittel an. Das heißt mit dem Bus, mit dem Taxi, mit dem Zug und so weiter, denn es liegt zentral am Hauptbahnhof.

One of the Examining Groups has a series of pictures as the stimulus to a conversation. Two examples are given here.

(a) You should imagine that you are the young man being sent shopping by your mother. Sometime later you will recount the story of what happened to a friend, who is the examiner.

You should expect to be interrupted, and questions may be asked at any stage. You are not allowed to make notes beforehand.

(b) The boy and girl in this family receive skis for Christmas. The whole family goes off skiing and the boy breaks his arm. Imagine you are the boy or girl and tell this story about your family's skiing holiday to a friend, who is the examiner, when you get back home. You can expect to be asked questions about any part of your story.

You can do a lot of preparation on your own for these two accounts. The sort of questions you could be asked by the examiner will depend of course on what you say, but they might be something like this:

(a) Was mußtest du kaufen?
Was wollten deine Freunde spielen?
Wie lange hast du Fußball gespielt?
Was hat deine Mutter gesagt?
Warum war deine Mutter so zornig?

(a)

(b)

(b) Wie war die Reise mit dem Auto?
Konntest du schon Ski laufen?
Wie war das Wetter?
Was ist auf der Piste geschehen?
Wie war der Patient im Krankenhaus?

SCOTLAND

In Scotland the speaking test forms the final proficiency test. It is taken in March of the final year of the course for the Standard Grade Examination. It is taken in addition to the ongoing internal assessment of speaking which will be carried out through a series of speaking activities in the final year. The final proficiency test will last for up to 15 minutes. Five tasks will be set by the board for each candidate. These tasks will be stated in English. Candidates will know what the tasks are to be on the day before the examination and they will receive guidelines and ideas on how the tasks set might be developed. It will not be possible to learn what to say off by heart. You will be assessed by your own teacher who will play the role of the foreigner. **Note.** The speaking test is double weighted as compared to listening and reading comprehension.

Here is an example of the kind of tasks which might be set in the final proficiency test: speaking. The situation you have to imagine is:

You are on holiday in Germany and you go on an excursion by train to Cologne. On the journey you start talking to a young German in your compartment. (The teacher/examiner will play the part of the young German.)

Task 1

Introduce yourself and say where you are going.

You will have to introduce yourself. You might talk about the journey, where you are going and why. Ask where the young German is going.

Task 2

The young German suggests that you might like to accompany him/her to Cologne. He/she will show you round. You accept the invitation.

You might want therefore to talk about what you will do together in Cologne: visit the cathedral, go shopping for souvenirs or presents, go to a café or restaurant.

Task 3

Talk about yourself and your holiday so far.

You might want to say, for example, where you are staying and who with, how long you've been there, why you chose that place and what it is like, where you came from and what it is like, how it compares with Germany, what you do at home, etc.

Task 4

You and your new friend are now in Cologne. You go to a café; discuss what you are going to have to eat and drink.

You might want to: offer to pay, ask what your friend would like, discuss the different kinds of coffee and gâteaux, discuss the prices, decide what to have, order what you want, decide where you are going next, say what sort of presents you would like to buy and for whom.

Task 5

Talk about the rest of your holiday.

You may want to say, for example: what you would still like to see and do, where you would like to go, when you intend to return home, how you will be travelling, whether you like being abroad and how you like best to travel, whether you would like to return, etc. You may want to discover the same sort of information about your new friend.

At all times throughout the 15 minutes that this test lasts you must be prepared to respond to questions as well as offering information. You can, of course, make up things about yourself. You will be provided with any necessary flashcards such as the menu in the café.

The day before the examination you are allowed to see the paper with the guidance for preparation details on it as set out above, but you are not allowed to have this paper in the test, just the list of tasks.

It is impossible to give a suggested script for this type of very open-ended extended role play, but the following should give any candidate help in their preparation on the night before the examination itself.

Task 1

Hallo! Entschuldigung! Ich heiße...Ich bin...Ich fahre nach Köln. Dürfen wir uns duzen? Gut, also, wohin fährst du? Wie lange dauert diese Fahrt? Ich mache einen Ausflug nach Köln, um eine Stadtbesichtigung zu machen und einige Souvenirs zu kaufen. Ich bin Schotte/Schottin. Im Augenblick verbringe ich zwei Wochen bei meinen Brieffreund (meiner Brieffreundin) in der Nähe von Bonn.

Task 2

Das wäre schön, wir können vielleicht den Dom besuchen und auch ein paar Einkäufe machen. Gibt es gute Warenhäuser in der Nähe von dem Dom? Ich möchte auch eine Dampferfahrt auf dem Rhein machen, wenn es möglich ist? Ich habe nichts mit zu essen oder zu trinken, so können wir in eine Konditorei gehen?

Task 3

Ich wohne im Moment in Beuel, einer kleinen Stadt nicht weit von Bonn entfernt. Ich wohne bei meinem Brieffreund Hans Kettel. Leider ist er krank heute und deshalb konnte er nicht mitkommen. Ich bin seit einer Woche da. Hans hat mich eingeladen, zwei Wochen bei ihm zu verbringen. Er wohnt in einem kleinen Einfamilienhaus. Deutschland scheint mir viel sauberer als Schottland. Man sieht wenige Abfälle. Die Gebäude sind meistens moderner als zu Hause. Zu Hause wohne ich in (Aberdeen). Zu Hause mag ich gern Schallplatten spielen, Sport treiben...

Task 4

Warme Getränke

Sonntags nur Kännchen

Kaffee mit reiner Sahne   Endpreis

Tasse Kaffee	2,20
Kännchen Kaffee	4,40
Tasse Kaffee Hag	2,30
Kännchen Kaffee Hag	4,50
Kännchen Mocca	5,80
Kännchen Mocca spezial	6,80
Irish-Coffee (mit Whisky)	7,50
Café noisette (mit Kirschwasser)	6,50
Rüdesheimer Kaffee (4 cl Asbach)	8,80
Capuccino	3,30

Tee

Portion feinster Blattmischungen, mit Kandis,
Zitrone oder Sahne:

„Assam" ostfriesische Art	4,80
„Darjeeling" blumiges Hochgewächs	4,80
„Sweet Orange"	4,80
„Earl Grey" für Kenner	4,80
Glas Tee, Darjeeling oder Ceylon	2,30
Glas Pfefferminz- oder Kamillentee	2,10

(div. Teesorten am Büffet zum Mitnehmen)

Schokolade *mit Schlagsahne*

Tasse Schokolade	2,40
Kännchen Schokolade	4,70
Russische Schokolade (mit Weinbrand) ...	5,50
Tasse Diabetikerschokolade	2,60

Heißgetränke

Glas Glühwein mit Zitrone	5,—
Glas Rum - Grog	5,—
Glas heiße Zitrone	3,60
„Eisbrecher" (Rum und Rotwein)	6,80

Preise incl. MWSt. und Bedienung

Torten - Kuchen - Konfitüren

Am Kuchenbüffet
finden Sie stets eine reichhaltige Auswahl frischer Torten, Kuchen und haltbarer Spezialitäten

Aus unserem Angebot:

Torten
Schwarzwälder Kirsch, Kapuziner, Jamaica-Rum, Käsesahne, Nußsahne, Dobus, Himbeer-Johannisbeer, Herrentorte, Schoksahne, Eistorten, div. Obsttorten (saisonbedingt)

Desserts
Nußkrem, Dobus, Erdbeersahne, Schwarzwälder Kirschrollen, Holl. Kirsch, Baumkuchendessert, Reistörtchen, Masarinen, Eierschecke, Mohnstreusel, Butterkuchen, Florentiner, dänischer Plunder, Obstschnitten (saisonbedingt) etc.

(In the examination you would see the menu in the form of a flashcard.)

Ich werde zahlen. Was möchtest du, es gibt eine große Auswahl hier nicht wahr? Wir könnten ein Kännchen Kaffee mit Sahne haben. Wie wäre das? Ich möchte auch ein Stück Schwarzwaldtorte und du? Herrentorte? Also, Herr Ober, ein Kännchen Kaffee mit Sahne und ein Stück Schwarzwaldtorte und ein Stück Herrentorte für meinen Freund/meine Freundin. Das wird 14,40 DM zusammen kosten. Diese Torte schmeckt aber lecker. Was machen wir heute nachmittag? Ich möchte einige Geschenke kaufen, für mein Mutter eine kleine Flasche Parfüm, für meinen Vater ein illustriertes Buch über Köln, für meine Schwester/meinen Bruder eine Schallplatte. Hoffentlich habe ich genug Geld, sonst muß ich in die Bank gehen, um einen Scheck einzulösen.

Task 5

Nächste Woche möchte ich gern nach Bonn gehen. Vielleicht können wir auch eine Rheindampferfahrt machen. Mein Brieffreund Hans hat übermorgen Geburtstag. Wir werden zu einer Diskothek gehen. Das wird schön sein. Am nächsten Wochenende werde ich nach Schottland zurückfahren. Ich werde mit dem Flugzeug fliegen. Ich fahre am liebsten mit dem Zug und mit dem Schiff, aber nach Aberdeen ist das eine sehr lange Reise, zu lang. Ich möchte nächstes Jahr zurückkommen. Ich habe Deutschland so gern, das Wetter ist schöner als in Schottland. Bist du je in Schottland gewesen? Möchtest du nach Aberdeen kommen? Was denkst du von Schottland?

7 WRITING GERMAN

Writing German forms part of the syllabus for all the GCSE Examining Groups in England, Wales and Northern Ireland, although it is not an essential part of the test for the lower grades of all the Examining Groups. Find out what the position is with your own Group. In Scotland it is an optional supplement designed for the Credit Level of the Standard Grade examination. (See pages viii–xi for details of each Group's requirements.)

Basic Level

At Basic or General (i.e. the more elementary) Level the types of writing in German which may be expected are listed below. You will of course check carefully which of these exercises are required by your own Examining Group. Many of the writing tests at Basic Level are closely directed.

(a) A short message conveying information, with specific mention of a number of listed items, perhaps in the form of a note or message left for a friend or relative. The number of words varies usually between 20 and 30.

(b) A letter, formal or informal, again with the requirement to convey specific items of information. The number of words varies between 60 and 80, depending on the particular Examining Group.

(c) Completing a simple form.

(d) Writing a postcard (informal), usually with the items of the message specified. Approximately 30 words.

(e) Filling in the gaps in a letter or similar.

(f) Lists.

(g) Giving directions, e.g. based on a street plan.

Any letters, postcards or such messages may be replies to letters or postcards addressed to you in German.

To score any marks at all at the Basic Level you will have to communicate the required message or messages clearly, so that the person for whom the message or instruction is intended will understand exactly what you mean. At the very lowest level you may be able to do this, even if your German contains some errors of grammar or spelling. However, accuracy in the language used is not something separate from the message. Your message will be clearer if you choose the appropriate words and use them correctly. The highest marks at Basic Level will go to those who can do this, even though there will be some reward for just getting the message across.

As with other parts of the examination you will be helped in your preparation for the writing of German by the information provided by your Examining Group. You will probably know in advance which topics will be examined and what sort of vocabulary you will be expected to use. This will mean that you can practise the kind of task likely to appear in the examination. (Details of the topic areas are given in the vocabulary section of this book on pp. 55–108.)

Here is an example. One of the Examining Groups tells you that you may have to send a simple message of about 30 words by postcard. One of the listed topics of this Group is **Holidays**. At the Basic Level you are told that you should be able to do the following things:

(a) Describe your holidays and holiday periods and how you spend them, e.g. where you go, with whom, for how long, what you normally do.

(b) Obtain similar information from others.

(c) Describe a recently spent holiday with details of where you went, for how long and what you saw or did.

(d) Say whether you have been abroad, to Germany or a German-speaking country, giving details, if applicable.

(e) Talk about holiday plans.

(f) Understand information in brochures and letters of reply.

Naturally this list of things you should be able to do covers speaking, reading and listening as well as writing, but you can easily pick out the items which might be part of a writing test.

A possible 'postcard' question might read like this:

You are on the first day of a holiday in Britain. On the blank postcard below write about 30 words to your German penfriend, telling him or her where you are, when you arrived, what kind of accommodation you have and some of the things you are going to do. You need not use complete sentences. Also write a German-style address in the space provided.

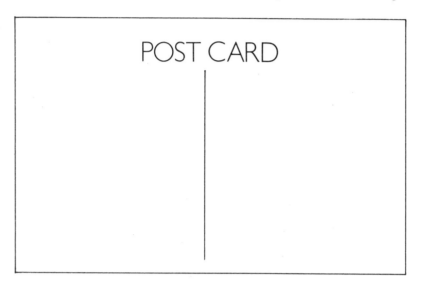

Both for postcards and letters you will have to learn the ways in which the Germans themselves write. You will find this mentioned in greater detail later in the unit. If you were writing the postcard described in the above question you would gain most marks by beginning in the German style, perhaps with the words:

Lieber Helmut/Liebe Erika, or **Lieber Helmut!/Liebe Erika!**

Viele Grüße aus Cornwall!

By starting like this you have both shown your knowledge of a real German convention and dealt with the first item of information.

The question directs you quite closely to the next point by telling you that you are on the first day of the holiday. You can interpret this in two ways – either that you arrived 'yesterday' or that you arrived 'earlier today'. You are not compelled to write a full sentence, so a very few words with just the verb would suffice, e.g.

Kam/Kamen gestern abend an or even a phrase without a verb: **Seit gestern abend hier.**

You now have some 23 words for the rest of the message. This is where you will have more choice over what you will write. Take advantage of this freedom to *use what you know.* Do not invent ideas in English and translate them into German. Ask yourself what German you have learnt to fit this situation and stick to it. For instance, you might write: **Habe ein Einzelzimmer mit Dusche. Bleibe heute im Hotel am Freibad. Abends gibt es Disko. Morgen mit der Familie nach Penzance. Samstag wieder nach Hause.**

There are several ways of ending a letter or message informally. Here, perhaps, you could write simply **Herzlichst** or **Nochmals herzliche Grüße** (as you began with **viele Grüße**). After that you simply sign the card with a Christian name.

You can invent similar exercises for practice from the information given by your Examination Group. Instructions appear on pages 162–7.

The skill of writing other simple notes or messages is very much like that of writing postcards. Concentrate on transmitting the essentials in good German without creating difficulties for yourself by attempting to use words or constructions which are new to you. Even simple messages should be carefully checked after they have been written. The method of checking is less complicated here than for full sentences, but checking is just as important at Basic Level. You should ask yourself the following questions:

1 Have I chosen the right vocabulary from the stock of German words known to me?

2 Where there are genders or cases, have I got them right?

3 Where there are adjectives, have I given them the right ending?

4 Where there are verbs, are they in the right form for this tense and person?

5 Above all: Have I conveyed the necessary message clearly to the person who will read it – probably someone whose native language is German?

List-making at Basic Level is simply a matter of learning whatever vocabulary may be specified at that level by the Examining Group and using the appropriate words. It is not difficult to work out which lists might be based on the topics in the syllabus. The question might be something like this:

You are sharing the shopping with a German friend who will go to the fruiterer and the grocer. Make a list of twelve things you might ask him/her to buy.

The following possible items appear in the vocabulary list at Basic Level for at least two of the major Examining Groups:

Lebensmittel	Obst unde Gemüse	Amounts/Numbers
Zucker	Apfel/Apfel-	Kilo/Kg
Butter	Apfelsine	Pfund
Margarine	Orange/Orangen-	halb/Halb-
Marmelade	Traube	All the cardinal numbers
Kaffee	Pfirsich	Tüte
Tee	Pflaume	Päckchen
Kakoa	Banane	Tafel
Keks	Tomate	Flasche
Wein	Kopfsalat	Liter
Weißwein	Zitrone	Glas
Rotwein	Kartoffel	Schachtel
Limonade	Erdbeere	
Mineralwasser	Himbeere	
Saft		
Käse		
Schokolade		
Praline		
Chips		
Cola		

The most basic list might read:

Zucker	Weißwein	Kartoffeln
Butter	Limonade	Kopfsalat
Käse	Äpfel	Tomaten
Marmelade	Bananen	Orangen

It would be more ambitious to include some amounts or numbers:

ein Kilo Zucker	Kopfsalat für fünf Personen
ein Glas Marmelade	ein Pfund Tomaten
ein Pfund Käse	fünf Tüten Chips
ein Liter Weißwein	eine Schachtel Pralinen
zwei Flaschen Limonade	eine Tafel Schokolade
zwölf Bananen	

If you know how to form compound nouns you can go a step further with words like *Erdbeermarmelade, Orangenmarmelade, Apfelsaft, Traubensaft*. Once again use what you know to be correct.

Writing letters

Some form of letter writing may be required at Higher Level by all the Examining Groups and at Basic Level by five of them. For one of the latter this may be a very short 20-word letter. Instructions are given in either German or English, or you will have to reply to a letter printed on the question paper. Letters may be formal or informal.

BEGINNING AND ENDING LETTERS

You must know how to begin and end both formal and informal letters.

The informal letter will usually be written to a friend, a penfriend or a relative. In such cases you would start your letter as follows: **Liebe Brigitte!** or **Lieber Hans!**

If you are writing to two people you can use both Christian names: **Liebe Antje! Lieber Max!** or you can write **Ihr lieben Zwei!**

If you are writing to more than one, for example to a whole family, you can begin your letter with **Ihr Lieben!**

Many people now use a comma instead of the exclamation mark. If you decide on the comma you must begin the first sentence with a small letter, *not* a capital unless the first word would normally have a capital letter, e.g.

Lieber Max!	Lieber Max,	Lieber Max,
Herzliche Grüße . . .	herzliche Grüße . . .	Grüße . . .

There are many ways of ending the informal letter:

Mit (vielen) herzlichen Grüßen (auch an Deine Eltern) . . .
Herzlichst . . .
Mit den besten Grüßen . . .
Dir und Deinen Eltern/Deiner Familie viele liebe Grüße . . .
Sei (*to one person*) Seid (*to more than one person*) herzlich gegrüßt . . .
Herzliche Grüße von uns allen . . .
Tschüß . . . (*a very informal ending, usually between young people*)
Alles Gute . . . (*all the best*)
So, Schluß für heute! . . . (*means something like 'Well that's enough for today!'*)

Different ways of asking your correspondent(s) to write again soon:

Schreib (bitte) bald (*for one person*)
Schreibt (bitte) bald (*for more than one person*)
Laß bald mal von Dir hören (*for one person*) Laßt bald mal von Euch hören (*for more than one person*)

Some of the above expressions can be combined, e.g. **Schreib bald! Herzlichst.**

When you sign an informal letter you must remember to give the possessive adjective (the word for 'your') the right ending, e.g. **Dein Jürgen; Euer Heinz; Deine Maria; Eure Barbara.**

When signing for two people: **Deine Franz und Peter; Eure Gudrun und Georg.**

If you are writing an informal letter to one person, you must address that person throughout as *Du* spelt with a capital letter. Remember that this applies to all the forms of **Du – Dein** (your), **Dich**, **Dir**. In an informal letter to more than one person the same applies to **Ihr – Euer** (your), **Euch** (dative and accusative).

The forms of address and endings for formal letters (business letters, letters to hotels, etc.) are of course different. In addressing the correspondent you should use the correct form of **sehr geehrt**, e.g. **Sehr geehrte Herren** (Dear Sirs); **Sehr geehrter Herr Braun; Sehr geehrte Frau Schmidt; Sehr geehrtes Fräulein Müller; Sehr geehrter Herr Direktor.**

The most formal endings to business letters are: **Hochachtungsvoll** or **Mit vorzüglicher Hochachtung** followed by the signature.

Slightly less formal endings, perhaps to a business colleague who is not a friend or to someone you don't know well, are: **Mit freundlichen Grüßen** or **Mit freundlichem Gruß.**

In formal letters you will address you correspondent(s) as **Sie** with the appropriate related forms: **Ihr** (your), **Sie, Ihnen.**

ADDRESSING ENVELOPES AND POSTCARDS

When the question paper carries the diagram of a postcard you may be asked to write the address in the German style of the person to whom you are writing. It is useful to know how to do this for your own purposes as well as for the examination.

First remember that **Herr** with a proper name must be in the dative form **Herrn**, e.g. **Herrn Franz Fischer**. The street name comes on the second line as in English, but the house number follows the name of the street, e.g. **Goethestraße 2.**

The post code (**Postleitzahl**) in the Bundesrepublik comes *before* the name of the town or village. If you are writing to West Germany from another part of Europe you should place D before the post code of the town. There is a European postal agreement to use the same international signs as for motor vehicles. It is a good idea to learn a few post codes for German towns and villages, e.g.

D6000 Frankfurt
D8000 München
D7834 Herbolzheim

The large towns also have numbered postal districts which follow the name of the town, e.g.

D6000 Frankfurt 4
D8000 München 13
D5000 Köln 51

Here is an example written out in full:

Herrn Franz Schmidt
Am Pumpenkamp 12
D8000 München 10

LETTERS AT BASIC LEVEL

If you are asked to write a letter at Basic Level you will be given detailed guidance over the content. Once again the letter will deal with a topic or topics from those listed by the Examining Group and you will be able to use vocabulary from the Examining Group's list.

Aim at conveying clearly the points which are required. Once again *do not* think out your letter in English and then try to translate it. Use the German you know. *Do not* try anything you have not learnt. Check what you have written, using the check for German from page 161. Read the instructions and follow them carefully. Count the number of words and state this accurately if you are asked to do so.

The following question is from a 1991 GCSE examination paper.

You receive this letter from your Austrian friend.

> Graz, den 14. April
>
> Hallo!
>
> Ich möchte Euch allen für den wunderschönen Urlaub danken. Nun mußt Du mir sagen, wann Du uns besuchen kannst. Dieses Jahr noch vielleicht? Wie war die Rückfahrt vom Hafen? Du wolltest doch den Krimi im Fernsehen anschauen. Habt Ihr den Film gesehen oder seid Ihr zu spät nach Hause gekommen? Ich kann meine Brieftasche nicht mehr finden. Vielleicht hab' ich sie bei Euch oder bei Deiner Tante liegenlassen. Hat sie Dir die Brieftasche gegeben?
>
> Du gehst erst nächste Woche wieder in die Schule. Was machst Du bis dann? Wie wirst Du Dein Geburtstagsgeld ausgeben? Hoffentlich war es ein guter Tag! Laß bald von Dir hören!
>
> Alles Gute!
>
> S.

Write a letter in German in reply. You must write 60–70 words and refer to four points only made in the letter. The last point must come from the second paragraph and should be answered at greater length.

N.B. Be sure to begin and end your letter properly and to sign it.

LEAG, summer 1991

LETTERS AT HIGHER LEVEL

The letters you may have to write at Higher Level are more demanding.

They will also be related to the topics specified by the Examining Groups. All the Examining Groups may require Higher Level candidates to write a letter – in some cases either formal or informal. The length of most of these letters is approximately 100 words, although one

Examining Group asks for a 200-word letter of thanks. Sometimes the letter will be a response to a letter received; sometimes there will be a stimulus in English with mention of the items to be included.

As at Basic Level, you must always read the instructions carefully. One of the essential elements in assessing your work will be the extent to which you have clearly transmitted whatever message is specified. The accuracy of your German will also be most important at Higher Level. Make sure you know what grammar is specified by your Examining Group and check your written German carefully point by point, following the instructions on pages 170–1.

The third element in assessing your letter writing at Higher Level will be the appropriateness, range and variety of your language. At Higher Level you must be more ambitious than at Basic Level. Make your German more interesting by varying your sentence construction and vocabulary, and introducing suitable idiom. Remember that the freedom which gives you the chance to show what you know also holds certain dangers. You must not stray from the point. You will lose marks if you introduce irrelevant material. *Do not* use any German unless you are sure of it. The advice given for Basic Level still holds good. *Do not* work out your letter in English and then translate it into German. Ask yourself what German you know which is appropriate to the situation.

The forms of address, the beginning and the ending of letters have already appeared on pages 162–3.

An informal letter at Higher Level

The following question is similar to some of those which may be asked at Higher Level.

You are going away for a few weeks when you receive a letter from a friend who would like to visit you next week. Reply to your friend explaining the situation.

Here is a possible answer:

Lieber Rudi/ Liebe Uschi,

vielen Dank für Deinen letzten Brief, den ich heute erhalten habe.

Es tut mir leid, daß Du nächste Woche nicht kommen kannst. Leider muß ich meinen Onkel und meine Tante in Schottland besuchen.

Am Wochenende soll ich mit dem Auto nach Aberdeen fahren. Ich werde vom nächsten Sonntag ab zwei Wochen bei meinen Verwandten verbringen. Als mein Onkel letztes Jahr bei uns war, hat er mich dazu eingeladen. Also muß ich dahin, sonst werden sie unzufrieden sein. Es ist wirklich schade, daß ich Dich diesmal nicht sehen kann. Hoffentlich wirst Du uns im nächsten Urlaub besuchen können.

Herzliche Grüße

Dein Robert/Deine Mary

You will see that the above letter is in the proper form. It has variety of tense, using modal verbs correctly. There are different kinds of sentence construction. There are some common idioms. It contains nothing that a Higher Level candidate might not reasonably be expected to know. In fact virtually everything is listed in the syllabus of one of the major Examining Groups. The only exceptions are *Schottland* and *unzufrieden*, but *zufrieden* is listed, and it is not too much to expect a Higher Level candidate to know the names of the countries which form the British Isles. There is, of course, no reason why you should limit yourself to the material listed by the Examining Group as long as you are sure of what you are writing.

A formal letter at Higher Level

Here is a possible question:

You have to spend three days in Cologne next month, working in the office of the local newspaper (Express). In about 100 words write to the manager of the Kolpinghaus Hotel, saying that the hotel has been recommended by a colleague who lives near Cologne. Ask to reserve a single room with bath or shower. Tell him when you will arrive by train and when you will depart from the main railway station. Ask how much the room will cost and whether an evening meal is available in the hotel.

Your letter might read like this:

Sehr geehrter Herr Direktor,

nächsten Monat soll ich drei Tage in Köln verbringen, um bei der Express-Zeitung zu arbeiten. Ein Kollege, der in der Nähe von Köln wohnt, hat mir das Hotel Kolpinghaus empfohlen.

Darf ich bitte ein Einzelzimmer mit Dusche oder Bad für vier Nächte ab Montag dem 8. September reservieren? Ich werde am 8. September so um 18 Uhr mit dem Zug in Köln ankommen, fahre dann am 12. um sieben Uhr dreißig vom Hauptbahnhof wieder ab.

Ich möchte jeden Abend im Hotelrestaurant essen – ist das möglich? Könnten Sie bitte diese Reservierung bestätigen und die Kosten angeben?

Hochachtungsvoll

Peter Müller

This letter contains two words, **bestätigen** and **angeben**, which are not to be found in the vocabulary lists of most Examining Groups. They are, however, the correct words for this situation, and you would be well advised to learn the expressions used in this kind of letter. After all, the vocabulary lists of the Examining Groups are there for your guidance and you will not lose marks by using more ambitious words correctly.

Today many Germans would use the somewhat less formal **Mit freundlichen Grüßen** in a letter of this kind.

Other useful expressions which may not always be listed by Examining Groups are:

ich wäre sehr dankbar, wenn Sie . . . könnten;
ich würde gern(e) wissen, ob . . .;
ich möchte gern(e) wissen, ob . . .;
uses of **mitteilen** – to inform;
mit umgehender Post – by return of post
in Beantwortung auf Ihren Brief/Ihr Frage – in reply to your letter/your question.

Accounts based on a series of pictures

All the Examining Groups include at Higher Level the possibility of accounts or narratives based on a sequence of pictures. You will probably be asked to tell the story as if you were one of the main characters taking part.

The advantage of choosing this form of writing in German is that the story line is set out for you, but the disadvantage is that you are tied to the vocabulary dictated by the pictures. With this option you must take special care to write in the past tense. This will normally be the imperfect for a story of this kind. Remember above all not to change the narrative tense in mid-story. You can, of course, use a different tense in direct conversation.

Before starting to write, look very carefully at the pictures, notice all the details, make sure you are clear about the story line and which details to include. Make notes of any phrases, points of vocabulary, etc which spring to mind before you start. If you know any expressions or idioms which fit the story, then make full use of them, but do not drag in irrelevant material which you have learnt in advance. This is always too obvious. Once again *do not* compose your story in English and then translate it into German.

As with the letter at Higher Level you will be assessed on three main points:

(i) The clarity with which you have conveyed the story.

(ii) The accuracy of your German.

(iii) The appropriateness, range and variety of your language.

Check your final version with the method on pages 170–1.

Here is a possible question:

Your teacher asks you to write an account in about 200 words of a recent day's outing. Base your account on the pictures provided, as if you were one of the four young people involved.

Here is a possible version of the story in pictures on page 168:

Ich heiße Hans Meyer. An einem schönen Sommermorgen schlug ich eine Fußwanderung auf das Land vor. Meine Schwester Inge und die Nachbarskinder, Anna and Peter, sollten mitkommen, und sie freuten sich sehr darauf. Nachdem wir die Rucksäcke mit Proviant für den ganzen Tag vollgepackt hatten, sagten wir den Eltern, Auf Wiedersehen und machten uns auf den Weg.

Drei Stunden lang schritten wir lustig durch herrliche Wälder und an grünen Feldern und alten Bauernhöfen vorbei. Gegen halb eins machten wir unter den Bäumen halt, um das Mittagessen zu bereiten. Wir aßen frisches Brot mit warmen Würstchen, die Anna über dem Feuer gebraten hatte, und tranken Limonade dazu. Im Freien schmeckte alles besser als zu Hause.

Als wir noch einmal unterwegs waren, bemerkten wir am Himmel dunkle Wolken, die jede Minute größer wurden. Bald fing es an zu regnen. Leider hörte der starke Regen nicht auf, und wir wurden endlich durchnäßt. Die Wanderung machte uns keinen Spaß mehr.

Sobald wir im nächsten Dorf ankamen, rief Inge meinen Vater an. Etwas ärgerlich holte er uns mit dem Auto von der Telefonzelle ab. Wir bedankten uns und fuhren so schnell wie möglich nach Hause zurück.

The above story is simple, relevant to the pictures, accurate and reasonably varied in its German. Note the ways in which this variety is achieved. A number of sentences begin with adverbs or adverbial phrases like **bald, leider, an einem schönen Sommermorgen, drei Stunden lang**. Each one of these is followed by inversion of the subject and verb. There is a range of subordinate clauses beginning with simple conjunctions: **nachdem, als, sobald**. The occasional relative clause appears. There is one phrase with **um . . . zu** + infinitive. Simple, relevant idioms and other common German expressions are well represented: **auf das Land** – into the country; **sich darauf freuen** – to look forward to it; **sich auf den Weg machen** – to set out; **im Freien** – in the open air; **unterwegs sein** – to be on one's way; **machte uns keinen Spaß mehr** – was no longer any fun for us; **sich bedanken** – to say thank you.

If you apply the check for written German (pages 170–1) you will see that the language is correct. The approach used for this picture story could be applied to all written accounts or reports required in the Higher Level examination.

Other possible questions at Higher Level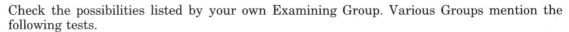

Check the possibilities listed by your own Examining Group. Various Groups mention the following tests.

(a) A straightforward account or report written in response to a simple title or instruction, e.g.

(i) Mein letzter Kinobesuch

(ii) You have recently spent a holiday in Germany. The local paper there has asked you to write a report of your most interesting day in about 150 words.

(b) A report or account based on notes previously made, perhaps with an accompanying diagram.

(c) Individual pictures on which you have to answer questions in German.

For accounts, stories or reports based on a straightforward title or instruction the advice for picture stories can be adapted with very little change, i.e. Consider the steps in the story or report in relation to the number of words allowed. List the words and phrases you have learnt which fit this particular situation. Remember that the question will be based on one of the topic areas specified. Above all *do not* attempt to translate into German a narrative or other version which you have first worked out in English.

Use one past tense consistently for the actual events. This will usually be the imperfect. Count the number of words carefully. Apply the check for accuracy of German given on page 170.

One Examining Group asks you to answer questions in German about five to seven unconnected individual pictures. To score marks here you will obviously need to know various types of German question and the kind of information with which they should be answered. Full sentences are not required. Here is a typical example.

1 Wo sitzen diese Leute?

2 Wat tut die junge Dame?

3 Warum sieht sich der alte Herr die Speisekarte an?

Possible answers:

1 In einem/In dem/Im Restaurant.

2 Sie trinkt (Wasser)/(Wein)/(Mineralwasser).

3 Weil er das Essen (die Gerichte) wählen will.

Here is some information about types of question and the answers they require:

Wer? indicates a person or persons in the nominative.

Wen? indicates a person or persons in the accusative.

Wem? indicates a person or persons in the dative.

Wen after a preposition, e.g. **für wen?** – the person or persons following the preposition take(s) the accusative.

Wem after a preposition, e.g. **mit wem?** – the person or persons following the preposition take(s) the dative.

Was? may require an answer to be either in the nominative or the accusative according to the question, e.g.

Was steht im Hintergrund? – Ein Baum (steht im Hintergrund).

Was sieht man im Hintergrund? – Man sieht einen Baum im Hintergrund.

Was tut/macht . . . ? requires you to describe an action.

Wo? requires a place in the answer.

Warum? requires a reason, which may be given in a **weil** clause or, where appropriate, with **um . . . zu** + infinitive.

Wie ist/sind . . . ? requires a description.

There are, of course, other question forms, but these are the most likely ones for this particular written test.

General advice for writing German

1 Find out the exact requirements of your own Examining Group, including the number of words expected and the amount of time allowed. Take account of both of these when planning your answers. Try to look at as many specimen questions or former question papers as possible.

2 Use the German you have learnt. *Do not* think out your version in English and then try to translate it into German. Draw on your own stock of words, phrases and constructions. The basis of this stock can come from the guidelines of your own Examining Group, but you must extend it as widely as possible from your own reading, listening, speaking and regular learning. *'If you haven't used it before, don't use it now!'* is good general advice.

3 When you use your linguistic stock, you must do this with relevance to the situation. Reproducing material learned by heart without reference to the situation in the examination will lose marks.

4 Read the instructions on the question paper carefully, particularly when the question asks you to list specific items of information or details.

5 Be consistent in the narrative tense you use and over the word for 'you'. Many marks have been lost in the past by candidates who have switched from imperfect to perfect for the events in the main storyline or by those who have changed from **du/Du** to **Sie** or vice versa. This applies also to many who have carelessly forgotten to keep up the capital letter of **Sie** in all its forms. You may, of course, change the tense when you introduce direct speech.

6 If you have time, make a rough draft first. In any case, apply the following check either to the rough draft or to your final version.

(a) Is the required message/storyline/detail conveyed clearly?

(b) Verbs: Check the tense, the person, and that you have used the correct form.

(c) Nouns and pronouns: Check
  (i) the case (subject, direct object, indirect object and case after prepositions);
  (ii) noun plurals;
  (iii) the correct words for 'you/your' if you have used them.

(d) Adjective endings: Check that you have used the right set of endings and that you have chosen the right endings for the case in question.

(e) Word order: Check
  (i) infinitives – are they in the right place?
  (ii) past participles – are they in the right place?
  (iii) Is it necessary to invert the order of subject and verb?
  (iv) Is the main verb in the right place in all the subordinate clauses?

(v) Are direct and indirect noun or pronoun objects in the right order?

(vi) Are adverbs and adverbial phrases in the right order (time, manner, place)?

The above check is intended for writing German at the Higher Level. A check for Basic Level appears on page 161.

Practice letters

1 Write a letter of about 100 words to your German penfriend. Tell him/her how you had a skiing accident during the holidays, which resulted in a short stay in hospital. Say how this will affect your future plans to visit this penfriend.

2 Sie sind neulich nach einem Aufenthalt bei Ihrem deutschen Brieffreund/Ihrer deutschen Brieffreundin nach Hause zurückgekommen. Schreiben Sie einen Dankbrief an seine/ihre Eltern: beschreiben Sie Ihre Heimreise – die Überfahrt, die Zollkontrolle, die Leute, mit denen Sie gesprochen haben.
(*about 100 words*)

3 Sie bekommen den folgenden Brief von einem deutschen Freund. Schreiben Sie eine passende Antwort darauf.

Lieber Chris!

Wie geht es Dir? Hoffentlich gut. Wie war es zu Ostern in Wales? Ich habe das Abitur gut bestanden, und jetzt möchte ich ab September ein Jahr in Großbritannien arbeiten, bevor ich auf die Universität gehe. Hast Du eine Idee, was für eine Arbeitsstelle ich bekommen könnte? Kann ich leicht eine Wohnung finden?

Ich würde mich freuen, wenn Du inzwischen zu uns nach Deutschland kommen könntest. Was meinst Du?

Meine Schwester Eva möchte gern eine englische Brieffreundin. Vielleicht kennst Du ein passendes Mädchen?

Viele Grüße!

Dein

Martin

(*100 words*)

Practice picture stories

1 You are writing a letter to your German penfriend. You include in your letter a description of an incident you were involved in last week, when you were locked out of your house. You were one of the two young people shown in the pictures below.

Write about 100 words in German. Do not write out the whole letter, but only write about the incident.

SEG German, Summer 1988

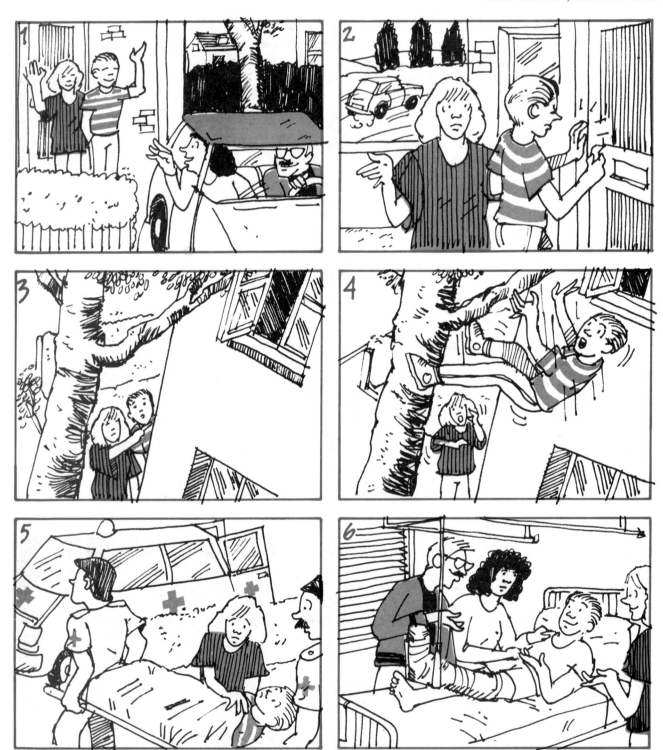

2 Your penfriend asks you to describe the best event of your holidays. Write your account in German based on the pictures printed below.

3 Tell the story which appears in the series of pictures on page 156 as if you were the boy doing the shopping.
(*about 140 words*)

SIMPLE TITLES FOR PRACTICE

1 Ein Picknick auf dem Lande.

2 Der Tag, wo ich mich verlaufen habe.

3 Ein Tanzabend oder ein Konzertabend mit meinem Freund/meiner Freundin.

8 SUGGESTED ANSWERS TO EXAMINATION PRACTICE QUESTIONS

Listening Comprehension – Basic Level

MULTIPLE-CHOICE ITEMS

1 B In the bag.
2 C Tomorrow at 7.30 a.m.
3 D 15 minutes.
4 A An umbrella.
5 C 1,20 DM.
6 C Two coffee spoons.
7 B 8.15.
8 B Go by bus.
9 C Two men have stolen fifty cameras.
10 C Take the fourth street on the right.

SHORT ITEMS

1 Do you want to pay?
2 Is this your case?
3 From platform 13.
4 She has left her bikini at home.
5 Can you describe your camera?
6 Could you help me with the washing up?
7 He/she has toothache.
8 One moment please! Hold the line.
9 Will you spell that please?
10 3,50 DM.

LONGER ITEMS

1 (a) It is not very big. It has a lovely view over the lake.
   (b) The lake, beautiful trees, sailing boats.
   (c) On the right near Paul's room.
   (d) A shower and toilet.
   (e) 8.30 a.m.
   (f) In the kitchen.

2 Name: Schmidt.
   Wieviele Personen: Four.
   Wohnwagen/Zelt: Tent.
   Datum: 11 August.
   Wieviele Nächte: One night.
   Preis: 15,50 DM.
   Geld/Scheck: Cheque.

3 (a) A single to Hamburg. (c) Platform 15.
   (b) 1.30 p.m. (d) 20,50 DM.

4 *Section 1*
(a) 7.30 a.m.
(b) As many suitable things as possible at reduced prices.

Section 2
(c) By train and by tram.
(d) Because a lot of people were already waiting for the doors to open.
(e) At 8 o'clock.
(f) The ladies' department.

Section 3
(g) A short red dress and a long blue dress.
(h) A green dress.
(i) In the sports department.
(j) In France.

Section 4
(k) Vests and socks.
(l) She rang him at the office.
(m) Shoes and suits.
(n) Go to the sales.
(o) You would go to the sales straight after lunch.

Listening Comprehension – Higher Level

1 Weather forecast

(a) 8 April
(b) In the North.
(c) 2 degrees.
(d) In the South.
(e) 5 degrees.
(f) In the central region.
(g) From the north-west.
(h) No change.

2 The road accident

Section A
(a) A boy has just been knocked over by a car.
(b) No.
(c) He rode out of a side street into the main road.
(d) The boy, because he did not look.
(e) He braked and skidded.
(f) He could not stop, nor avoid the boy.

Section B
(g) He has gone to ring for the police and an ambulance.
(h) The car ran over both his legs.
(i) Hold the crowd back.
(j) You can hear their sirens.
(k) About five minutes.

Section C
(l) He is trying to get the people to step back and let the ambulance through.
(m) Five or six years old.
(n) Both legs are broken.
(o) He is lucky to be alive.
(p) Boys of this age should not be riding bikes alone in these traffic conditions.
(q) The boy could have been knocked down by a bus or a lorry.

3 A guided tour

Section A
(a) One and a half hours.
(b) The main station and the Schnoorviertel.
(c) Narrow streets and old houses.

Section B
(d) In the buildings around the market place.
(e) The statue Roland.
(f) Since the year 1404.

Section C
(g) The townhall, the Ratskeller, the Cathedral.
(h) The old restored buildings.
(i) Flowers.
(j) It is a Hansestadt and the smallest state in the Federal Republic.
(k) It is a pedestrian zone. The tram goes through it.

Section D
(l) 1405 to 1409.
(m) No. It dates from the Renaissance, 200 years later.
(n) Guided tours on weekdays are at 10, 11, 12 o'clock from March to the end of October.
(o) It is one of the oldest wine cellars and was built in 1408.

Section E

(p) In the seventeenth and eighteenth centuries.

(q) This is an area where people work.

(r) Two of: architects, writers, potters, glass-blowers.

(s) It is old and quaint. There is plenty to see, especially craftsmen at work, and you can buy beautiful and inexpensive souvenirs.

(t) All the best!

SHORTER ITEMS

1 (a) In 30 minutes.

(b) Platform 8.

2 You should take the tablets *three times a day, with water.*
You should stay in bed *two or three days.*
You should eat *not much/only a little.*
You should drink *lots of warm drinks.*
You have probably got *a touch of the flu.*

3 The receptionist said they had only two single rooms available and neither had a bath or a shower.

4 Inge will arrive in *two weeks' time.*
She will arrive by *train* at *2.00 p.m.*
She will be wearing *a blue hat* and *anorak* and *yellow trousers.*
She will be carrying *a brown case* and *a green bag.*
Under her arm she will also be carrying *a magazine.*

5 (a) (i) Sailing on the sea in a sailing boat belonging to Hans' parents.

(ii) We should ring up Hans.

(b) Hans and his parents are going to Holland for three weeks, leaving tomorrow.

6 (i) Train crash or collision.

(ii) One train ran into another stationary train.

(iii) 22 dead (including 5 children).

(iv) He ran to pull people out of the train/helped/witnessed or saw the accident.

(v) Horror/thought it was terrible/he was shocked/he felt like crying/he helped/thought it was a bomb.

(vi) There was chaos/the situation was bad/many were in hospital or being operated on.

(vii) Blood/blood donor.

Basic-level reading

(a) Multiple Choice (elements in English)

1 A
2 C
3 C
4 B

(b) Multiple choice (elements in German)

1 D
2 B
3 A

(c) Tick the box (elements in English)

1 Your teacher
2 On a train
3 Variable cloud, but dry

(d) Tick the box (elements in German)

1 Eßsaal
2 Herrenmode
3 Zahnarzt

(e) Ticking yes/no

1 Yes for the following: curried sausage, chips, breadrolls, potato salad. **No** for the others.

2 Can you buy training shoes there?   YES
Can you buy gifts and presents there?   YES
Can you buy furniture there?   NO
Do students get 21% discount?   NO

3 All the answers are **Yes** except the last, which is **No**. (It is not mentioned how many the Berghof can accommodate.)

(f) Open-ended questions

1 (i) Chemist's (1)

    (ii) Train departures (½ + ½)
    (iii) Detour (1)
    (iv) No parking (1)

2 A red (½) briefcase (½), needed for an examination (½).

3 Any four from: Sunny mountains
                Relaxation
                Good company
                Families welcome
                Nature Park
                Tennis
                Riding
                Mini-golf (pitch and putt)
                Fishing
                Chairlift

4 It is prohibited to hitch-hike on motorways etc., where it is too dangerous for cars to stop. (1)
It is safer to hitch-hike at filling stations (½) and in carparks (½).
If possible, don't hitch-hike at weekends. (1)

5 **(i)** On the first floor. (1)
    (ii) There are in total two washrooms (1), each of which has two showers (½) and toilets (1).
(i.e. one washroom for area A and an identical one for B)
    (iii) Any four from:
Large dining/day room (for 80 people)
Common room for 30 people
Common room for 15 people
Cloakroom
Shoe room
Day-toilets/washroom
Canteen
Washing-up area
Catering kitchen
    (iv) Table tennis
Pool
T.V.
Reading

6 **(i)** Man in car (½) is talking to attendant (½).
    (ii) He is saying the attendant is new (1) at this job (1).

7 **(i)** Any three from:
Squash
Cross-country running
Swimming
Listening to music
    (ii) Her English is weak. (1)
    (iii) 15 (½) or over (½).

8 **(i)** Her elder brother. (1)
    (ii) He takes her (½) glass when she wants a drink (½).
    (iii) She doesn't know how. (1)

9 **(i)** A letter. (1)
    (ii) Their dog, Aika, had pups. (1)
    (iii) She's not looking forward to it. (1)

Answers to higher-level reading

(a) Multiple choice (elements in English)

1 **(i)** C
    (ii) A
    (iii) D

2 **(i)** A
    (ii) B

3 C

(b) Ticking yes/no

1 Is the indoor pool open all year round?   YES
Is the outdoor pool open all year round?   NO
Is the indoor pool open to all swimmers for the whole of Monday?   NO
Is the outdoor pool open daily from 8.00 to 20.00 or dusk, whichever is the
earlier?   YES

2 Is the welcome party in the afternoon?   NO
Do we go to the flax market on Sunday?   NO
Is there an organized programme for Sunday and Monday?   NO
Is Monday a Bank Holiday?   YES

(c) Open-ended questions

1 **(i)** Doing a sightseeing tour of Palermo (1) with other holidaymakers (1).
   (ii) They were all full.
   (iii) She had to fly back home (1) immediately (1).
   (iv) She herself paid. (1)

2 **(i)** In a chemistry lesson. (1)
   (ii) He retaliated, striking his assailant (1) (friend) with an umbrella (1).
   (iii) Writing out 100 times (1) 'I must not hit Herbert on the head with my umbrella'. (1)
   (iv) 2 hours detention. (1)
   (v) He thinks the teacher will give him a grade 6. (1)

3 *Section 1*
   (i) 2 days.
   (ii) Buy provisions (1) for (the next stage of) his journey to China (1).
   (iii) Some came from Australia. (1) Others are going to Thailand. (1)
   (iv) One week (eight days). (1)
   (v) The hurricane season is beginning. (1)

   Section 2
   (i) Stop sailing. (1) Spend a day repairing it. (1)
   (ii) It is the first single-handed yacht (1) to be allowed into China (1).
   (iii) The hurricane is 600 miles to the north of him.
   (iv) He has a fever (1) and needs to recover (1).
   (v) He's sailing against the wind. (1)

4 **(i)** She realizes she won't be able to play tennis all her life. (1)
   (ii) A career in television. (1)
   (iii) She likes writing (1), although she finds it difficult (1).
   (iv) She doesn't regret leaving school (1) at 16 (1).
   (v) She singles out learning the guitar. (1) She hasn't time to practise and practise. (1)

5 **(i)** Sweden (1) and France (1)
   (ii) 7/8/9 June 1985 (1)
   (iii) Any *two* from: At the youth centre (1)
                           Camping in the park (1)
                           In a hotel (1)
   (iv) 15 marks
   (v) Mr W Schrick

6 **(i)** The west (1)
   (ii) The Peters-Portal (1)
   (iii) 157.38 metres (1)
   (iv) 97.25 metres, 509 steps (1)
   (v) North (1)

7 **(i)** A cycling holiday. (1)
   (ii) On a beautiful campsite (1) right by the beach (1).
   (iii) The water is very dirty. (1)
   (iv) In a field (1) or in a little village. (1)
   (v) They looked everywhere for them. (1)
   (vi) A woman had taken them (1) and *either* put them in a shed (1) or put them away for safety (1).
   (vii) Fresh (½) milk (½) and warm (½) rolls (½).

8 **(i)** Any two from: Monkeys/snakes/crocodiles. (1 mark each)
   (ii) They behaved quite badly. (They annoyed the crocodiles.) (1)
   (iii) They looked at the other animals. (1)
   (iv) They went for an ice-cream. (1)
   (v) He sends his greetings to her (1) and tells Klaus to give her a big kiss from him (1).

GERMAN– ENGLISH VOCABULARY

A

abbrechen, to break off
der **Abend** (-e), evening
das **Abendessen** (-), evening meal, dinner, supper
abfahren, to depart, leave
die **Abfahrt** (-en), departure, start
abgeben, to hand in
abgerissen (*adj.*), torn off
abholen, to fetch, collect, meet
abliefern, to hand over, deliver
abmachen, to arrange
abrollen, to roll off
absetzen, to stop, pause
abspringen, to jump
der **Absprung** (ˉe), jump
das **Abspülen** (-), washing up
abspülen, to wash up
der **Abstieg** (-e) descent
die **Abteilung** (-en), department
abwaschen, to wash up
die **Abwesenheit** (-en), absence
ach, oh, ah, alas
Achtung!, attention! look out!
der **Agent** (-en), (secret) agent
die **Agentur** (-en), agency
alle, everyone
allein(e) (*adj.*), alone
alles, everything
allgemein (*adj.*), general
als, when; than
alt (*adj.*), old
der **Amerikaner** (-), American
amerikanisch (adj.), American
ander (*adj.*), other
anderthalb (*adj.*), one and a half
die **Änderung** (-en), change
anfahren, to run/drive into
der **Anfang** (ˉe), beginning
anfangen, to begin
anfangs (*adv.*), in the beginning
der/die **Angestellte** (-n), employee
der **Angriff** (-e), attack, assault
die **Angst** (ˉe), fear, anxiety
   Angst haben, to be afraid
   vor Angst, for fear
anhaben, to wear, have on
anhalten, to stop
ankommen, to arrive
anmachen, to switch on
der **Anorak** (-s), anorak
anrufen, to phone, call
anscheinend, apparent(ly)
ansehen, to look at
die **Anspannung** (-en), strain, exertion
die **Anstrengung** (-en), exertion, effort
die **Antwort** (-en), answer, reply
antworten, to answer, reply
anziehen, to put on
der **Apfel** (ˉ), apple
der **Apparat** (-e), apparatus, equipment
die **Arbeit** (-en), work
   sich an die Arbeit machen, to set to work
arbeiten, to work
der **Architekt** (-en), architect
ärgerlich (*adv.*), angrily
sich **ärgern**, feel angry, annoyed
arm (*adj.*), poor
die **Armbanduhr** (-en), wristwatch
der **Ast** (ˉe), branch, bough
atemlos (*adj.*), breathless
auch (*adv.*), also
auf und ab gehen, to walk up and down

der **Aufenthalt** (-e), stay, stop
aufgeben, to give up, abandon
aufgeregt, excited
aufheben, to raise, lift up
aufhören, to cease, stop
aufpassen, to pay attention
aufregend (*adj.*), exciting
aufsetzen, to put (clothes) on, dress
aufstehen, to get up
der **Aufstieg** (-e), ascent
aufstoßen, to push open
das **Auge** (-n), eye
der **Augenblick** (-e), moment, instant
aus (*prep.+dat.*), out of
die **Ausfahrt** (-en), exit (*e.g. motorway*)
der **Ausflug** (ˉe). excursion, outing
der **Ausgang** (ˉe), exit, way out
ausrauben, to rob
ausrufen, to call out
der **Ausschank** (ˉe), bar, tavern
aussehen, to look, appear
außen (*adv.*), (on the) outside
   nach außen, outward(s)
die **Aussicht** (-en), view
aussteigen, to get out
aussuchen, to search for
ausziehen, to take off (clothes)
australisch (*adj.*), Australian
das **Auto** (-s), car
der **Autobus** (-se), bus
der **Autofahrer** (-), car driver
automatisch (*adj.*), automatic

B

die **Bäckerei** (-en), baker's shop, bakery
das **Bad** (ˉer), bath
der **Badeanzug** (ˉe), bathing-costume
das **Badezimmer** (-), bathroom
der **Bahnhof** (ˉe), (railway) station
die **Bahnhofsuhr** (-en), station clock
der **Bahnsteig** (-e), platform
bald (*adv.*), soon
der **Balkon** (-s), balcony
die **Banane** (-n), banana
die **Bank** (-en), bank
bauen, to build
der **Bauernhof** (ˉe), farm
der **Baum** (ˉe), tree
der **Beamte** (-n), official
bedenken, to think about
bedenklich (*adj.*), doubtful
beenden, to end
befehlen, to command
(sich) **befreien**, to free (onself)
begegnen (*+dat.*), to meet
beginnen, to begin, start
begleiten, to accompany
begrüßen, to greet, welcome
bei (*prep.+dat.*), with
beide (*adj.*), both
das **Bein** (-e), leg
beißen, to bite
bekommen, to get, receive
belebt (*adj.*), busy, crowded (street)
Belgien, Belgium
bemerken, to notice
beobachten, to observe, watch
bequem (*adj.*), comfortable
die **Beratung** (-en), consultation, conference
bereit (*adj.*), ready, prepared
bereiten, to prepare

bereuen, to regret
bergab (*adv.*), downhill
berichten, to inform s.o. of sth., to report
der **Beruf** (-e), profession, trade, occupation
    von Beruf, by profession, etc.
beruhigen, to calm, soothe
berühmt (*adj.*), famous
Bescheid sagen, to inform s.o.
beschließen, to resolve; decide
beschreiben, to describe
besonders (*adv.*), especially
besorgt (um), worried (about)
bestimmt, certain(ly)
der **Besuch** (-e), visit
besuchen, to visit
betrachten, to watch, contemplate
betreten, to enter (room etc.)
das **Bett** (-en), bed
beunruhigen, to disturb, trouble, worry
bevor, before
die **Bewegung** (-en), movement, motion
    (sich) in Bewegung setzen, to set going,
      set in motion, start
bewundern, to admire
bezahlen, to pay (for)
das **Bier** (-e), beer
der **Bikini** (-s), bikini
das **Bild** (-er), picture
billig (*adj.*), cheap, inexpensive
der **Biologielehrer** (-), biology master
bis, until
ein **bißchen** (*adv.*), a bit, a little
bitte, please
bitten, to ask
blau (*adj.*), blue
bleiben, to stay
der **Blick** (-e), glance, look
blicken, to glance, look
blond (*adj.*), blond, fair
bloß (*adv.*), only, merely; just
das **Blumenbeet** (-e), flowerbed
der **Blumenmarkt** (⁻e), flower market
die **Bluse** (-n), blouse
das **Blut** (*no pl*), blood
der **Boden** (⁻), ground
die **Bodenübung** (-en), floor exercise
böse (*adj.*), angry; bad, wicked
    böse auf (+*acc.*), angry with
brauchen, to need
braun (*adj.*), brown
braungebrannt (*adj.*), suntanned
brechen, to break
bremsen, to brake
der **Brief** (-e), letter
die **Brille** (-n), (pair of) glasses, spectacles
bringen, to bring, take
das **Brot** (-e), bread
das **Brötchen** (-), bread roll
der **Bruder** (⁻), brother
brummen, to speak in a deep voice,
    growl, mumble
das **Buch** (⁻er), book
die **Buchhandlung** (-en), bookshop
buchstabieren, to spell
sich **bücken**, to bend (down), stoop
bummeln, to stroll
die **Bundesbahn**, Federal Railway(s)
die **Bundesrepublik** (-en), Federal Republic
    (*of Germany*)
der **Bürgersteig** (-e), pavement
das **Büro** (-s), office

C

der **Champignon** (-s), mushroom
der **Chauffeur** (-e), chauffeur, driver
der **Chef** (-s), manager, boss

D

da (*adv.*), there
dafür (*adv.*), for it, for that
dagegen (*adv.*), against it, that
    ich habe nichts dagegen, I have no objection (to it)

dahin (*adv.*), there, to that place
damals (*adv.*), then, at that time
die **Dame** (-n), lady
damit (*adv.*), with it, that; so that, in order to
danach (*adv.*), afterwards
vielen **Dank!**, many thanks!
darin (*adv.*), in it, that
daß, that
dauern, to last
davon (*adv.*), of it, of that
dazu (*adv.*), to it, to that
denken (an), to think (of, about)
denn, for
derselbe, dieselbe, dasselbe, the same
desselben, of the same
dessen, whose
der **Detektiv** (-e), detective
deuten auf (+*acc.*), to point at
deutsch (*adj.*), German
der/die **Deutsche** (-n), German
der **Dieb** (-e), thief
dieser (*used as a noun*), this one; he
diesmal (*adv.*), this time; for (this) once
der **Doktor** (-en), doctor
der **Dom** (-e), cathedral
Donnerwetter! good gracious! my word! hang it all!
das **Doppelzimmer** (-), double room
das **Dorf** (⁻er), village
dort (*adv.*), there
sich **drängen**, to force oneself
draußen (*adv.*), outside
der **Dreck** (*no pl*), dirt, filth (*fig.*); trash
drehen, to turn
dreijährig (*adj.*), three year(s) old
dreiwöchig (*adj.*), three week(s) long
dringend (*adj.*), urgent, pressing
der **Drogist** (-en), chemist
drüben (*adv.*), over there
dumm (*adj.*), stupid
dunkel (*adj.*), dark
dünn (*adj.*), thin
durch (*prep.*+*acc.*), through
durchgehend (*adv.*), continuously
durchnässen, to drench
durchnehmen, to go through, over
die **Dusche** (-n), shower

E

eben (*adv.*), just
die **Ecke** (-n), corner
das **Ei** (-er), egg
eigentlich (*adv.*), really
eilen, to hurry
der **Eimer** (-), bucket
die **Einbahnstraße** (-n), one-way street
einbiegen, to turn into
der **Einbrecher** (-), burglar
der **Einbruch** (⁻e), burglary, housebreaking
einfach (*adj.*), simple, single (*ticket*)
der **Eingang** (⁻e), entrance
einige (*adj.*), some; several
der **Einkauf** (⁻), purchase
einkaufen, to buy, go shopping
das **Einkaufen** (-), shopping
die **Einkaufstasche** (-n), shopping bag
einladen, to invite
einpacken, to pack up, wrap up
einreißen, to tear
einsteigen, to get in
einverstanden (*adj.*), agreed
der **Einwohner** (-), inhabitant
das **Einzelzimmer** (-), single room
die **Eltern** (*pl.*), parents
die **Empfangsdame** (-n), receptionist
empfehlen, to recommend
das **Ende** (-n), end
    am Ende, at/in the end
endlich (*adv.*), finally
eng (*adj.*), narrow
entdecken, to discover
entlang (*prep.*+*acc.*), along
entstehen, to arise

entweder ... oder, either ... or
die **Episode** (-n), episode
die **Erde** (-n), earth; ground
das **Erdgeschoß** (-sse), ground floor
erfahren (von+*dat*.), to learn (of, about)
der **Erfrischungskiosk** (-e), refreshment kiosk
erhalten, to receive
sich **erheben**, to rise, get up
sich **erholen**, to recover
erkennen, to recognize
erklären, to explain
erlauben, to allow, permit
erleichtert, relieved
erreichen, to reach
errichten, to erect
erscheinen, to appear
erschießen, to shoot (dead)
erschreckend (*adj*.), alarming, startling
erschrocken (*adj*.), frightened, terrified
erst (*adj*.), first
erst (*adv*.), firstly; not until
erstaunt, astonished
erstens (*adv*.), first, firstly
der/die **Erwachsene** (-n), grown up, adult
erweisen, to prove
erwidern, to reply, retort, answer
erwischen, to catch, trap
erzählen, to tell, recount
das **Essen** (-), meal, food
essen, to eat
der **Eßsaal** (-säle), dining hall
das **Eßzimmer** (-), dining room
die **Etappe** (-n), stage
etwa, about; roughly; approx.
etwas (*adv*.), somewhat; something
etwas Unhöfliches, something impolite
die **Europazentrale** (-n), European central office
die **Ewigkeit** (-en), eternity

F

das **Fach** (-̈er), school subject
fahren, to drive, travel
das **Fahrrad** (-̈er), bicycle
die **Fahrt** (-en), journey
fallen, to fall
falls (*adv*.), in case
der **Fallschirm** (-e), parachute
die **Fallschirmsportlergruppe** (-n), group of parachutists
das **Fallschirmspringen** (-), parachuting
die **Familie** (-n), family
der **Familienurlaub** (-e), family holiday
das **Farbphoto** (-s), colour photograph
der **Farmer** (-), farmer
die **Fassade** (-n), facade
fast (*adv*.), almost, nearly
fehlen, to be missing, absent
der **Feierabend** (-e), finishing/closing time
das **Fenster** (-), window
die **Ferien** (*pl*.), holidays
der **Fernsehapparat** (-e), television set
fernsehen, to watch television
der **Fernseher** (-), television set
fertig (*adj*.), ready
mit etwas fertig sein, to have finished something
fertigmachen, to get ready
fest (*adj*.), firm, solid
festhalten, to hold tight
das **Fieber** (-), fever
Fieber haben, to have a temperature
finden, to find
der **Fingerabdruck** (-̈e), fingerprint
das **Fleisch** (*no pl*.), flesh; meat
der **Fleischer** (-), butcher
die **Fleischerei** (-n), butcher's shop
fliegen, to fly
der **Flugplatz** (-̈e), airfield, aerodrome
das **Flugzeug** (-e), aeroplane, aircraft
folgen (+*dat*), to follow
folgend, following
fortfahren, to go away

das **Fotogeschäft** (-e), photographic shop
die **Frage** (-n), question
eine Frage stellen, to ask a question
fragen, to ask
Frankreich, France
der **Franzose** (-n), Frenchman
das **Französisch**, French (*the language*)
auf französisch, in French
die **Frau** (-en), wife; woman, lady
der **Freifall** (-̈e), freefall
freiwillig (*adj*.), voluntary
fressen, to eat (*used of animals*)
der **Freund** (-e), friend
die **Freundin** (-nen), friend
freundlich (*adj*.), friendly, cheerful
frisch (*adj*.), fresh
froh (*adj*.), glad
früh (*adj*.), early
das **Frühstück** (-e), breakfast
frühstücken, to (have) breakfast
frühzeitig (*adj*.), early
fühlen, to feel; be aware of
die **Führung** (-en), guided tour
das **Fundbüro** (-s), lost property office
ein **Fünfziger** (-), ⎫
der **Fünfzigmarkschein** (-e), ⎬ 50 DM note
für (+*acc*), for ⎭
fürchten, to fear, dread
der **Fuß** (-̈e), foot
der **Fußball** (-̈e), football
die **Fußgängerzone** (-n), pedestrian precinct

G

die **Gabel** (-n), fork
ganz (*adv*.), quite, entirely
der **Garten** (-̈), garden
die **Gasse** (-n), street
die **Gaststätte** (-n), restaurant, café
die **Gaststube** (-n), guest room, hotel lounge
geben, to give
es gibt, there is, there are
der **Gebrauchtwagenverkäufer** (-), second hand car salesman
der **Gedanke** (-n), thought
die **Gefahr** (-en), danger
gefährlich (*adj*.), dangerous
gegen (*prep*.+*acc*.), towards; against
der **Gegenbesuch** (-e), return visit
der **Geheimagent** (-en), secret agent
gehören (zu), to belong (to)
gelb (*adj*.), yellow
das **Geld** (-er), money
der **Geldschein** (-e), bank-note
genau (*adj*.), exact
genau (*adv*.), exactly
die **Gepäckaufbewahrung** (-en), left luggage office
gerade (*adv*.), just
das **Gerät** (-e), implement, instrument
gern (e) (*adv*.), willingly, gladly
das **Geschäft** (-e), shop
geschehen, to happen
es geschieht ihm recht, it serves him right
das **Geschenk** (-e), present, gift
die **Geschichte** (-n), story
geschickt (*adj*.), skilful, clever
das **Gesicht** (-er), face
gestohlen (*adv*.), stolen
gesund (*adj*.), healthy
das **Getränk** (-e), drink
das **Gewicht** (-e), weight
gewinnen, to win
das **Gewissen** (-), conscience
ein schlechtes Gewissen, guilty conscience
gewöhnlich, usually
die **Gitarre** (-n), guitar
das **Glas** (-̈er), glass, jar
der **Glasbläser** (-), glass-blower
glauben, to believe
gleich, immediately, at once, presently
gleich darauf, immediately afterwards
gleichgültig (*adv*.) indifferently
das **Gleis** (-e), railway line
die **Gleisnummer** (-n), track number

glitschig (*adj.*), slippery
das **Glück** (-sfälle), luck, fortune
glücklich (*adj.*), happy
glücklicherweise (*adv.*), luckily, fortunately
der **Grad** (-e), degree
die **Grenze** (-n), frontier
die **Grippe** (-n), influenza
groß (*adj.*), big, large
die **Großmutter** (-), grandmother
grün (*adj.*), green
die **Gruppe** (-n), group
der **Gruß** (-e), greeting
grüßen, to greet
günstig (*adv.*), favourable
gut (*adj.*), good, (*adv.*) well
gutmütig, good-natured

H
der **Hals** (-e), neck
halten für, to regard as; take to be
die **Haltestelle** (-n), stop
der **Hamster** (-), hamster
die **Hand** (-e), hand
der **Handschuh** (-e), glove
hängen, to hang
hängenbleiben (**an**+*dat*), to get caught
(up) (on/in)
der **Hauptbahnhof** (-e), central/main station
die **Hauptstraße** (-n), main street
die **Hausaufgabe** (-n), homework
das **Häuschen** (-), small house
zu **Hause**, at home
die **Haustür** (-en), house door; front door
heben, to lift, raise
die **Heimfahrt** (-en), journey home
heißen, to be called
heiter (*adj.*), clear, bright (*weather*)
helfen (+*dat*), to help
das **Hemd** (-en), shirt
herabsetzen, to reduce
herausziehen, to pull out
die **Herrenmode** (-n), men's fashion
herrlich (*adj.*), splendid, magnificent
herrschen, to control
herunter, down; downstairs
der **Herzenswunsch** (-e), heart's desire
heute, today
heute nacht, tonight
hier (*adv.*), here
hierher (*adv.*), here, hither
die **Hilfe** (-n), help, assistance
der **Himmel** (-), sky
Himmel!, (good) heavens
hinauslehnen, to lean out
hinter (*prep.*+*dat*/*acc.*), behind
hinüber (*adv.*), over (there), across
hin und zurück, return (ticket)
hinuntersteigen, to climb down
das **Hobby** (-s), hobby
hoch (*adj.*), high
die **Hochdruckzone** (-n), high pressure zone
hocken, to crouch, squat
hoffen, to hope
die **Höhe** (-n), height; altitude
auf halber Höhe, half way up
der **Höhenmesser** (-), altimeter
höher, higher
holen, to fetch
hören, to hear
die **Hose** (-n), trousers
hübsch (*adj.*), pretty
der **Hund** (-e), dog

I
die **Idee** (-n), idea
identifizieren, to identify
ihr, ihre, her
der **Imbiß** (-sse), snack
immer (*adv.*), always
immer noch, still
die **Innenstadt** (-e), town centre

das **Innere** (*no pl.*) inside, interior
das **Inserat** (-e), advertisement
der **Inspektor** (-en), inspector
interessant (*adj.*), interesting
inzwischen (*adv.*), in the meantime, meanwhile
irgend jemand, someone, anyone
Italien, Italy

J
ja (*adv.*), yes
die **Jacht** (-en), yacht
die **Jacke** (-n), jacket
das **Jahr** (-e), year
das **Jahrhundert** (-e), century
jawohl, yes; yes indeed
jedesmal (*adv.*), each/every time
jetzt (*adv.*), now
die **Juliwoche** (-n), week in July
jung (*adj*), young
der **Junge** (-n), boy

K
kabeln, to cable
der **Kaffee** (-s), coffee
Kaffee kochen, to make coffee
kalt, cold
die **Kamera** (-s), camera
der **Kamerad** (-en), comrade, companion, friend
der **Kamin** (-e), fireplace
die **Karotte** (-n), carrot
die **Kartoffel** (-n), potato
die **Katze** (-n), cat
kaufen, to buy
das **Kaufhaus** (-er), department store
kaum (*adv.*), hardly
kennenlernen, to get to know; make s.o.'s
acquaintance
das **Kind** (-er), child
der **Kindergarten** (-), kindergarten, nursery school
der **Kirchhof** (-e), cemetery
klar (*adj.*), clear
der **Klassenlehrer(in)** (–(-nen)), form teacher
das **Kleid** (-er), dress, (*pl.*) clothes
der **Kleiderschrank** (-e), wardrobe
klein (*adj.*), small
klettern, to climb
klug (*adj.*), clever, intelligent
der **Koffer** (-), (suit) case; trunk
die **Kohle** (-n), coal
der **Kohlenhändler** (-), coal merchant
der **Kollege** (-n), colleague
komisch (*adj.*), funny
kommen, to come
können, to be able to
er konnte kein Französisch (Deutsch).
he could not speak French (German)
der **Kopf** (-e), head
der **Kopfweh** (-e), headache
das **Kopfnicken** (*no pl.*), nod
das **Kopfschütteln** (*no pl.*), shake of the head
die **Kopfverletzung** (-en), head injury
der **Korb** (-e), basket
kosten, to cost
kräftig (*adj.*), powerful, strong
das **Krankenhaus** (-er), hospital
der **Krankenpfleger** (-), male nurse
der **Krankenwagen** (-), ambulance
die **Kreuzung** (-en), crossing
die **Küche** (-n), kitchen
das **Küchenfenster** (-), kitchen window
die **Küchentür** (-en), kitchen door
kühl (*adj.*), cool
der **Kunde** (-n), customer
die **Kündin** (-nen), customer
kurz (*adj.*), short
die **Küste** (-n), coast

L
lächeln, to smile
lachen, to laugh

laden, to load
die **Lage** (-n), position
landen, to land
lang (*adj.*), long
lange (*adv.*), long; for a long time
langsam, slow
sich langweilen, to be bored
der **Lärm** (*no pl.*), noise
lassen, to allow, let
der **Lastkraftwagen** (-)/**LKW**, lorry
der **Laternenpfahl** (¨e), lamp post
lauern, to lurk
laufen, to run, walk; go by
laut, loud
    so laut er konnte, as loud as he could
der **Lautsprecher** (-), loudspeaker
das **Leben** (-), life
    ums Leben kommen, to lose one's life; die
leben, to live
das **Lebensmittelgeschäft** (-e), grocer's shop
leer (*adj.*), empty
lehnen, to lean
der **Lehnstuhl** (¨e), armchair; easy chair
der **Lehrer** (-), teacher; instructor
leicht (*adv.*), easily
leid: es tut mir leid, I'm sorry
leider (*adv.*), unfortunately
die **Leine** (-n), line; cord
leise, low, soft, gentle
die **Leiter** (-n), ladder
lernen, to learn
lesen, to read
das **Lesestück** (-e), reading passage
letzt (*adj.*), last; final
leuchten, to shine, gleam
die **Leute** (*pl.*), people
liegen, to lie
der **Liegestuhl** (¨e), deckchair
die **Limonade** (-n), lemonade; soft drink
die **Limonadeflasche** (-n), lemonade bottle
die **Linie** (-n), line, route (*bus*)
link (*adj.*), left
links, on the left
die **Liste** (-n), list
das **Loch** (¨er), hole
der **Löffel** (-), spoon
das **Lokal** (-e), public house
die **Lokomotive** (-n), locomotive
los! go!
lügen, to (tell a) lie
lustig (*adj.*), merry, jolly

M
machen, to make, do
das **Mädchen** (-), girl
das **Mal** (-e), time
    zum ersten Mal, for the first time
man, one, you, they
der **Mann** (¨er), man; husband
der **Mantel** (¨), coat; overcoat
die **Mark** (-), coin; mark
der **Marktplatz** (¨e), market place
das **Meer** (-e), sea
mehr, more
    mehr als, more than
meinen, to think, believe; be of the opinion
die **Meinung** (-en), opinion
    seiner Meinung nach, in his opinion
die **Menge** (-n), crowd, a lot
der **Mensch** (-en), person, man, woman, (*pl.*) people
merken, to notice
messen, to measure
das **Messer** (-), knife
der **Meter** (-), metre
die **Metzgerei** (-en), butcher's shop
mild (*adj.*), mild
die **Minute** (-n), minute
mitkommen, to come along
mitnehmen, to take with/away
mitspielen, to play; join in a game
das **Mittagessen** (-), lunch
(jdm) etwas **mitteilen**, to tell s.o. sth.
das **Mitteleuropa**, Central Europe

das **Möbel** (-), furniture
der **Möbelpacker** (-), removal man
das **Möbelstück** (-e), piece of furniture
möglich (*adj.*), possible
die **Möglichkeit** (-en), possibility
der **Moment** (-e), moment
der **Morgen** (-), morning
morgens (*adv.*), in the morning
die **Morgenzeitung** (-en), morning paper
das **Motorrad** (¨er), motorbike
müde (*adj.*), tired
die **Mühe** (-n), difficulty, trouble
murmeln, to mumble, murmur
das **Museum** (-een), museum
müssen, to have to
mutig (*adj.*), brave, courageous
die **Mutter** (¨), mother
Mutti, Mummy

N
na, well! now!
der **Nachbar** (-n), neighbour
die **Nachbarin** (-nen), neighbour
die **Nachbarschaft** (-en), neighbourhood
nachdem, after, when
nachher (*adv.*), afterwards, then
der **Nachmittag** (-e), afternoon
die **Nachrichtenagentur** (-en), news agency
nachschlagen, to look up, consult
nachsehen, to look after
nächst (*adj.*), next
die **Nacht** (¨e), night
nächtlich (*adv.*), nightly
die **Nähe** (*no pl*), nearness, proximity, vicinity
    in der Nähe, close by
nämlich (*adv.*), namely
naß (*adj.*), wet
natürlich (*adv.*), of course, naturally
der **Nebel** (-), mist, fog
neben (*prep.+acc./dat.*), near, beside
die **Nebenstraße** (-n), side street
neblig (*adj.*), misty, foggy
der **Neckar**, river Neckar
nehmen, to take
nein (*adv.*), no
nervös (*adj.*), nervous
nett (*adj.*), nice
neu (*adj.*), new
nie (*adv.*), never
niederschlagen, to knock down
niemand, no one
noch (*adv.*), still
    noch nicht, not yet
der **Norden**, the North
die **Nordsee**, North Sea
der **Nordwesten**, north-west
der **Notausgang** (¨e), emergency exit
die **Note** (-n), note
der **Notfall** (¨e), case of need, emergency
das **Notizbuch** (¨er), note book
notwendig (*adj.*), necessary
die **Nummer** (-n), number
nur (*adv.*), only
nur eines, only one thing

O
ob, whether, if
oben, at the top
ober (*adj.*), upper
die **Oberhand gewinnen**, to win the upper hand
obwohl, (al)though
oft (*adv.*), often, frequently
offen (*adj.*), open
offensichtlich, manifestly, evidently
öffentlich (*adj.*), public
(sich) öffnen, to open
ohne (*prep.+acc.*), without
ohne weiteres, without any hesitation
in **Ordnung bringen**, to put in order
der **Ostermontag** (-e), Easter Monday
das **Ostern**, Easter
    zu Ostern, at Easter
Österreich, Austria

P

ein **paar**, a few, some
packen, to pack (up)
die **Packung** (-en), packing, packaging
das **Papier** (-e), paper
der **Park** (-e), park
der **Passagiere** (-n), passenger
paß auf! be careful
passend (*adj.*), suitable
passieren, to happen
die **Pause** (-n), pause, stop
die **Person** (-en), person
der **Photoapparat** (-e), camera
das **Picknick** (-e *or* -s), picnic
das **Piepsen** (-), squeaking
der **Pilot** (-en), pilot
die **Pistole** (-n), pistol, gun
der **Platz** (¨e), square; place
plaudern, to chat, talk
plötzlich, suddenly
die **Polizei** (-en), police
der **Polizeiwagen** (-), police car
der **Polizist** (-en), policeman
der **Preis** (-e), price
preiswert (*adj.*), inexpensive, cheap
das **Problem** (-e), problem
die **Propagandatafel** (-n), propaganda hoarding
der **Proviant** (*no pl*), provision
der **Prospekt** (-e), prospectus; brochure
der **Pulverkaffee** (-), instant coffee
pünktlich (*adj.*), punctual

Q

quittieren, to receipt (*bill*)

R

das **Rad** (¨er), wheel
das **Radio** (-s), radio
rasen, to rush, hurry, speed
der **Rasierapparat** (-e), shaver, razor
sich **rasieren**, to shave (oneself)
das **Rasieren** (-), shaving
raten, to guess, advise
das **Rathaus** (¨er), town hall
ratlos (*adj.*), puzzled; at a loss
der **Ratskeller** (-), town-hall wine bar
rauchen, to smoke
das **Raucherabteil** (-e), smoking compartment
reagieren (auf), to react (to)
die **Rechnung** (-en), bill
recht (*adj.*), right, correct
recht haben, to be right
nach dem Rechten sehen, to see/attend to a thing; see fair play; put things right
rechts (*adv.*), on the right
der **Rechtsanwalt** (¨e), lawyer, solicitor
der **Regen** (-), rain
der **Regenschauer** (-), rain shower
regnen, to rain
regnerisch (*adj.*), rainy
die **Reise** (-n), journey
der **Rentner** (-), pensioner
die **Rentnerin** (-nen), pensioner
die **Reparatur** (-en), repair
der **Reiseprospekt** (-e), travel brochure
rennen, to run, race
der **Rest** (-e), rest, remainder
restauriert (*adj.*), restored
richtig (*adv.*), correctly
richtig (*adj.*), proper, correct
riesig (*adj.*), gigantic, huge
die **Rippe** (-n), rib
der **Rock** (¨e), coat, jacket; skirt
die **Rocktasche** (-n), jacket pocket
rot, red
der **Rucksack** (¨), rucksack
der **Ruf** (¨), call, shout
rufen, to call, shout
ruhig (*adj.*), quiet, calm

S

die **Sache** (-n), thing
sagen, to say
der **Salat** (-köpfe), lettuce, salad
das **Salatblatt** (¨er), lettuce leaf
das **Salzwasser** (-), salt water
sauber (*adj.*), clean
schade!, a pity! too bad!
scharf (*adj.*), sharp
schätzen, to estimate, guess
schauen, to look
scheinen, to appear, seem
schicken, to send
schieben, to push
schießen, to shoot
das **Schiff** (-e), ship
der **Schirm** (-e), umbrella (*also short for* **der Fallschirm**)
der **Schlamper** (-), slovenly person
schlecht (*adj.*), bad
schleudern, to skid
schließen, to shut, close
schlimm (*adj.*), bad
der **Schluß (Schlüsse)**, conclusion, end
der **Schmerz** (-en), pain, ache
schmutzig (*adj.*), dirty
schneiden, to cut
schnell, quick, fast
schon, already
schon lange, for a long time
schön (*adj.*), beautiful
der **Schrank** (¨e), cupboard
schrecklich (*adj.*), terrible
schreiben, to write
der **Schreibtisch** (-e), (writing) desk
die **Schreibwaren** (*pl.*), stationery
schreien, to shout, call
der **Schriftsteller** (-), writer
der **Schuh** (-e), shoe
das **Schulbuch** (¨er), school book
die **Schuld** (*no pl*), fault, blame
es ist Ihre Schuld, it is your fault; you are to blame
schuldig (*adj.*), guilty, culpable
die **Schule** (-n), school
die **Schulmappe** (-n), satchel
die **Schulter** (-n), shoulder
die **Schüssel** (-n), dish
schweigen, to be silent
der **Schweizer** (-), Swiss
schweizerisch (*adj.*), Swiss
schwer (*adj.*), difficult
die **Schwester** (-n), sister
schwierig (*adj.*), difficult
die **See** (-n), sea
der **See** (-n), lake
das **Segelboot** (-e), sailing boat
sehen, to see
die **Sehenswürdigkeit** (-en), sight (*of interest*)
sehr, very
sei, *present subjunctive of* **sein**
sein/seine, his, hers
seit (*prep.+dat.*), for, since
seit einem Jahr, for a year
die **Seite** (-n), side, page
selb (*adj.*), same
selbst, self, personally
der **Sessel** (-), armchair
(sich) **setzen**, to sit down
sicher, certain, sure; firm
das **Silber** (*no pl*), silver
silbern (*adj.*), (of) silver
die **Silberschüssel** (-n), silver dish
sinken, to sink
die **Sirene** (-n), siren
sitzen, to sit
der **Ski** (-er), ski
das **Skilaufen** (-n), skiing
der **Skistock** (¨e), ski stick
sobald, as soon as
die **Socke** (-n), sock
das **Sofa** (-s), sofa
sofort, at once; immediately
sogar, even
der **Sohn** (¨e), son

solch (*adj.*), such
sollen, to be (supposed) to
der Sommerschlußverkauf (ːe), end-of-summer sale
der Sonderangebot (-e), special offer
der Sonderkorrespondent (-en), special correspondent
sonnig (*adj.*), sunny
sonst, otherwise
sorgfältig, carefully
sparen, to save
die Sparkasse (-n), savings bank
der Spaß (ːe), joke, fun
spät (*adv.*), late
der Spaten (-), spade
später, later
spazierengehen, to go for a walk
die Speisekarte (-n), menu
spielen, to play
die Spitze (-n), tip, top
der Sport (-e), sport; (*fig*) hobby
Sport treiben, to go in for sports
der Sportflieger (-), s.o. who flies for a hobby
sprachlos (*adj.*), speechless
sprechen, to speak, talk to
springen, to jump
der Sprühregen (-), drizzle
der Sprung (ːe), jump
die Stadt (ːe), town, city
stammeln, to stammer (out)
stammen, to come from
stattfinden, to take place
stecken, to stick
stehen, to stand
das Stehen (-), standing
aus dem Stehen, from a standing position
stehenbleiben, to stop
stehend, standing, upright
stehlen, to steal
die Stelle (-n), place, spot
auf der Stelle, on the spot
stellen, to place; stop (*a thief*)
still (*adj.*), quiet, still, silent
die Stille (-n), stillness, silence
die Stimme (-n), voice
das Stockwerk (-e), storey, floor
stolz (auf+*acc.*), proud (of)
die Stoppuhr (-en), stop-watch
stoßen, to push; thrust
der Strand (-e), beach
die Straße (-n), street, road
die Straßenbahn (-en), tram
die Stube (-n), room
das Stück (-e), piece
studieren, to study
die Stunde (-n), hour
suchen, to look for
der Süd (*no pl*), south
der Süden, the South
Südfrankreich, South of France

T
die Tablette (-n), tablet
der Tag (-e), day
eines Tages, one day
guten Tag!, good day!
täglich (*adj.*), daily
der Tannenbaum (ːe), fir tree
tanzen, to dance
die Tasche (-n), pocket; bag
das Taschengeld (-er), pocket money
tatsächlich, actual, real, in fact
tausend, a thousand
das Taxi (-s), taxi
der Teil (-e), part
das Telefonbuch (ːer), telephone directory
die Temperatur (-en), temperature
der Teppich (-e), carpet
die Terrasse (-n), terrace
das Tier (-e), animal
der Tisch (-e), table
das Tischtuch (-e), table cloth
der Tod (-e), death

die Toilette (-n), toilet
tönen, to sound, ring
der Töpfer (-), potter
das Tor (-e), goal
ein Tor schießen, to score a goal
tot (*adj.*), dead
der Totozettel (-n), football pools coupon
die Tour (-en), tour
der Tourist (-en), tourist
die Tragbahre (-n), stretcher
tragen, to carry
trampen, to hitch-hike
träumen, to dream
der Treffpunkt (-e), meeting point
die Treppe (-n), stairs, steps
die Treppe herab, down the stairs/steps
treten, to step
trinken, to drink
trocken (*adj.*), dry
tropfen, to drip, drop
trotz (*prep.+gen*), in spite of, despite
trotzdem (*adv.*), in spite of that
das Tuch (-e), cloth
tun, to do, make
der Tunnel (-), tunnel, subway
die Tür (-en), door
die Tüte (-n), paper bag

U
üben, to practise
über (*prep.+dat./acc.*), over; about
über vierhundert, more than 400
überall (*adv.*), everywhere
überdenken, to think sth. over
überfahren, to run over
überfallen, to assault
überqueren, to cross over
überraschen, to surprise
übersetzen, to translate
die Uhr (-en), clock, watch
um (*prep.+acc.*), around
um acht Uhr, at eight o'clock
um . . . zu (+*infin.*), in order to
die Umgebung (-en), surroundings
umgehen mit, to use something
die Umleitung (-en), diversion
der Umweg (-e), roundabout way/route; detour
auf Umwegen, in a roundabout way
der Umzug (ːe), move, removal
undeutlich (*adj.*), vague, indistinct, unclear
der Unfall (ːe), accident
ungefähr, approximately
ungewöhnlich (*adj.*), unusual
unhöflich (*adj.*), impolite
unruhig (*adj.*), uneasy
unschlüssig (*adj.*), undecided
unten, downstairs
sich unterhalten, to talk, converse
das Unterhemd (-en), vest
das Unternehmen (-), enterprise, operation
die Untersuchung (-en), investigation, examination
unterwegs (*adv.*), on the way
der Urlaub (-e), holiday
auf Urlaub, on holiday

V
der Vater (ː), father
sich verabschieden, say goodbye; take one's leave
verängstigt (*adj.*), scared
verbergen, to hide, conceal
verboten (*adv.*), forbidden
der Verbrecher (-), criminal
verbringen, to spend (*of time*)
zur Verfügung, at one's disposal
vergessen, to forget
vergeßlich (*adj.*), forgetful
verkaufen, to sell
die Verkäuferin (-nen), shop girl
verlangen, to demand, ask for
verlassen, to leave
verletzt, injured, hurt

die **Verletzung** (-en), injury
verlieren, to lose
   das verlor sich bald, that soon disappeared
vermeiden, to avoid
vermissen, to miss
vernehmen, to hear, learn
verpacken, to wrap up, pack up
verschwinden, to disappear
die **Versicherung** (-en), insurance
die **Verspätung** (-en), lateness
   Verspätung haben, to be late
verständigen, to inform, notify
verstecken, to hide
verstehen, to understand
der **Versuch** (-e), attempt
versuchen, to try attempt
verunglücken, to be killed
der **Verwandte** (-n), relative, relation
viel, much, a lot of
vielleicht (*adv.*), perhaps, maybe
völlig (*adv.*), fully
vor (*prep.+dat./acc.*), ago, before; in front of
   vor einigen Tagen, a few days ago
vorbeigehen, to pass, go by
vorher (*adv.*), before, previously
   ein paar Tage vorher, a few days before
vorig (*adj.*), last, previous
vorsichtig (*adj.*), cautious, careful
sich **vorstellen**, to introduce onself
die **Vorstellung** (-en), performance
vorüber (*adv.*), (*time*) over, gone by
   das Essen vorüber, when the meal was over
vorwärts (*adv.*), forward
jmd etwas **vorwerfen**, to accuse s.o. of sth.

W

der **Wagen** (-), car; carriage (railway)
die **Wagentür** (-en), carriage door
wahr (*adj.*), true
   nicht wahr?, isn't it?
während (*prep.+gen.*), during, while
wahrscheinlich, probably
der **Wald** (⸚er), wood, forest
die **Wand** (⸚e), interior wall
die **Wanderung** (-en), walk, hike
wann?, when?
wäre, *imperf. subjunctive of* **sein**
warm (*adj.*), warm
warten (auf), to wait (for)
warum, why
was, what
   was für (ein), what sort of (a); what (a)
waschen, to wash
   sich waschen, to wash oneself
   sich die Hände waschen, to wash one's hands
der **Waschraum** (⸚e), washroom
das **Wasser** (-), water
weg, away; gone; out
wegbleiben, to stay away
wegen (*prep.+gen.*), because of
wegtragen, to carry/take away
weh (*adj.*), sore
   weh tun, to ache, hurt
das **Weihnachten** (*no pl.*), Christmas
   zu Weihnachten, at/for Christmas
weil, because
weinen, to cry
die **Weintraube** (-n), grape; bunch of grapes
weiß (*adj.*), white
weit, far
   weit mehr, much more; far more
   er war so weit, he was ready
   nichts Weiteres, nothing more
weitermachen, to carry on, continue
welch, which
wem (*dat of* **wer**), to whom
wenig (*adj.*), little
   ein wenig nach vorn, forward a little
wenn, when, if
wer, who
werden, to become

werfen, to throw
das **Werkzeug** (-e), tool
wert (*adj.*), worth
   viel wert, worth a lot; valuable
weshalb, how
die **Westseite** (-n), west side
das **Wetter** (-), weather
der **Wetterbericht** (-e), weather report
die **Wetterlage** (-n), weather conditions
die **Wettervorhersage** (-n), weather forecast
wickeln, to wrap, wind
wie, how
wieder (*adv.*), again
   wieder einmal, once again
auf **Wiederhören!**, goodbye! (*on telephone*)
auf **Wiedersehen!**, goodbye!
wieviel (e) (*adj.*), how much, (how many)
der **Wind** (-e), wind
der **Windschutz**, windbreak
winzig (*adj.*), tiny
wirklich (*adv.*), really
die **Wirklichkeit** (-en), reality
wissen, to know (*a fact*)
wo, where; when
die **Woche** (-n), week
das **Wochenende** (-n), weekend
der **Wochentag** (-e), weekday
woher (*adj.*), from where
wohin (*adv.*), where (. . . to)
der **Wohnwagen** (-), caravan
die **Wolke** (-n), cloud
wolkig (*adj.*), cloudy
womit (*adv.*), with what
woran (*adv.*), about what
wozu (*adv.*), for what; why
der **Wohnsitz** (-e), residence
die **Wohnung** (-en), flat
das **Wohnzimmer** (-), living room; sitting room
das **Wort** (-e *or* ⸚er), word
wunderbar (*adj.*), wonderful
der **Wunsch** (⸚e), wish
wütend (*adj.*), angry, enraged

Z

die **Zahl** (-en), number
zahlen, to pay
zählen, to count
der **Zahn** (⸚e), tooth
der **Zahnweh** (-e), toothache
zeigen, to show
die **Zeit** (-en), time
der **Zeitpunkt** (-e), moment; time
die **Zeitschrift** (-en), magazine
die **Zeitung** (-en), newspaper
das **Zelt** (-e), tent
zelten, to camp
zerbrechen, to break
ziehen, to pull
   herausziehen, to pull out
die **Zigarette** (-n), cigarette
das **Zimmer** (-), room
zittern (**vor**+*dat*), to tremble/shake (with)
zögern, to hesitate
der **Zoo** (-s), zoo
zornig (*adj.*), angry
zu (*adv.*), closed, shut
zuerst (*adv.*), first (of all); at first
zufällig (*adv.*), by chance, accidentally
zufrieden, contented, satisfied
der **Zug** (⸚e), train
zugehen, to go up to, move towards
zugeknöpft, buttoned up
auf jdn **zukommen**, to come up to s.o.
zumachen, to close
zurückfahren, to drive/travel back
zurückhalten, to hold back
zurückkommen, to come back
zurückrollen, to roll back
zurücktreten, to step back
zwanzig, twenty
zweit (*adj.*), second
zweitens (*adv.*), secondly

ENGLISH–
GERMAN VOCABULARY

A
able: to be able to, können
about, (=*around*) um (+*acc.*); (*with time*) gegen (+*acc.*)
abroad (*adv.*), im Ausland
   to go abroad, ins Ausland fahren
address, die Adresse (-n), die Anschrift (-en)
afraid (*adj.*), ängstlich
   to be afraid of, Angst haben vor (+*dat.*)
after (*prep.*), nach (+*dat.*); (*adv.*) nachher;
(*conj.*), nachdem
again (*adv.*), wieder
ago (*adv.*), vor (+*dat.*)
alarm clock, der Wecker (-)
all, all, alle
all sorts of, allerlei
allowed, erlaubt
   to be allowed to, dürfen
alone, allein
already, schon
although, obwohl, obgleich
always, immer
and, und
angry, böse
angrily, zornig, wütend
to **arrive**, ankommen
as . . . as, so . . . wie
as (*conj.*), während, indem
to **ask**, fragen, bitten
at (*prep.*), (*place*) in, an, bei; (*time*) um, zu
at last, endlich
at least, wenigstens, mindestens
aunt, die Tante (-n)

B
bad, schlecht, schlimm
bank, die Bank (-en)
bathroom, das Badezimmer (-)
to **be**, sein
to **be situated**, sich befinden
because (*conj.*), denn, weil
bed, das Bett (-en)
bedroom, das Schlafzimmer (-)
to **begin**, beginnen, anfangen
beginning, der Anfang (-̈e)
behind (*prep.*), hinter (+*acc.* or *dat.*)
besides (*adv.*), außerdem
big, groß
black, schwarz
book, das Buch (-̈er)
bread, das Brot (-e) or (-sorten)
breakfast, das Frühstück (-e)
to **bring** (*with*), (mit)bringen
brother, der Bruder (-̈)
to **build**, bauen
building, das Gebäude (-)
bus, der (Auto)bus (-se)
to **buy**, kaufen
by (*prep.*), durch (+*acc.*); von (+*dat.*)
by train, mit dem Zug

C
café das Café (-s)
to **call**, rufen; (*on telephone*) anrufen
campsite, der Lagerplatz (-̈e)
car, das Auto (-s), der Wagen (-)
card, die Karte (-n)
to **cash** (*a cheque*), einlösen
cheque, der Scheck (-e or -s)
child, das Kind (-er)
Christmas, (das) Weihnachten
cinema, das Kino (-s)
clean, sauber

to **clean**, putzen
clear, klar
coast, die Küste (-n)
coffee, der Kaffee
cold (*noun*), die Kälte; (=*illness*) die Erkältung (-e);
(*adj.*) kalt
to **come**, kommen
comfortable, bequem
counter (*shop*), der Ladentisch (-e); (*pub.*) die Theke
(-n); (*bank*) der Kassenschalter (-)
countryside, das Land (-̈er)
to **cry** (=*shout*), schreien; (=*weep*), weinen
cup, die Tasse (-n)
curtain (*net*), die Gardine (-n); (*heavy*)
der Vorhang (-̈e)
to **cut**, schneiden

D
dad, Vati
date (*time*), das Datum (Daten)
daughter, die Tochter (-̈)
day, der Tag (-e)
to **decide**, beschließen, sich entscheiden
difficult, schwer, schwierig
dining-room, das Eßzimmer (-), das Speisezimmer (-)
dinner, das Abendessen (-)
distance, die Ferne
   in the distance, in der Ferne
to **do**, machen, tun
dog, der Hund (-e)
door, die Tür (-en)
   back door, die Hintertür (-en)
   front door, die Haustür (-en)
downstairs; to go downstairs, nach unten gehen,
die Treppe hinuntergehen
to **drink**, trinken
to **drive**, fahren, führen
duck, die Ente (-n)
during (*prep.*), während (+*gen*)

E
Easter, das Ostern
   at Easter, zu Ostern
Easter holidays, die Osterferien
to **eat**, essen; (*of animals*) fressen
to **eat up**, aufessen, auffressen
egg, das Ei (-er)
elder (*adj.*), älter
empty, leer
English, englisch
evening, der Abend (-e)
everything, alles
eye, das Auge (-n)

F
face, das Gesicht (-er)
family, die Familie (-n)
far, weit, fern, entfernt
farm, der Bauernhof (-̈e)
fat, dick
father, der Vater (-̈)
favourite, Lieblings-
   favourite subject, das Lieblingsfach (-̈er)
few, einige, ein paar, wenige
film, der Film (-e)
to **find**, finden
first, erst
   at first, zuerst
fish, der Fisch (-e)
flash (*in the phrase 'quick as flash'*), blitzschnell
flat (*adj.*), flach; (*noun*), die Wohnung (-en)

football, der Fußball (¨e)
for (*conj.*), denn; (*prep.*), für (+*acc.*)
to **forget**, vergessen
fortnight, vierzehn Tage
friend (*male*), der Freund (-e); (*female*),
    die Freundin (-nen)
friendly (*adv.*), freundlich
from (*prep.*), von (+*dat.*), aus (+*dat.*)
in **front of** (*prep.*), vor (+*dat./acc.*)
furniture, die Möbel (*pl*)

G
garden, der Garten (¨)
gateau, die Torte (-n)
Germany, das Deutschland
to **get** (=*become*), werden
to **get dressed**, sich anziehen
to **get undressed**, sich ausziehen
to **get changed**, sich umziehen
to **get up/to stand up**, aufstehen
girl, das Mädchen (-)
girlfriend, die Freundin (-nen)
to **give**, geben
glad, froh
glass, das Glas (¨er)
to **go**, gehen, fahren
to **go back**, zurückgehen, zurückfahren
to **go for a walk**, einen Spaziergang machen
good, gut
grandmother, die Großmutter (¨)
granny, die Oma (-s)

H
half (*adj.*), halb; (*noun*), die Hälfte (-n)
half an hour, eine halbe Stunde
hand, die Hand (¨e)
to **have to**, müssen
to **hear**, hören
to **help**, helfen (+*dat.*)
here, hier
holiday, der Urlaub (-e)
holidays, die Ferien (*pl*)
home (*as in to go home*), nach Hause gehen
hope (*I hope that, etc*), hoffentlich
to **hope for**, hoffen auf (+*acc.*)
hospital, das Krankenhaus (¨er)
hotel, das Hotel (-s)
hour, die Stunde (-n)
house, das Haus (¨er)
how, wie
however, aber
to be **hungry**, Hunger haben
hungry, hungrig
husband, der Mann (¨er)

I
idea, die Idee (-n)
if (*conj.*), wenn, ob
ill, krank
in (into), in (+*dat./acc.*)
interested: to be interested in, sich interessieren
    für (+*acc.*)
to **invite**, einladen
island, die Insel (-n)

J
to **jump**, springen
just (*adv.*), eben

K
kitchen, die Küche (-n)
to **knock at**, klopfen an (+*acc.*)
to **know** (*a fact*), wissen; (*a person*), kennen

L
lake, der See (-n)
large, groß
last, letzt
late, spät

to **laugh**, lachen
to **learn**, lernen
to **leave**, verlassen; (=*depart*), abfahren
letter, der Brief (-e)
to **lie**, liegen
light, das Licht (-er)
to **light**, anzünden
to **like**, gern haben
to **listen**, (zu)hören; (=*pay attention*), aufpassen
little, klein
to **live**, leben; (=*to dwell*), wohnen
long, lang
to **look**, blicken
to **look for**, suchen
to **look** (=*appear*), aussehen
to **look forward (to)**, sich freuen (auf+*acc.*)
to **lose**, verlieren
to **lose one's way**, sich verlaufen
a **lot**, viel, viele

M
man, der Mann (¨er)
many, viele
marvellous, wunderbar
midday, (der) Mittag (-e)
minute, die Minute (-n)
to **miss** (*e.g. a bus*), verpassen
money, das Geld
more, mehr
morning, der Morgen (-)
mother, mummy, die Mutter (¨), Mutti
mountain, der Berg (-e)
range of mountains, das Gebirge (-)
much, viel

N
nearly, fast
to **need**, brauchen
new, neu
newspaper, die Zeitung (-en)
next, nächst
nice, nett
night, die Nacht (¨e)
nothing, nichts
to **notice**, bemerken
now, nun, jetzt

O
of course, natürlich
old, alt
on, auf (+*dat./acc.*)
only, nur, erst
open, offen
to **open**, öffnen, aufmachen
to **order**, bestellen
other, ander
out of, aus (+*dat.*)
own, eigen

P
parents, die Eltern (*pl*)
park, der Park (-e)
particularly, besonders
to **pass** (*of time*), vergehen
passport, der Paß (Pässe)
past: to go past, vorbeigehen (an+*dat.*)
to **pay for**, bezahlen
people, die Leute
perhaps, vielleicht
person, die Person (-en)
pet, das Haustier (-e)
piece, das Stück (-e); (*of toast*), die Scheibe (-n)
pipe, die Pfeife (-n)
plan, der Plan (¨e)
please!, bitte!
pleased: to be pleased (*about*), sich freuen (über+*acc.*)
poor, arm
post office, das Postamt (¨er), die Post (-en)
present, das Geschenk (-e)
pretty, hübsch

Q

quarter, das Viertel (-)
quick, schnell, rasch
quickly, schnell, rasch
quite, ganz

R

radio, das Radio (-s)
railway, die Eisenbahn (-en)
to **reach**, erreichen
to **read**, lesen
ready, fertig
really, wirklich
reception (*desk*), die Rezeption (-en),
   der Empfang (-̈e)
to **remember**, sich erinnern an (+*acc.*)
to **repair**, reparieren
to **repeat**, wiederholen
to **reply**, antworten, erwidern
reply, die Antwort (-en)
to **reserve**, reservieren
restaurant, das Restaurant (-s)
to **return**, zurückgehen, zurückkommen
right, richtig
to **be right**, Recht haben
to **ring**, klingeln, läuten
to **run**, laufen

S

sandwich, das Sandwich (-es)
to **say**, sagen
scarcely, kaum
school, die Schule (-n)
sea, die See (-n), das Meer (-e)
seaside: at the seaside, an der See
to **see**, sehen
to **send**, schicken, senden
to **shine**, scheinen
shopping: to go shopping, Einkäufe machen
to **show**, zeigen
shower, die Dusche (-n)
since (*prep*), seit (+*dat.*)
since (*conj.*), seitdem; (*adv.*), seither
single, einzeln
sister, die Schwester (-n)
   brothers and sisters, die Geschwister
to **sit, be sitting**, sitzen
to **sit down**, sich setzen
slice, die Scheibe (-n)
slowly, langsam
small, klein
to **smile**, lächeln
so, so, also
some, einige, wenige
something, etwas
soon, bald
sorry! Verzeihung! Es tut mir leid
to **speak**, sprechen
to **spend** (*of time*), verbringen
spring, der Frühling (-e)
stamp, die Briefmarke (-n)
to **starve**, verhungern
station, der Bahnhof (-̈e)
   main station, der Hauptbahnhof (-̈e)
to **stay**, bleiben, wohnen
still (*adv.*), noch
to **stop**, anhalten; (=*to cease*), aufhören
story, die Geschichte (-n)
straight away, gleich
to **swim**, schwimmen
sugar, der Zucker (-)
summer, der Sommer (-)
sun, die Sonne (-n)
sure, sicher

T

table, der Tisch (-e)
to **take**, nehmen
to **talk**, sprechen
tea, der Tee
telegram, das Telegramm (-e)
telephone, das Telefon (-e)
to **tell**, sagen, erzählen

tent, das Zelt (-e)
terrible, terribly, furchtbar, schrecklich
than (*in comparison*), als
thanks, der Dank (*no pl.*)
   many thanks, vielen Dank
then, dann, denn, damals
there, da, dort
thermos flask, die Thermosflasche (-n)
thin, dünn, mager
thing, das Ding (-e)
to **think**, denken, glauben
to **think about/of**, halten von (+*dat.*)
through, durch (+*acc.*)
to **throw**, werfen
ticket, die Fahrkarte (-n)
ticket office, der Schalter (-)/derFahrkartenschalter (-
time, die Zeit (-en)
to (*prep.*), an (+*dat./acc.*), zu (+*dat.*)
toast, der Toast (-e)
today, heute
too (*adv*), zu
tooth, der Zahn (-̈e)
towards: he came towards me, er kam auf mich zu
town, die Stadt (-̈e)
town hall, das Rathaus (-̈er)
train, der Zug (-̈e)
   goods train, der Güterzug (-̈e)
   slow train, der Personenzug (-̈e)
   through/fast train, der D-Zug (-̈e)
traveller, der/die Reisende (-n)
traveller's cheque, der Reisescheck (-e or -s)
to **try**, versuchen

U

uncle, der Onkel (-)
under (*prep.*), unter (+*acc./dat*)
to **understand**, verstehen

V

very, sehr
view, die Aussicht (-en)
village, das Dorf (-̈er)
visit, der Besuch (-e)
to **visit**, besuchen
voice, die Stimme (-n)

W

to **wait** (*for*), warten (auf+*acc.*)
waiter, der Kellner (-), der Ober (-)
waitress, die Kellnerin (-nen)
walk: to go for a walk, einen Spaziergang machen,
   spazierengehen
to **walk**, zu Fuß gehen
to **want**, wollen
warden, der Wärter (-)
to **wash** (*oneself*), (sich) waschen
washroom, der Waschraum (-̈e)
water, das Wasser
weather, das Wetter (-)
week, die Woche (-n)
well: I am well, es geht mir gut
where, wo
while (*conj*), während
   after a while, nach einer Weile
white, weiß
window, das Fenster (-)
wish, der Wunsch (-̈e)
to **wish**, wünschen
with (*prep.*), mit (+*dat.*)
without (*prep.*), ohne (+*acc.*)
worry, die Sorge (-n)
to **write**, schreiben

Y

year, das Jahr (-e)
yes, ja, jawohl
yesterday, gestern
yesterday evening, gestern abend
yet, doch
young, jung
youth hostel, die Jugendherberge (-n)

INDEX